March, 2013
To Razilee,
Congratulations on your acceptance
to Milano!

I hope you will join us and
allow us to help you move
closer to your vision.

Mark Tilton

Guiding Growth

Guiding Growth

How Vision Keeps Companies on Course

Mark Lipton

Harvard Business School Press
Boston, Massachusetts

Printed in the United States of America
07 06 05 04 03   5 4 3 2 1

Requests for permission to use or reproduce material from this book should be directed to permissions@hbsp.harvard.edu, or mailed to Permissions, Harvard Business School Publishing, 60 Harvard Way, Boston, Massachusetts 02163.

Library of Congress Cataloging-in-Publication Data

Lipton, Mark, 1950–
    Guiding growth : how vision keeps companies on course / Mark Lipton.
        p. cm.
    Includes bibliographical references and index.
    ISBN 1-57851-706-0 (alk. paper)
    1. Corporations—Growth. 2. Strategic planning. 3. Industrial management. I. Title.
    HD2746 .L57 2003
    658.4'06—dc21

                                                    2002008878

The paper used in this publication meets the requirements of the American National Standard for Permanence of Paper for Publications and Documents in Libraries and Archives Z39.48-1992.

Dedicated to my parents

Esther Bashevkin Lipton

William L. Lipton

Contents

Acknowledgments

So many people were instrumental in bringing this project from concept to reality.

I first thank my many loyal and trusting clients who believed in me when I told them that working on vision was a waste of time—then believed in me again when I told them they *had* to invest time and energy in a vision. While some clients are featured in this book, the majority with whom I tested the vision framework model are not. I learned so much from each of you. I appreciate the opportunities to work with such smart and dedicated executives from the private, nonprofit, and public sectors, and I value the confidence you placed in me by allowing me to help you guide your growth.

I am grateful to colleagues at the New School University who encouraged me to share the results of my experiences and research and to cut back on many of the managerial roles I had assumed over the years. As I considered the research required to determine whether the ideas discussed in this book were supported by hard data, their encouragement for reducing these extraneous roles was critical. With 20/20 hindsight, it was sage advice that I wish I had heard much earlier. I am indebted to Jonathan F. Fanton, former president of New School University and now president of the John D. and Catherine T. MacArthur Foundation, for his unwavering support over nearly two decades. A number of deans throughout my twenty-two-year tenure helped me test my own managerial and entrepreneurial mettle by giving me enough rope to hang myself as

I developed new and often risky ventures within the university. Thankfully, I am still alive and the experience gleaned has become invaluable. Bryna Sanger, my colleague at the Milano Graduate School, strongly and consistently encouraged me to find my passion where the intersection of scholarship and applied management meet. She has been a wonderful role model.

I thank particularly Susan Cane. For over sixteen years she has been a valued academic colleague, a frequent consulting partner, and—most important—a great friend. Without her unconditional support during the past two years, I may not have been able to reach the finish line. I am indebted to her for handling the heavy lifting of my former administrative roles while I was on sabbatical and for running interference on sticky issues once I returned. Her keen ability to give me effective feedback on concepts that were not ready for prime time, to build my confidence when I became frustrated, and to lend an ear whenever I needed one were gifts.

My research and program assistants over the past four years have labored deep in the archives of management research and uncovered data that I could not discover on my own. They were not only great sleuths but also talented, insightful, and critical thinkers.

When I decided to write this book, I hoped that Harvard Business School Press would accept and publish it. I knew that I wanted a most respected publisher, and I admired the consistent quality of their publications. Little did I know the professional staff I would work so closely with would mirror this quality. My editors, Melinda Adams Merino and Sylvia Weedman, were ceaseless in their encouragement and support for some ideas that needed refinement. Each, in her own way, motivated me to continually focus on and reframe concepts to benefit the reader. Sylvia was consistently attentive, utterly reliable, and a joy to work with regularly. In her role as copyeditor, Cathi Reinfelder made fine recommendations for clarity and style, and was able to see "the warp and woof" of my thoughts as they were carried across chapters. As manuscript editor, Jill Connor seamlessly pulled everything—and everyone—together near the end of this project. I am grateful to all the editors for encouraging me to "speak" in the voice in which I prefer to write, rather than the stilted prose of the academic world. You helped me to become a more critical thinker and, in turn, a better writer.

A number of years ago, while I was working on a piece for *Harvard Business Review,* I had the pleasure to work with Regina Maruca, then an editor at the *Review.* Now, as a talented independent editor, Regina served as an invaluable "reality checker." She helped me test the clarity of concepts, consistency of language and style, and she gave me straight feedback when I needed it. She is also a fine cheerleader.

Cathy Masterson's patience, caring, understanding, and support—particularly during the early years of this project—were invaluable and appreciated more than she will ever know.

And to my family: You were always there when I needed you. Even at times when I didn't think I needed you (but you knew). My sister Claire Zimmers and her husband Mel, Joshua Katz, Debbie Katz Ragals, and her husband John have all been anchors. Thanks to the twins, Emily and Arielle, for choosing to not enter this world until the day after my edited manuscript was delivered to the publisher. Your timing was impeccable. My friend of thirty years, Tom Higginbottom, has been like a brother and I appreciate his continual presence—even at three thousand miles away. And to my mother, Esther Bashevkin Lipton, who—going on 93—continues to be a role model of energy, determination, and spirit.

Thank you all.

Introduction

Another Book about Vision?

A BOUT TEN YEARS AGO, MY CLIENTS STARTED asking me—one by one, with increasing frequency—to help them conceptualize and articulate vision statements. I turned them down and told them that I didn't believe in "vision," that I thought it was just another management fad du jour. But I began to wonder. And since I had written a controversial article in the 1980s about management fads, I wanted to be able to state with some authority that this "vision thing" was not only a fad, but had *no* positive impact on organizational performance. So I put organizational vision on my research agenda. Little did I know I was in for quite a surprise.

As it turned out, my original research hypothesis was dead wrong. Not only does vision have a positive effect on performance, I found, it is critical to the survival of most organizations.[1] As a result of my research, I evolved from being a cynic about organizational vision to an evangelical, born-again believer. And I have long since apologized to those well-intentioned clients I turned down a decade ago; my soul is cleansed.

The discovery that vision is so important naturally led to other questions: If vision does make a difference, then what does an effective vision have to include? What organizational variables must the

1

content address? And what's the process by which an effective vision gets developed and implemented? Jim Collins and Jerry Porras arrived at the same conclusions about the importance of vision at about the same time that I did; their findings are published in their excellent book, *Built to Last*.[2] But these questions were not answered by Collins and Porras or by others. So I launched a second major research project on the heels of the first, the results of which were summarized in an article I wrote for *Sloan Management Review* in 1996.[3] The *Sloan* piece generated interest from senior managers in the private, public, and nonprofit sectors and became a primer on vision in many M.B.A. programs around the world. But an article can only go so deep; it did not quench the thirst. While there were a few shelves-worth of books related to vision in the management section of my local mega-bookstore, none adequately addressed the difficulties that executives face once they decide to implement a vision process. Most published works hover around at twenty thousand feet. None tackled the nitty-gritty details.

What's more, I was continuing to encounter even more questions about the how's and why's of successful visions in my consulting work. The time was ripe for further study. For a researcher intrigued by the dynamics of organizational growth and decline, the 1990s was a fertile decade. In places like Silicon Alley in New York City—my backyard at the time—the laboratory bench for examining these phenomena was stacked high and wide.

Consultant and Researcher

In the 1990s, so many organizations were growing at a torrid rate. And so many seemingly sound firms were imploding. I became increasingly intrigued by the somewhat paradoxical realization that growth can kill an organization. In the last decade particularly, when venture capital flowed and a good idea one day would become a multimillion-dollar organization the next, the rate of failure accelerated. While the hot money available during the mid-to-late 1990s may have obscured the need for rigorous analysis of the business models funded, I believed that the wholesale attribution of so many failures to a poor or insufficiently developed model was too easy an explanation for the crash of so many well-endowed firms.

Hot money chasing after ill-conceived business plans was just too simplistic an explanation to generalize over so many failures. How could it provide insight to entrepreneurial firms showing solid profits for a decade but failing as the scaling process accelerated?

I began to lay plans for a book that would explore the challenges of growth and link successful growth to the importance of vision. And so I honed my research still further, incorporating in-depth interviews and a major exploration of the disparate academic studies. Some of this had been done before, but too much of this literature, I believe, remained inaccessible to the senior practitioner, and the threads linking many of these studies had never been tied together. This included, but was not limited to, a broad and deep review of existing literature, assessment of my own client work from the past decade, and studies (coupled with surveys) of existing firms experiencing growth and, often, simultaneous decline.

I found, at that point, what I had expected: that reliance on naïve, one-dimensional explanations for organizational failure during periods of torrid growth turned out to be a chimera. When I analyzed the organizations that successfully managed expansion during periods of aggressive growth, they, too, benefited from venture capital (VC) funding and initial public offerings (IPOs). Clearly, other variables—with vision emerging first and foremost among them—were accounting for the success of some and the failure of many.

Challenging consulting engagements provided a catbird seat to several firms that found torrid growth a formidable endeavor. But my observations of clients, along with my research subjects and the marketplace at large, were also grounded by my other professional role—that of management professor. For over fifteen years I directed two large graduate programs at the New School University's Milano Graduate School of Management and Urban Policy in New York. Two decades as a scholar observing organizational phenomena and as a researcher trying to make rational sense of what I was seeing kept me focused on "data" rather than the hype as I moved forward.

Three Streams of Inquiry

The case I build in these pages is based on the outcome of three broad streams of inquiry. The first is my own research over the past decade, projects that involved both quantitative and qualitative data collection. (I should note that my research has always cut across the for-profit, nonprofit, and public sectors. I see organizational behavior generically, and while I acknowledge differences in the corporate, nonprofit, and government worlds, I also see common phenomena inherent in them all.)

The second stream is a series of meta-analyses of the research conducted by others in related areas: entrepreneurship, organizational growth and decline, leadership competency, strategy, organization structure, human resources management, and organizational culture. I wove together the findings from these targeted meta-analyses in areas where overlaps in the data and constructs were found. For example, I noted data suggesting a significant correlation between a particular type of organizational structure and its impact on organizational innovation and growth, since important economic and organizational theory and research tells us that growth is an imperative for most firms. Staying with this example, I looked at the interaction effect of organizational innovation and growth and found that the moderating variable—the single most important element facilitating both innovation and sustained growth—was a successful vision process. In many cases, the analyses of multiple studies representing areas directly or indirectly related to growth have never been conducted—or at least never published—for the benefit of practitioners and the intellectually curious.

Ultimately, the studies by other scholars in management and economics led me to a substantiated belief that most organizations must grow to survive. And the odds of surviving the trauma, bumps, and pains that come with growth are increased when a robust vision process is at work. That research also helped me to better understand what I was experiencing in the field—my third stream of inquiry. I was finding that few organizational leaders—particularly those struggling with the consequences of torrid growth—were able to hunker down and manage this "vision thing." Working with vision, I was finding, is a counterintuitive and frustrating process that goes against the grain of what most managers are trained to do. Over the years I have refined my approach to helping executives embrace this process, and my most recent findings are discussed here.

(Some who read earlier drafts of this book have told me that this is really a book about leadership since arguably the quintessential responsibility of a leader is to set direction and build commitment among followers to pursue that direction. The thought has merit. The overwhelming majority of executives fail with the vision process, and in this book I explore the ways senior managers can use this process not only to create an organization better positioned for growth but also as a way to enhance their own leadership effectiveness. But I will rarely use the word "leadership" in these pages. While I agree that vision and leadership are inextricably linked, I make no claims beyond the fact that this is a book about organizational growth and how the vision process can successfully guide that growth.)

While the professional balance of researcher and consultant can be a difficult one, it can also be liberating. Consultants are invariably pulled in different directions. They're yanked one way to do what is best for the client, to provide interventions grounded in substance (which for me equates to valid and reliable research generated by impartial people), and to manage the client's resistance so the organization can embrace what is difficult. But consultants are also pulled in another direction as they try to minimize resistance. Inadvertently, they may collude with the client's desires, rather than what is right. I don't present myself as a paragon of consultant virtue but only as someone particularly sensitive to the difficulty of bridging the worlds of academe and consulting. This has been a separate interest of mine and those readers intrigued by the relationship dynamics between consultants and their clients might find two articles I wrote for *The Journal of Management Consulting* of interest—"When Clients Make You Crazy" and "When Clients Resist Change."[4]

If a client's best intentions are not strong enough to motivate the behavior necessary for helping her do what is right for managing her organization's growth, if I cannot reduce the client's resistance to these necessary behaviors, and if all she wants is a consultant to sanction an ill-conceived organizational strategy, then I wish her well and bid her adieu. I love organization development consulting, but it is not my sole calling. It provides the living laboratory to bring substantiated research findings to life. Helping executives with their complex organizational issues is immensely more satisfying than residing full-time in the ivory tower.

The Vision Framework Model among Others

My model, which I refer to as the *vision framework,* and the guidelines you'll see here, emerged from my earliest research into the core themes a vision must address if it's to be viable. After scrutinizing over one hundred firms that not only had a vision, but used it as a process for guiding their growth, I was able to expand further on the three core themes—raison d'être, strategy, and values—and modify them over the years. The more I was able to field-test the model with clients, the more I was able to see other common elements of visions that work; for example, the development of reward structures for all employees that reinforce the key elements of a vision's strategy and values.

The vision framework model has some overlap with other conceptions of organizational vision, but what makes this one distinctive is its strong roots in research, application across many types of organizations, relative ease of implementation, and intuitive appeal to executives. Its closest cousin, I believe, is a vision model developed by the Ashridge Strategic Management Centre in the United Kingdom.[5]

Why don't most other interpretations of what it takes to create a good corporate vision fit the bill? First, many of the guiding principles provided in the innumerable books on leadership generally, and those on organizational vision more specifically, have not been tested to determine whether they actually yield the desired effect. While they may seem genuinely appealing on an intuitive level, some models simply don't achieve the desired results. Second, while some models may accurately reflect broad themes considered important, they may not be presented in a way that is helpful to executives as they struggle to overcome the potentially incapacitating resistance inherent in the process.

The components that compose the model for a "growth vision," as outlined and recommended in this book, have been tested in real organizations, and they work. The model for a growth vision, and the processes by which it is woven into the organizational fabric, are based not on consulting trial-and-error but on research. Testing this in the field came last. Fortunately, most managers who have used the model find it has strong "face validity"—it makes sense. This face validity goes a long way toward minimizing resistance and facilitating progress. I hope it will also resonate with you.

Who Will Find This Book Valuable?

I wrote this book to be of value to a few groups. Entrepreneurs involved in start-ups, seasoned executives wrestling with the conundrums of organizational growth, and others trying to understand why a growth initiative may have failed will all find this book of interest. In a perfect world, entrepreneurs would read this book *before* they started an organization because it is rich in guidance for building an organizational foundation that facilitates growth rather than one that becomes frayed by growth. Seasoned executives who have led organizational–growth initiatives have often done so with a personal "mental model" to guide their approach. Whether the model was successful or not, a set of guiding principles, grounded in research and the experiences of others, is helpful to add to one's repertoire. The vision framework model discussed here is intended to help executives develop and implement a vision but it has also been used as a diagnostic model to understand why vision initiatives fail. Whether it is used in a post-mortem analysis, or to help the intellectually curious better understand another dimension of organization dynamics, *Guiding Growth* can serve multiple requirements. Early drafts of the manuscript reviewed by entrepreneurs and seasoned executives evoked the same comment: "Why didn't you bring this book out *before* I made all the mistakes that I'm now trying to work around?"

This book is based on research and my experiences applying the research, but it is written for the practitioner in a relatively informal style. Many senior managers I have worked with from across the United States, Europe, and South Africa who participated in the leadership development programs I designed and facilitated were continually asking for a comprehensive yet user-friendly resource to support them through the vision development and implementation process. Participants in these programs, like those I worked with inside organizations, struggle constantly with "vision inertia" and are stymied in their ability to keep so many dimensions of their organizations in alignment.

My graduate students helped me realize the extent to which this book fills a gap in the resources available for advanced management courses in entrepreneurship, strategy, and organization change management. While it is neither intended nor written as an academic book, its base of research, intuitively appealing models, and case vignettes make it an appropriate secondary text for graduate programs.

Finally, the title implies that it is a "business" book, but I use the term loosely. My work with fast-growing nonprofits has convinced me that the organizational dynamics inherent in scaling are identical to those of their for-profit cousins. And, while we are in desperately short supply of vision-driven public agencies, I am happy to report that some do exist. A number of years ago, for example, a talented young precinct captain for the New York City Police Department participated in my year-long leadership development program for high-potential senior-level officials in New York City government. He created a compelling vision for managing a difficult precinct in Manhattan and, through the process, was able to dramatically improve morale, community involvement, and the ever-important crime-related performance metrics established by headquarters. Research findings and applications in the book are equally relevant to the for-profit, nonprofit, and public sectors.

Direction of the Book

Part I of *Guiding Growth* explores what many people have found to be the most challenging and thought-provoking issues involved in the vision process: understanding what an organizational vision is, how it relates to sustainable growth, and why there is such a natural resistance on the part of executives to embrace the process. Insight into the notion of vision and what composes one is a prerequisite to grasping why it is so important for sustained growth. But an intellectual grasp is a far cry from practical implementation and overcoming the resistance inherent in the process. Part I, therefore, provides first a concise overview of the entire book (chapter 1), a foundation for the validity of the vision concept and a sense of what elements of effective visions look like (chapter 2). It then illustrates the linkage between a well-designed and fully implemented vision and the increased probability for preparing an organization for sustained growth (chapter 3). With the linkage established, the work begins: Understanding the processes available for vision development and overcoming the natural resistance to these processes are addressed fully in chapter 4. Part II of the book provides a detailed map for implementing the vision framework. But implementing ideas across an organization that may exist only as notions on a piece of paper is the conversion point at which most vision initiatives fail. "From Paper to Practice" (chapter 5) examines what is required at the personal level to succeed with this process.

Ironically (or perhaps not), the flow of the first part of the book parallels my own journey: I first needed to believe that vision made a difference, then I had to understand what an effective "vision" was. Yet, even after drawing connections from research data on the relationship of vision to growth, I often remained stymied in my attempts as a consultant to help clients overcome their own resistance. Even in the face of supporting data and their own gut instinct that it was important, they just couldn't "do it."

Part II "unpacks" the vision framework—elements of the organizational infrastructure and process that must be aligned with the vision. Without alignment, you end up with a nicely worded document hanging on the conference room wall that people occasionally snicker at. Vision is an ongoing "process," and the way in which the message of the vision becomes woven into the fabric of day-to-day organizational life starts with those who are most accountable—the executive group (chapter 6). This group articulates the vision and serves as its torchbearer. The members of this group are also ultimately responsible for ensuring that three core organizational elements are continually aligned with the vision: culture (chapter 7), structure (chapter 8), and people processes (chapter 9). These three elements, along with the executive group, constitute the framework that creates a guided organization prepared for the challenges of growth.

About the Stories and Metaphors

In recent years, social scientists have come to appreciate what political, religious, and military figures have long known: that the use of stories and metaphors constitutes a uniquely powerful currency in human relationships. I would suggest further that stories and metaphors of identity—narratives that help individuals think about and feel who they are, where they come from, and where they are headed—are among the most powerful tools in a leader's toolkit. As you will see, visions describe who we (those of us in an organization) are, where we come from, and where we are headed. Social science research, as well as personal experience, helps us understand why some of the most effective visions leverage these tools.

Although I will discuss these tools in chapter 4 as a means for conceptualizing a vision, I'll take it one step further. My clients have found metaphors indispensable in thinking about their organizations and in conceptualizing the vision. In many cases, the power of metaphor has led to significant breakthroughs in thinking about an organization's purpose, strategy, and values. In this spirit, I use in this book several metaphors for organizational phenomena to not only help you understand the concepts but also illustrate how metaphors can be used. You may find them helpful, but you may also find that not every metaphor works for you. At the risk of employing more metaphors than may be typical in a book of this genre, I hope they serve as examples for how they can be used in your organization.

Finally, I present here a model—the vision framework—as a means for conceptualizing and creating an organization that can sustain growth. While you will find in this book many examples of organizations that embody elements of the framework, no organization does it all perfectly. (Please note that when I use an organization as an example, I am not endorsing the organization as it exists today, nor am I suggesting that it is or will be infallible in the future. I'm simply offering an illustration that has value, and is worth your consideration in the context in which it occurred.) This book is about a process that is challenging to implement, but can be extraordinarily effective the closer one comes to implementing it. The model looks different for every firm, and it is rare that any firm follows it with precision, but my findings suggest that it is an ideal worth striving for. For example, Oakley, a company based in Southern California, has developed an organization infrastructure and process that meets the criteria of the framework, but has not articulated a formal vision. As you will see, Oakley's vision is simply part of its "organizational DNA" that gets played out every day, in a myriad of activities. From its origin, Oakley was able to identify and implement elements of the vision framework even though its vision was not explicitly written into a document. Other examples will delve into an organization's vision and the extent to which it has directed some—but perhaps not all—of the vision framework variables. Examples from the field have helped me better understand how some executives have been able to succeed and how others failed at this vision thing. I believe the examples discussed here will not only bring the concepts to life but will make them particularly relevant to your unique organizational context.

Part I

Vision and Sustained Growth

Chapter One

Growing with Vision

I N 1977, I BOUGHT A 225-YEAR-OLD FARM ATOP A
small mountain in western Massachusetts. The winters
are rough there, and my office in the house—situated at the end of
an ell, the last stop on the business end of the central heating duct-
work—was vulnerable to the elements. When the weather was
frigid, so was my workspace.

It was 1981 before I decided to do something about it. A
woodstove, I thought, would be the perfect solution. So I followed
my instincts to the manufacturer I had heard was producing the
highest quality, most efficient, and best-looking stoves on the market: Vermont Castings.

I bought one of its models, installed it, and began having problems within the first year. Complaints to the dealer were met with
commiserations that the manufacturer "just wasn't putting out the
quality they had grown their reputation on." I was frustrated, the
dealer was angry, and both of us were mystified about why quality
and service were slipping so quickly.

As it turned out, what had happened was simple. The company's founder and leader had retired, taking his vision with him.

Duncan Syme started Vermont Castings in the midst of the
1970s' energy crisis, when the demand for good woodstoves far
outstripped the supply and when virtually all high-quality woodstoves were being imported from Europe. Syme's vision was to
make the best woodstoves in the world. (So obsessed was he about

realizing that dream that he hovered over his production lines to ensure that every stove met his precise standards.)

Soon after its launch in 1975, the company became the fastest growing in the industry. Within a few years, it had reached annual sales of $29 million. What's more, Syme's margins often hit an enviable 60 percent. But his job was exhausting. And he was burning out quickly. So he stepped away from the daily grind of the business and turned everything over to a management team he hired from outside. Syme left, the pros took over, and things began to fall apart.

The company's quick downturn wasn't all the fault of the new managers, however. Without Syme, there was no guiding principle to help the new top managers stay focused. Absent such focus, the company aggressively pursued product extensions (after all, the market was there) and nudged down the quality standards on its woodstoves (in the rational interests of cost reduction).

Apparently, I wasn't the only dissatisfied customer. Sales and profits leveled; the innovative culture eroded, causing new products to miss their mark; and employees (those who didn't leave) agreed that Vermont Castings had lost its greatness. In entrepreneurial ventures particularly, employees want to be part of something great.

The happy ending was not that Syme returned to run the business (which he did) but that on his return, instead of guarding his vision as its sole caretaker, he initiated a process to ensure that it would endure without him. He began by creating a vision statement, which he called "The Vermont Castings Statement." But more important, he began an aggressive campaign to embed in the organization the values, beliefs, and strategies articulated in the statement, so that they would inform every operational decision going forward, regardless of whether or not he was there to oversee things. Vermont Castings was sold subsequently to a Canadian manufacturer of related products, and I have no doubts that Syme's new approach toward vision was a critical factor in making the company a very attractive acquisition prospect.

Many people, assessing what happened at Vermont Castings when Syme left, would be tempted to point to poor strategic planning, and to say something along the lines of: "He left without providing clear goals and a map detailing the strategy necessary for achieving them." Or, "He should have reexamined his products and their position in the market before he left, then created one-year and longer-term strategic plans that the new management team could revise and update regularly with new numbers, new planning targets, and new objectives."

The notion, however, that more formal planning alone would have kept the company on course is wrong. Vermont Castings needed a viable mechanism to infuse the higher-level beliefs and values that, sans Syme, it just didn't have.

Planning, according to Henry Mintzberg, management theorist and researcher from McGill University, is about *probabilities*. It entails looking at factors like the economy, your industry, and customer trends, placing bets on what will happen, and changing course as needed to pursue the position of lowest risk or highest return.[1] But without a vision that permeates the organization, even the most carefully crafted strategy will quickly falter because vision is the rudder that guides the strategy. Vision is the higher order, and it's all about *possibilities*—idealistic notions, the difference an organization and its people plan to make in the world. A vision does *not* fluctuate from year to year, as a strategy will, but instead serves as an enduring promise. A successful vision tells a lucid story about the organization and, though future-based, is always in the present tense, as if it were being realized now.

A vision is a vivid picture of a specific destination, a desired future, that is both descriptive and challenging. It also specifies the way an organization is going to work and the essence of what people can expect if they are going to work there.

It's worth clarifying up front that, as I see it, "vision" and "mission" are not and should not be the same thing. A *mission* is about what an organization does. It describes its activities. A graduate school of management, for example, might have a mission as simple as, "We educate students to receive a high-quality M.B.A." A *vision* is about purpose. That same school's vision, then, might begin with the statement, "Our graduates will have the capacity and drive to improve organizations and the communities in which they exist. Their impact on people, organizational processes, and ultimately the society in which they live will be profound and positive."

Vision and Growth

Vision is a tough concept to understand. Most people dismiss it as "soft," "amorphous," or "nice to think about but not essential to the nitty-gritty details of running a business." And it's even harder to embrace. Especially when the going gets tough, the overwhelming majority of business leaders are hard-wired to focus on external scapegoats like market forces rather than looking inward.

But vision is an essential ingredient to the success of any company, and particularly to those that are attempting rapid growth. Why? Because a comprehensive vision provides the driving force that can get a company through the growing pains it will inevitably encounter.

Vision is a basic "shape" of the future that allows an organization the flexibility of means to build around it. It expresses optimism and hope about possibilities and desired futures. In a way, vision acts as a "clearing agent" in organizational worlds characterized by tensions driven by conflicting interpretations. Visions articulate a view of a realistic, credible future for the organization that is in some way better than the present state. It is a target that beckons.

A vision guides the action an organization will take in the face of ambiguity and surprise. It also gives people the feeling that their lives and work are intertwined and moving toward recognizable, legitimate goals. How will the company think about whether to pursue a new line of business? What characteristics do we want in our employees? What will characterize our management style? How should the corporate culture support the business model? What do we think of our customers? The vision guides these processes.

Put another way, an organization's vision must speak to three core themes that address the questions people want answered in the organizations they commit to.[2]

First, the vision must articulate an organization's purpose to encapsulate its very reason for being—its *raison d'être*—and to determine *why* it gets involved in various activities. The raison d'être represents the organizational equivalent of the sobering, existential questions some individuals grapple with throughout life:

Why do we, as an organization, exist? For whose benefit are all these efforts? What difference can we make on the world?

Second, the vision must define a *strategy,* but not simply from a business planning or classical strategic-planning standpoint. The strategy must help establish the organization's identity and the distinctive characteristics that differentiate it significantly from anyone else. It speaks to the question: How will the raison d'être be achieved?

In this context, strategy is not a one- or three-year plan for accomplishing equally short-term goals, but a way to articulate the operational logic for what the organization hopes to accomplish. If the raison d'être is to change the way people make decisions about how they manage their inventories, then the strategy must explain the principles that will make this possible. Strategy defines the distinctive competencies or competitive advantages the organization currently has or plans to develop. Strategy, as it is embedded in the vision for Charles Schwab, for example, includes being "fair, empathetic, and responsive in serving our customers; striving relentlessly to improve what we do and how we do it; always earning and being worthy of our customer's trust; delivering high-quality, reliable ethical products and services at a fair price."[3]

The ultimate worth of the vision as a management process is undermined if the vision is nothing more than a statement of purpose and a strategy for getting there. Purpose and strategy, therefore, lack the power to guide performance unless they can be converted into action, policy, and job-related behavioral guidelines. So, the vision must finally address the *values* that identify what the organization stands for. Explicitly stated values provide the underpinnings for a deliberately determined culture, which in turn establishes the unwritten rules for behavior.

This third theme or principle, which I refer to under the umbrella of *values,* embraces the key assumptions, attitudes, and beliefs embodied by the organization and represented in the daily flow of activities necessary for moving it closer to the raison d'être and for supporting the strategy. Organizational values serve as the foundation that directs and sustains this behavior.

In organizations that manage torrid growth, these principles (figure 1-1) provide the basis for a process that guides day-to-day

FIGURE 1 - 1

Principles of a Vision

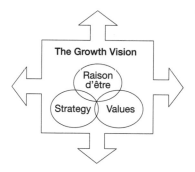

management. In chapter 2, I'll elaborate on these principles as the three major principles that an effective vision needs to clarify.

Go Ahead, Be Suspicious

I was very suspicious about the whole "vision thing." As I noted in the Introduction, when I first set out to learn more about vision, it was with the expectation that I would be debunking a myth and proving that vision *does not* work, not that it *does*.

I knew, going into my research, that many CEOs are either skeptical about vision to begin with or lose faith quickly when they hear about the capacity of a vision to manage growth. I also knew that while most organizational leaders who try to develop and implement their visions do so with good intentions, the overwhelming majority fail miserably.

But what I found, in extensive surveys and interviews with one hundred industry leaders, was that most top companies *do* have visions and *have* made explicit efforts to ensure that these visions are much more than carefully worded inspirational statements bolted to their conference room walls. The positive impact that a well-implemented vision had on so many organizational outcomes—many related to growth—startled me.[4]

At the same time I was becoming a vision convert, Stanford University professor Jerry Porras and consultant Jim Collins were analyzing organizations that maintained continuous growth over at least four decades. *Built to Last,* the well-known and worthy culmination of that impressive study, also provides compelling data in support of vision (data that also flew in the face of most existing business school doctrine). For example, Collins and Porras did not find that "maximizing shareholder wealth" or "profit maximization" was the dominant driving force or primary objective for firms with a long history of success. Those firms tended to pursue a cluster of objectives, of which making money was only one and typically not the primary one. For them, business was more than an economic activity, "more than just a way to make money."[5]

In their detailed pair-by-pair comparison of long-lived, continually growing companies, Collins and Porras made an ironclad case showing the more successful of each pair (in seventeen of eighteen pairs) had been driven overwhelmingly by *ideology* and less by pure profit. Does that mean that those successful companies do not care about economic success? Hardly. Of course organizations that maintain sustainable growth pursue profits. But it is their vision and the way in which it transcends immediate economic considerations that accounts for their success.

The proof is there. So what's the problem? Put simply, there is a huge "disconnect" between believing in vision and knowing how to create one and put it to use in an organization. Even the most ardent supporters of vision find themselves swimming against the tide when it comes to implementation. ("We believe in it; we just won't do it," one CEO confessed to me on behalf of himself and other CEOs he knew.) Why? Because what has to be done to implement a vision in an organization, in large part, isn't natural, instinctive behavior.

The Binary Response

In the mid-1990s, Korn/Ferry conducted an exhaustive study of 1,500 senior leaders, 870 of them CEOs, from twenty different countries. When these managers were asked: "What are the key traits or talents that CEOs should possess by the year 2000?" the most frequently chosen response was "the ability to convey a strong sense of vision." Specifically, 98 percent saw that trait as the most important for CEOs—by a 20 percent margin over any other skill.[6]

Another study examined senior managers' comfort levels at working with the vision process. More than 90 percent reported a lack of confidence in their own skills and ability to conceive a vision for their organizational unit—and they were uncomfortable engaging in the vision development process.[7]

Intellectually, most CEOs acknowledge the need. Many even love the idea of creating a vision to guide their organizations and leaving that vision as their legacy. But most loathe the thought of taking vision from paper to reality. Smart—even brilliant—managers are often paralyzed by the process. Consultant Gary Hamel and consultant/scholar C. K. Prahalad found in the mid-1990s that less than 3 percent of senior management's energy is typically devoted to building a collective perspective on the future—a dangerously inadequate amount.[8]

While we could shrug our shoulders and write off this "vision inertia" with a dismissive "they just don't get it," despite the avalanche of data supporting its role in laying a critical path to organizational growth, I believe the disconnection reaches more deeply into the human psyche. I call this phenomenon the "binary response." The *binary response* to the vision process relates to the human tendency to fall back on what is familiar and to avoid those behaviors—and ways of thinking—that are not part of our familiar repertoire. When we encounter a problem or challenge, we naturally fall back on our practiced approaches. But with vision, most managers have no practice, no historical context of experience to fall back on. When the challenge hits, they choose to deal with the discomfort by avoiding the problem altogether.

The binary response works against successfully implementing a vision because it allows senior managers to ignore that which they can't put their arms around and fall back instead on the kinds of factors and measures they're comfortable with—sales reports, economic indicators, and the like. It allows them to make decisions based on market pressures or the attractive prospect of technology (customer relationship management software that promises to "do it all" comes to mind). Those decisions might seem strategically sound at the time—but they're made without due consideration about whether the action taken is right for the organization over the long term.

The binary response can also cause a leader to be far too timid even when he or she does try to create a vision-driven organization, emerging with a mental model of their company that does not *allow* it to change strategic course to adapt to market conditions. The organization may emerge rigid, fighting the same battle over and over again even as new battles on other fronts have already begun.

The other side of this binary response is when leadership is able to articulate a vision and impregnate it into the day-to-day belief systems and life of the organization. While there may never even be a formal vision statement printed anywhere, it often takes on a more tangible life than those carefully reduced to a few paragraphs, engraved on plaques, hung on walls, and printed in the annual report.

What Vision Looks Like When It's Done Right

Consider, for example, Oakley, the high-style, high-priced eyewear company (and one of *Fortune*'s "100 Fastest Growing Companies" for 2002). In 2000, Oakley was getting hammered by competition and the economy in its niche market. Then, in late 2001, Luxotica, a powerful Italian eyewear company and a key Oakley competitor, purchased Sunglass Hut—which happened to be the largest outlet for Oakley's glasses. Almost immediately, Sunglass Hut, once the close partner, stopped selling the Oakley brand so it could retail the products their new parent designed and manufactured. Almost overnight, 28 percent of Oakley's sales pipeline was shut down.[9]

The folks at Oakley did not freak out, but it wasn't because they were "very cool" people. They didn't freak because they didn't— and don't—think of themselves as being in the eyewear business (even though Wall Street did; the week the news broke, Oakley's stock tumbled). Oakley's vision has created an organization that "is driven to seek out problems, create solutions, and wrap those solutions in art."[10] The firm's focus on innovation has built a foundation of science, sculpture, and defiance of conventional thinking.

The passion that shook up the optical industry has now migrated to high-performance footwear, wristwatches, apparel, and accessories. And Oakley's strategy for carefully selecting retailers for their ability to add value through service and image and its decision to focus on selective distribution helped the company survive the Sunglass Hut rejection while others would probably have floundered. Wall Street, by the way, saw Oakley's flexibility and innovative response, and the stock took only four months to rise above where it was before the news.

In most companies, the process of creating a vision begins when the senior team reaches consensus that a vision is important and decides to come up with a vision statement (usually at an off-site executive retreat). The effort yields a few pages of print peppered with bullet points indicating agreement around some core principles the organization stands for. Maybe someone fiddles with the jumble of ideas, tries tying all words and phrases together, and emerges with a brief statement typically crammed with trendy management phraseology that sounds like a Dilbert cartoon strip. Then the statement gets printed, laminated, and bolted to conference room walls; it gets boiled down to a short paragraph and printed on the back of everyone's business card; it may even have its own link on the company's Web site.

The steps required to implement this bunch of words remain a mystery, however. Even worse, the bunch of words may have no meaning to others in the organization. The problem with these "faux" vision statements is that they leave so much open to interpretation. If they're not, in fact, *mission* statements (i.e., about what the organization does), they are often so lofty that they fail to provide the crucial connection for the very people they are intended to impact. And that's where the process stops.

Vision-driven organizations distinguish themselves by moving far beyond a slick statement with no resonance. They design organizational structures and operating systems that continually reinforce the *meaning* of the vision. They establish tracking mechanisms to provide feedback on whether the company is moving toward the realization of the vision. Vision thus becomes an everyday reality that continually raises and maintains performance standards because it is supported by mechanisms and processes that motivate people to stay focused on it.

More often than not (and sometimes without realizing it), companies ask: "What functions should we perform that fit our current structure and organization?" The vision-driven organization asks: "What structure will best enable us to carry out our vision?"

What's the critical difference? In the first instance, employees, succumbing to the pull of the binary response, will quickly become nonadaptive. When people find a certain approach to something that works for them, they tend to lock into that chosen process and stop searching for alternatives—even if they're working in an organization that is trying to scale quickly and continually needs to develop and deploy new ways of doing things. And established processes often take on lives of their own. They cease to be a means to an end and become ends in themselves.

People follow the processes not because they are efficient or effective, but because they are well known and comfortable. Once a process becomes routine, once it becomes ingrained as "the way things are done around here," it prevents employees from considering new ways of working to cope with the by-products of growth.

In the second instance, vision acts as a strong *defense* to inertia, making it easier for people to change even the most comfortable of processes because they have embedded a longer-term view of what their company is trying to accomplish. Work, in a vision-driven company, doesn't stop with completing today's tasks or meeting this month's goals. Instead, it is about constantly moving toward a higher aspiration.

How can senior managers overcome the negative drag of the binary response? By working outward, from an intellectual context in which they're comfortable, to establish and continually strengthen an organizational framework that supports their company's vision. (Subsequent chapters of this book are devoted to explaining this framework and working through the vision-creating process; here, to introduce the concept, I'll lay it out in broad strokes.)

The Warp and the Woof: Making Vision Actionable

Articulating a vision that captures the three themes noted earlier (raison d'être, strategy, and values) is a major accomplishment in beating the tough odds inherent in the binary response. But that is only part of the battle. Unless the vision is brought to life and made actionable, until the time it is woven into the day-to-day fabric of the organization's processes, it may not represent much more than the veritable one-page statement that remains disconnected from the organization.

The most vivid, memorable visions often utilize the power of metaphor. To understand a successful vision and what it means for executives to overcome the binary response, consider for a moment not only the metaphor of organizational "fabric," but how fabric, or a tapestry, is created.

Weaving—a rug, tapestry, nearly anything—requires two sets of threads. The first set—called the "warp"—is attached to the loom itself. The warp threads are strung vertically and remain flat and taut through the entire weaving process. But they also attach, in groups, to different pedals, so that you can raise some of them by pressing one pedal, and others by pressing another pedal. The warp takes a long time to thread through little needles on the treadles; doing so, and setting the pedals, requires concentration. But once those tasks are complete, your pattern—however complex—has been defined.

But bringing the tapestry from a design in your mind to physical reality is where the second set of threads—called the "weft threads," or, commonly, the "woof"—comes in. These create the real texture of the material. Woof threads are wound around a device called a shuttle; the shuttle is "thrown through the warp" (i.e., in the space between the raised and lowered warp threads). And then the weaver pulls the batten close against the warp and woof to ensure that the two sets are pressed tightly together as they should be. As the shuttle is thrown, with the woof being woven through the warp, the pattern and material come to life, millimeter by millimeter.

Historically, warp and woof had social and symbolic meaning in many cultures. In China, for example, where the word for *warp* also means "king," the warp attached to the loom represented the immutable forces of the world, and the woof, as it moves back and forth between warp threads, stood for the transient affairs of humans. In India, the woof strands relate to the stages of life, whereas the warp threads represent the external factors that shape a person.

Stay with me here.

This process of weaving, I believe, provides an equally symbolic and insightful metaphor for the simplicity and complexity, as well as the development and deployment, of a vision.

Starting with the warp threads, you weave your own distinctive tapestry of how you want the organization to be—that is, the warp threads lay down all the essential strands of your vision. So the warp is your definition of why the organization exists, the contributions it will make to its environment, and the strategies that articulate your distinctive competencies and sources of competitive advantage. The warp also identifies the values that establish what the organization stands for and provides guidelines for how each individual should engage in his or her work.

The warp configuration, then, is the metaphorical equivalent of your organization's unique raison d'être, strategy, and values. But, while the parameters and pattern of the vision are in place, the warp alone is not a tapestry. In fact, if left alone, it remains an unfinished, useless creation. It is only a concept in the eyes of those who created it. It has no "texture," no impact on anyone else. Warp threads, even when carefully strung and threaded, even with the pedals of the loom set perfectly in place, only represent *potential*.

That's where the woof comes in. The woof threads, to stick with our metaphor, are the intersecting elements that create a pattern for the lives of people in the organization; they breathe life into the vision. And the shuttle, the device "thrown" relentlessly over and over again to weave the warp and woof together is the metaphorical equivalent of an organization's executive group—the ones accountable for bringing the vision into every nook and cranny of the organization's being.

Vision development is the "warp" phase. The "woof" is how and where it becomes effectively woven and ultimately the "fabric" of the growing organization. Without the woof, an organization may have a compelling vision but it is not connected to employees' thinking and the behaviors that lead to collective action. It's like trying to wear clothing from fabric that only has a set of strands going one way.

The Vision Framework: Bringing Vision to Life

A vision standing on its own is not much more than intellectual warp; it's an intangible concept. But an effective vision has a strong infrastructure that will make it come to life, is apparent to everyone in the organization, and is actively maintained by the organization's leaders.

I call this infrastructure the *vision framework;* it might be useful to think of it as the woof threads that provide a resilient supporting weave for the warp threads of the vision. Much as a building's frame holds its shape together and enables it to function as its designer and structural engineer intend, the framework provides the load-bearing support to ensure that a growth vision evolves into an organizational process rather than remaining a useless declaration.

The vision framework, therefore, is the integration of those key elements that hold the organization together and give it strength. It is not only the vision but also *how* the vision comes alive in the way critical elements of the organization are fashioned. The framework

FIGURE 1 - 2

The Vision Framework

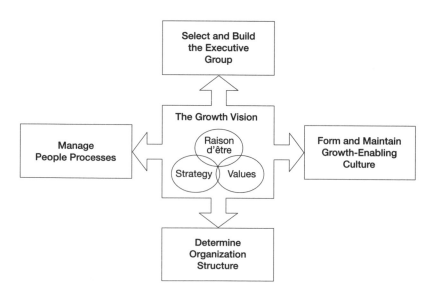

guides (1) selection and building of the executive group, (2) formation and maintenance of a growth-enabling culture, (3) organization structure, and (4) management of people processes. These four organizational elements draw their strength and direction from the vision (see figure 1-2). While a vision alone is worthless, the key organizational elements that compose the framework can work at cross-purposes if they are not guided by, and aligned with, a vision. As you will read in later chapters, a firm's continued growth, if not its actual sustainability, is at risk when these elements are not in alignment.

In addition to the vision itself, the vision framework consists of four major elements.

The Executive Group

Martin Luther King, Jr. once observed that "people cannot become devoted to Christianity until they find Christ, to democracy until they find Lincoln and Jefferson and Roosevelt, to Communism until they find Marx and Lenin."[11] People often become committed to great ideas through a person or people who personify those ideas. In my experience, and with supporting data from others' research, the champion of an organizational vision is not one person. That "champion" is what I call the *executive group*. It is composed of the senior-most managers and has a central leadership role. While there is of course still a CEO with ultimate responsibility, the ideal executive group works far more collaboratively and communicates more effectively than the typical collection of executive officers. Group members are diverse in their viewpoints and thinking, they look out for the growth and welfare of the entire organization (rather than protecting only their silo), and they are critical to deploying the vision across the organization. Their job of promoting the vision is essential, and they must continually elicit and manage conflict as they strive for consensus around the nature of the strategic choices they make. If elements such as continuous improvement, innovation, and entrepreneurship are improvised or managed in an ad-hoc fashion, they will die quickly. Organizational processes, particularly those associated with successful growth, require the continual attention and guidance of the firm's senior leaders—they are accountable for implementing the vision. Further, this group must develop short-range strategies, model the competencies required of all managers as well as employees in general, continually scrutinize how well the organization is aligned with its vision, and both monitor and manage the often painful consequences of growth. In chapter 6 I will explain why the senior-most group of managers is not expected to function as a team, but as a cohesive group representing diverse perspectives who may not always agree but share a modus operandi focused on the vision. They are the torchbearers of the vision and of the need for innovation embedded within the vision. Without the executive group working in concert to deploy and manage it, the vision process will flounder.

The Culture

A company's culture is distinctive and reinforces the vision in a way that cannot be bought or copied. When a company's culture is consistent with stated values and other elements of the vision and is embedded across the organization, it influences the growth and evolution of that organization more than any formal system. When the culture, the management structure, and formal systems are aligned, that combination expands to a formidable platform for sustainable growth. Managing the culture is an ongoing process and responsibility must rest at the top. The executive group sets the course for the emerging culture and takes responsibility for ensuring it is aligned with the vision.

Organization Structure

Organization structure determines the way in which people are organized or grouped in an organization. Structure can either support or erode the vision. In a classic study of organization structure, since replicated over the decades, Paul Lawrence and Jay Lorsch discovered that organizations always face a paradox of encouraging various groups to be both different enough to manage a variety of tasks and integrated enough to achieve coordination among the different groups and the overarching vision of the firm.[12] Indeed, the most successful organizations had groups that were both more distinct in orientation and skill *and* more able to integrate these differences than were less successful firms.[13] In reality, this is a tough design act to pull off and, as I discuss in chapter 8, managing the structural paradox is conditional to realizing guided growth.

People Processes

People processes are associated historically with traditional human resources (HR) functions, but they are also a significant distinguishing characteristic of successful scaling initiatives. How new people are recruited, selected, socialized, developed, and retained are decisive factors contributing to a firm's sustainability. For this reason, people processes are the responsibility of all managers and not just a series of transactional tasks buried in a department. Too often, people leading HR functions in an organization are well aware of the people processes required but, due to lack of authority or resources, find themselves incapable of implementing their beliefs. Ultimate responsibility for people processes lies with the executive group, and, if an effective HR unit exists, they work in close collaboration.

Where Strategy Fits In

If you're still tempted to fall back on the (understandable) logic that vision is ethereal and believe strategic planning alone is the key to success, you're in good company. Harvard University's Michael Porter maintains that formal planning will provide the discipline to pause occasionally to think about strategic issues. But, consider for a moment the wisdom of Henry Mintzberg, Porter's ideological counterbalance, who believes that reliance on planning has only aggravated the very problem it was intended to solve, further detaching managers from the broader context. In his exhaustive examination of strategic planning, Mintzberg concluded that underlying the essential concept of strategic planning was really a plea for leadership and direction.[14]

I'm in Mintzberg's camp. Executives of scaling organizations need to understand the turbulent environment in which they operate and how their organization will have the capacity to bob and weave in response to the punches and opportunities thrown at it. But because classical strategic planning is universally viewed primarily as a means for making strategic decisions, people imagine that a formal process can generate strategy. Unfortunately, this is the wrong solution to the problem. In all the firms Mintzberg and others have studied, strategic *vision* from above was crucial to the planning process for every organization. Strategic planning cannot provide this strategic vision on its own, and—in all but the shortest term—it is totally useless without a vision. I found in my consulting that managers who consistently thought about strategy solely at the planning level, rather than on the broader dimension of the vision, were far more likely to become victims of the binary response.

Mintzberg argued passionately in his influential book *The Rise and Fall of Strategic Planning* that strategic planning is an oxymoron.[15]

- Planning is about analysis, and strategy is about synthesis.
- Planning is about facts, operations, and budgets, while strategy requires creative *thinking* about vision and how to gain competitive advantage.
- Planning is an approach to consider probabilities of what we *think* is going to happen, rather than consideration of the possibilities of what we *want* to happen.[16]

The demise of formal strategic planning has led some organizations to say that their strategic objective is essentially to make money. Departments are given annual budgets, financial targets, market share objectives, and new product launch dates. Here, the shift in planning moves too far on different time and strategy dimensions. It makes no assumptions that the internal actions required and the complex organizational needs of a growing organization are in alignment.

Maximizing shareholder wealth or profit has *not* been the driving force or primary objective for organizations that have sustained growth over decades. While this may seem an anomaly, the reason for the absence of financial targets as the principal goal is that they provide no clue about the internal functions required of the organization to achieve them. Shareholder wealth and profit are the metaphorical equivalent of the oxygen, food, and water that the body requires. They are not the point of life, but without them, there is no life.

Does strategic planning still hold up as the essential process for managing the future? The classic approach is a complex process requiring that executives spend time on the development of a five-year plan and pray that the world around them remains relatively static during that period. For obvious reasons, that approach has taken a significant hit over the past decade; firms involved in disruptive technologies are lucky if they have visibility into the next year. As we have seen since the late 1990s, the rules of some industry games have changed dramatically. New entrants in digital technology can serve customers in ways not even dreamed of by more established firms with carefully scripted plans. Start-ups engage in seemingly irrational tactics—like giving stuff away—in their drive to grab market share. And for long-established firms committed to staying competitive, it means adopting bleeding-edge technology and integrating it seamlessly into daily business. Whatever the industry or tactical spin, the common denominator among all is unrelenting rapid change.

Larry Downes, one of the anti-strategic planning torchbearers, found in his studies that it is not poor planning that derails promising projects, but poor execution. "The No. 1 cause of death for e-business ventures inside traditional and established companies," he finds, "turns out to be the annual budget process. It tends to treat every IT initiative as a major effort, requires return-on-investment proof in twenty-four months or less, and offers little flexibility to quickly scale up (or down) if market conditions change dramatically between budget cycles."[17] These execution obstacles, for the most part, are either internal to the company or generated by outside forces within the industry. "Internal issues test the flexibility of companies to launch initiatives that represent significant departures from long-standing assumptions about who they are and what they do."[18] In the overwhelming majority of these cases, the culprit that led to failure of a scaling initiative within a nonscaling established firm was the overreliance on strategic planning and lack of a robust "growth vision."

The main point here is not that strategic planning is a waste, but engaging in this activity without a strategic vision from above will lead to a flawed planning process. Planning is critically important; just be sure it is guided by a vision.

From Strategic Planning to Managing with a Vision

The late Dave Case, CEO of San Francisco's fabled investment bank Hambrecht & Quist, which became part of J.P. Morgan Chase, reflected in 2001 on the inability of technology firms to sustain their scaling.

> They brought their technologies this far, but now they have to build foundations for endurance. We call it "wind sprints in the marathon," which means that sometimes you have to speed up but you can never slow down. The most important quality we look for as investment bankers is whether a company has a long-term, sustainable advantage and whether it has people with the will and the skill to execute against that.
>
> I worry that the Lego-construction-set approach to companies has gone too far. I worry that human ability to adapt and change and build teams and own a culture—and do that again and again, disconnecting and reconnecting—is reaching some kind of limit. If you look at the people who built great companies over long periods of time, they usually had great products and a great ability to spot a market. But what really made them scale was their unending commitment to finding and hiring great people who could work together—and their ability to take the long view.[19]

In the "old days," maybe twenty years ago, you could set a direction for your business, define a value proposition, then lumber along pursuing it. Today, you still need to define how you're going to be distinctive. But we now know that simply making that set of choices will not protect you unless you're constantly absorbing all of the available means to improve on your ability to deliver.

A lasting, winning strategy must involve differentiating an organization's value proposition from that of others. But broad, long-term strategies are not the result of analysis, technique, and simple tools. They are the product of a vision and the aspirations of the organization's leadership. This does not necessarily follow an obvious value proposition. Anyone who shops at Wal-Mart can experience Sam Walton's strategy, which came about because of his deep belief about the social desirability of helping people in small communities purchase popular retail goods at prices lower than they were accustomed to. Walton's emotional belief happened to be profitable, but that was secondary; he did not scour the competitive landscape in search of the most economically feasible value proposition.

Staying focused on an organization's purpose from a perspective of twenty thousand feet up, rather than on next quarter's revenue projections (i.e., from one hundred feet up), has often been characterized as the visionary approach, and the hard data from many studies over the past decade provide convincing evidence that vision is far from the "soft" side of management. On the contrary, organizations that leverage a growth vision are extraordinarily effective when measured by the typical financial metrics. Among its benefits, this approach provides a more flexible way to deal with the uncertain world of the scaling enterprise by establishing the broad outline of strategy, while leaving the details to be worked out. In other words, the expansive perspective is both deliberate and articulate, but the specific operating tactics are allowed to emerge. When the unexpected happens, assuming the vision is sufficiently robust, the organization can adapt.

Organizations that rely heavily on planning have a higher propensity to respond to changes appearing chaotic in a chaotic fashion, while firms more dependent on a vision react to the changes as part of the normal course of business. Mintzberg framed this more starkly: "If you have no vision but only formal plans, then unpredicted change in the environment makes you feel like your sky is falling."[20]

It is a myth that successful companies make their best moves by brilliant and complex strategic planning. Counterintuitive to standard business dogma is the realization that vision-driven companies find some of their most successful opportunities through experimentation, trial and error, opportunism, and sheer accident. Firms that meet the criteria for being "visionary" find their success in unpredictable ways, *not* through strategic planning. What looks in retrospect like brilliant foresight and preplanning was often the result of "Let's just try a lot of stuff and keep what works." In this sense, visionary companies mimic the biological evolution of species.

Our understanding about what works in contemporary organizations that have scaled successfully requires a philosophy that goes beyond the relatively limited framework of long-term planning. It compels individuals throughout the organization to have a sense of purpose and strategy, which involves identifying the unique values that must guide their collective behavior. We now realize that many of the bureaucratic controls intended to direct peoples' efforts had a profoundly negative impact on them and, particularly, on the scaling enterprises as a whole. If we can embrace a different approach that will help employees understand what the organization is trying to accomplish and provide guidelines for how they need to work day to day, they will be significantly more effective at making decisions and managing themselves without bureaucratic controls. We also know they will be more motivated, satisfied, and committed to the organization's need for growth.

Guiding Growth with a Vision

Building a venture today may seem like a cruel twist on the classic tortoise-versus-hare tale. However safe and convenient it would feel to move slowly, build a solid foundation, and keep the feel of a large but close family, it is a luxury few firms today can afford.

But scaling is enormously difficult. Forget the books showing smooth, linear line graphs that predict aggressive growth as an unbroken trajectory or a series of nicely rounded, proportionately formed oscillating waves. The experience of scaling an organization over time has about as much smoothness as sitting in a capsule atop an Atlas booster rocket as it launches from the pad and fights its way through earth's gravitational pull. The graceful curvilinear arc that observers on the ground admire in no way represents what it feels like sitting in that capsule.

Organizational growth is far from a smooth process. In a now-classic theory on organizational growth originally published in 1972 in *Harvard Business Review,* Larry Greiner described accelerated growth as nothing short of a *revolution.*[21]

The vivid picture painted by results from research dating back to the 1960s shows clearly how extended periods of growth are characterized more by near-catastrophic turbulence than by a universally smooth and predictable experience. Growth periods *are* times of revolution in the organization, typically distinguished by the unintended impact of management's practices, a serious upheaval in those practices, or both. The way management does its job, perhaps once acceptable for a smaller size and lower rate of growth, is no longer acceptable. Frustrated top-level managers and disillusioned lower-level supervisors now react to the strain and respond to the stress.

It is not simply a cruel irony that rapid growth can so weaken an organization; the real killer is not just growth but more specifically the aggressive *rate* and the length of *time* the scaling process is pursued. Rapid growth often stretches an organization's infrastructure past the breaking point and takes a tremendous toll on the human dimension of the firm. The image of being hurled through earth's atmosphere takes on a more tangible meaning to those who are in the midst of scaling-up.

The critical task for management during the revolution is to establish and maintain a set of organizational practices that will enable the firm to withstand the speed and long period of ascent. The need to hire employees, for example, accelerates the necessity to create new structures for accommodating large staff increases and meeting the ever-increasing skill sets while simultaneously keeping the organization nimble. Creating organizational structure while maintaining flexibility begins to feel like a sardonic oxymoron.

And if the organization can cope with this revolution and win in the short term, there still remains a forbidding probability that the subtle or obvious wear and tear of scaling will continue to strain the human systems. These signs may be apparent to everyone suddenly, with a precipitous fall in quarterly revenue, public image, or internal stability. But more often the danger signs are barely noticeable, evolving slowly, imperceptibly, over weeks, months, or years. They are generally unintentional on the part of management. But perhaps not: Danger signs may be passively allowed when they could be prevented, or they may be actively—though usually covertly—supported if key managers see them as furthering their personal agendas.

Inevitably, the revolution feels like a battlefield and, for most organizations, the scars of battle become apparent. Too often, the well-meaning management team will encounter symptoms of this revolutionary period, but it cannot recognize them as harbingers of larger problems. The whole is obscured by attention to isolated events and by failure to analyze them as indications of broader implications. The scaling organization usually becomes adept at handling crises by establishing elaborate problem-solving routines. The organization's real vulnerability, however, lies in its failure to monitor and identify many of these crises as part of a much larger picture representing the collateral damage from scaling.

A few large organizations are able to handle the perils of scaling. While hundreds of well-funded dot-coms cratered in 2000 and 2001, eBay expanded into new markets, grew revenues astronomically, and made a consistent profit.[22] It executed flawlessly in the wake of the crises that torrid growth brought on. It has stayed focused on a vision and has a talent infrastructure that understands and continually monitors the bigger picture.

Conventional wisdom has led us to believe that consistent growth in the long term is a chimera. It may be an intuitively appealing notion to account for the vast number of failures, but the truth is that relentless growth can be achieved. Case in point: A recent study examined companies with unbroken rates of growth. It started by identifying 3,700 U.S. and non-U.S. firms with revenues greater than half a billion dollars and found that while sustained growth is very difficult, achieving it is worth surviving the battle.

- Only 3.3 percent (122) had consistent profitable growth in the top line, bottom line, and shareholder returns for the 1990–1997 period.
- Less than 1 percent (21) had sustained this level of growth over the past twenty years.[23]

The data support the axiom that survival through a long period of consistent growth separates the fittest from all others. Yet it also provides insight to the value of accomplishing the seemingly impossible: These twenty-one highly successful growth companies outperformed the S&P 500 during the same time period with a 26 percent compound annual market cap growth as compared to an average 13 percent for all S&P companies. Their return to shareholders was twice the index. High risk—high reward.

Vision, while not a cure-all, goes a long way toward helping companies survive the growth process and positioning them for that long-term success.

The risk, of course, is that when an organization adapts a growth vision as its guide, it may lose some of its people. When the organization takes a strong stand on defining what it is, what it believes in, and how it will change the world, some people may leave. For the person who does not fit, the vision and the systems, structures, and practices that are influenced by it will serve as relentless reminders of the mismatch. The vision declares, "Here's what we're all about so you can decide if it's something you can commit yourself to. We're not determining that you have to commit; you decide whether or not you want to." It creates a transparent screening process in which people either find something meaningful in which to invest their energy and commitment—or they choose to leave. The important difference when compared to organizations operating without such a framework is that individuals here are in the position to *choose* whether they want to join the organization, help it realize its vision, and conduct their work in a way that everyone understands and agrees with.

The forward reach of an organization depends on how people in it perceive the need for growth. Both the vision that leadership sets out for them and the enthusiasm with which it is conveyed create a gap between what is (the current state) and what could be (the vision). From this comes the desire to create change. Leaders can crystallize and convey the raison d'être of an organization that wins commitment from others *if* they understand the business environment and the practices that will work for the people in their organization. They learn what works, what members of the organization find meaningful, and what the customer wants.

If the vision framework seems too burdensome for the CEO of a scaling operation, then reconsider Duncan Syme and Vermont Castings. Syme represents the typical entrepreneur struggling with the typical entrepreneurial conundrums of growth. Although he may have been perceived as a visionary leader, the dependency of everyone on him for the vision grossly reduced his effectiveness as leader. He had a vision—but the company he originally created did not. Everything depended on him. A real vision becomes the property of the entire organization and is infused throughout it by focusing on elements of the vision framework in such a way that it remains hardy and intact well after an individual leaves daily operations. In effect, the growth vision becomes embedded into the nooks and crannies of organizational life. When Syme created the "Statement" and infused it within the culture and daily decision processes, he created a mindset for Vermont Castings. The pressure on him lessened—because the vision could stand on its own.

Chapter Two

The Principles of Growth-Guiding Visions

Let's Start with Semantics

Whole Foods Market, founded in 1980 as a small store in Austin, Texas, has grown to become the world's largest retailer of natural and organic foods, with 122 stores in twenty-two states and the District of Columbia. "We are a grocery store," is how Whole Foods identifies itself in its brief company "description" on its Web site.

But the company's vision, officially titled the "Declaration of Interdependence," goes far beyond that bare-bones definition. First articulated and documented in 1985 by sixty employees who volunteered their time, it has been updated in 1988, 1992, and 1997. Whole Foods Market's vision includes phrases such as:

- "We earn profits every day through voluntary exchange with our customers."

- "We know that profits are essential to create capital for growth, job security and overall financial success. They are the 'seed corn' for next year's crop."

- "We see the necessity of active environmental stewardship so that the earth continues to flourish for generations to come."

- "We are not a fully self-sustaining ecosystem. There are hundreds of other businesses that we depend on to assist us in creating an outstanding retail shopping experience for our customers. We view our trade partners as allies in serving our stakeholders. We treat them with respect, fairness and integrity, and expect the same in return."

- "Satisfying all of our stakeholders and achieving our standards is our goal. One of the most important responsibilities of Whole Foods Market's leadership is to make sure the interests, desires and needs of our various stakeholders are kept in balance. We recognize that this is a dynamic process. It requires participation and communication by all of our stakeholders. It requires listening compassionately, thinking carefully and acting with integrity. Any conflicts must be mediated and win-win solutions found. Creating and nurturing this community of stakeholders is critical to the long-term success of our company."[1]

These phrases tell you a lot more about the company than "we are a grocery store." This vision statement outlines points that sound practical, even actionable. It's a document from which the entire company (its strategy, policies, processes, and people) can draw strength and direction. But the word *vision* on its own rarely conveys that kind of Monday-morning weight. Which brings me to a mundane but nonetheless important issue: choosing the right word for vision at your company. I use the term *vision* in this book only because it is the most general one for naming the construct. Many organizations, however, abstain from using the word because of negative connotations it has built up over the years from its misuse. Others want to distinguish their vision from other organizations' by putting a different label on it. Johnson & Johnson, for example, has referred to its vision as "The Credo" since the early 1940s; for Hewlett-Packard, it was "The HP Way" since 1957.

Call it what you will; the key point is to choose a label that makes sense to you and your peers in the organization and avoid labels that carry negative connotations, or "baggage." And read on with the following thought in mind: If a vision is to resonate with everyone in your organization, it must first make sense to you.

The Three Principles of Effective Visions

As I mentioned in chapter 1, an effective vision needs to articulate the organization's position on three core themes. These are the principles that guide the vision process.[2] While they may at first appear to be relatively independent, their interdependence becomes evident once the articulation process begins.

- Raison d'être—the organization's purpose, or reason for being
- Strategy—how that raison d'être will be achieved
- Values—the key assumptions, attitudes, and beliefs embodied by the organization and represented in the daily flow of activities necessary for moving it closer to the raison d'être and for supporting the strategy

Raison d'être

An organization's raison d'être is the essential reason why it exists and carries out its activities. "I think people assume, wrongly, that a company exists solely to have money," said Hewlett-Packard founder, David Packard, expressing his sense of the relationship between financial goals and purpose in an organization. "While this is an important result of a company's existence, we have to go deeper and find the real reasons for our being."[3]

Thinking about raison d'être in this context contrasts the theme with a term it is often confused with: mission. Let's clear up this point right away. The basic difference is that *mission* describes what the organization does, while *raison d'être* speaks more to *why* the organization exists and what it will look like as it works toward that high-level goal. While a mission may be a declaration of purpose and broad objectives, it is not one of direction. Missions commonly describe what business the organization is in and the markets and customers it serves. Although missions may rarely change over time, their delimiting nature has the impact of erecting borders around organizational activities and thereby has the potential to decelerate growth.

Taco Bell, for example, once defined itself as being in the Mexican fast-food business (a mission). To the people at Taco Bell, that definition came with a certain mindset regarding the delivery of their product. Fast food meant a free-standing "box" restaurant. Over the course of a decade, though, beginning in 1984, CEO John Martin pulled the firm's self-definition away from a particular product or market to being in "the business of feeding people" (more of a raison d'être). (To give in and use the pun, Martin helped the company think "out of the box.") This enabled the company to stake out new markets with thousands of new "points of access," such as stalls and kiosks in airports, malls, convenience stores, and the cafeterias of high schools and colleges. This simple shift away from a product-oriented mission that focused on a business domain (Mexican fast food) has had a dramatic bearing on new avenues for growth.[4]

A notion that originated in the business strategy field that I have found helpful to expand reflection on a firm's raison d'être is known as "outside in" thinking. Typical mission statements invariably represent "inside out" thinking: Executives see the future through the lens of current products and customers. This perspective starts with current assets, an organization, a core competence, perhaps a brand—and tries to build on it. The mission response can only be "What are we doing now and how can I explain it so it leads us to doing more of it?"

An outside-in perspective looks at the drivers of change. What are the needs of a current market and markets perhaps not even conceived of yet? What do people out in the world *need*? How are their needs changing? Many looking through this lens realize—with discomfort—that these changes imply that goods or services being produced today are on their way to being obsolete or becoming a subset of some new need. Companies with an enviable record of sustainable growth look at themselves from the perspective of their present and future customers. They ask what is happening in their marketplace, how needs are changing, what is causing the changes, and where the resulting opportunities lie.

Noel Tichy and Ram Charan, both well-known academics, consultants, and authors, have studied a number of huge organizations that continue to lumber along the growth path despite their size. They assert that "the greatest source of risk in a business is failure to understand the needs of the customer or end user. If people don't look from the outside in, external change will overtake them, no matter how much energy they lavish on their business. . . . Reach into your customers' thoughts, see their needs, and work backward. The rest is execution."[5]

I use a simple test to keep executives honest in determining whether they have really defined their raison d'être or whether they have merely engaged in a writing exercise that states a mission. They must continually ask: "Is this *what* our organization or division does, or is it clarifying *why* we are in business?" "What" tends to be about mission. "Why" is the vision.

The satirical cartoonist Roz Chast published one of her pieces in the *New Yorker* that she labeled, "The Tunnel of Why."[6] In the cartoon, an adolescent girl is facing her mother on the living room couch, and the dialogue bubbles above both their heads form a cyclic spiral:

DAUGHTER: Can Debbie sleep over?

MOTHER: No.

DAUGHTER: Why?

MOTHER: Because it's not a good night for a sleep over.

DAUGHTER: Why?

MOTHER: Because Grandma and Grandpa are coming.

DAUGHTER: Why?

MOTHER: Because we haven't seen them for a while.

DAUGHTER: Why?

MOTHER: Because they live far away.

DAUGHTER: Why?

. . . and on it goes, until—in excruciatingly small print—the mother ultimately reaches what I refer to as the "terminal answer." Anyone who has spent time with children can appreciate the Tunnel of Why. I am always amused that children are so motivated to find the terminal answer and so skilled at understanding what is required to get it. In most cases, it requires asking "why" three or four times in response to the initial answer. While some authors have formalized this technique as The Four (or Five) Whys, in my experience I find it is best used to the extent that it helps unravel a statement of mission to get at the true purpose behind it.[7] If a raison d'être describes *what* the organization does, then the resulting vision will be too constrained. If it describes *why* the organization is involved in its business activities, then a more challenging and far-reaching purpose is communicated.

Whole Foods Market, while casually referring to itself as a "grocery store," states in its Declaration that "our vision goes far beyond just being a food retailer." They see themselves as a dynamic leader in the quality food business, and success is "measured by customer satisfaction, Team Member excellence and happiness, return on capital investment, improvement in the state of the environment, and local and larger community support."[8] While some of the success metrics might be considered practical and measurable, others may be considered unrelated to business, if not downright sappy. But they are quantifiable and they all work because the performance metrics keep people focused on the larger purpose of the organization's existence.

Strategy

Too often, but understandably given the pressures of Wall Street and other stakeholders, not to mention the press, organizations formulate strategies in a knee-jerk reaction to current events and over time look back to assess the success of these strategies based solely on how well they matched subsequent events. The test should not be how well a strategy stands up to external events but *how well it enables the organization to remain viable and sustain its growth*. The driving force for strategy should be the raison d'être because without this larger purpose, strategy is limited to tactical maneuvering designed to win the current round of the game.

Whole Foods Market's strategy, as stated in its vision, includes the following:

- "Continually experiment and innovate in order to raise our retail standards. . . . Create store environments that are inviting, fun, unique, informal, comfortable, attractive, nurturing and educational. We want our stores to become community meeting places where our customers come to join their friends and to make new ones."

- "Design and promote safe work environments where motivated Team Members can flourish and reach their highest potential. And no matter how long a person has worked or plans to work with us, each and every Team Member is a valued contributor."

- "Grow at such a pace that our quality of work environment, Team Member productivity and excellence, customer satisfaction, and financial health continue to prosper."[9]

The vision also connects the company to its external environment:

- "[Our business is] intimately tied to the neighborhood and larger community that we serve and in which we live. The unique character of our stores is a direct reflection of the customers who shop with us. Without their support, both financial and philosophical, Whole Foods would not be in business. . . . We donate 5% of our after-tax profits to not-for-profit organizations. We have a program that financially supports Team Members for doing voluntary community service."

- "Satisfying all our stakeholders and achieving our standards is our goal. [Our leadership makes] sure the interests, desires and needs of our various stakeholders are kept in balance. We recognize this is a dynamic process. It requires participation and communication by all of our stakeholders. It requires listening compassionately, thinking carefully and acting with integrity. . . . Creating and nurturing this community of stakeholders is critical to the long-term success of our company."[10]

So, if looking from the outside-in yields a new set of needs demanded by the marketplace, then what is a different way of producing the product or delivering the service? How can these needs be met before anyone else develops the capacity? Can new needs be created?

United Parcel Service (UPS) would probably be aghast at seeing itself described as "the package delivery company." Its senior managers have unobtrusively been executing a far-reaching strategy to become much more than just a package handler. Over the years, they have put the company at the center of every crucial logistics step of its corporate clients' operations, from shipping the raw materials for a product to processing the payment for its final sale. Their strategy, in the spirit of a vision-related strategy, is to leverage technology so powerfully that they will morph into an organization that helps companies manage their supply chain, store their inventory, repair their products, answer their phones—and deliver their parcels. By 2002 this strategy, emanating from a noncore business, had already accounted for 25 percent of revenue and remains one of UPS's distinctive competencies.[11]

Values

How are values defined? What do they look like? They might be written down; more likely, though, they are part of the "genetic code" of an organization. They are the "norm"—"the way we do things around here."

For Whole Foods, values are seamlessly woven throughout its Declaration and they "are not values that change from time to time, situation to situation or person to person, but rather they are the underpinning of our company culture."[12] A small sample of its stated values includes the following:

- "We value experiments. Friendly competition within the company helps us to continually improve our stores. We constantly innovate and raise our retail standards and are not afraid to try new ideas and concepts."

- "We take responsibility for our own success and failures. We celebrate success and see failures as opportunities for growth."

- "We believe knowledge is power and we support our Team Members' right to access information that impacts their jobs. We also recognize everyone's right to be listened to and heard regardless of their point of view."[13]

The description of the firm's values is long and specific. The vision also provides direct linkages to action. For example, the organizational structure component of Whole Foods is guided by the following statement within its vision:

The fundamental work unit of the company is the self-directed Team. Teams meet regularly to discuss issues, solve problems and appreciate each others' contributions. Every Team Member belongs to a team.[14]

These values get passed down from one generation of management to the next. (It's no surprise that successful organizations with strong, working visions do a lot of "promoting from within.") They become an integral part of the selection, reward, and promotion mechanisms of the firm, and those who prosper do so because there is a natural fit between their abilities, their values, and the type of behavior that brings success in that particular organization. They do not prosper merely by being sycophants.

An intriguing question posed by researchers, including myself, is why the values of long-lived, continually growing organizations have remained stable and relevant over the years (I will examine this question further in the chapters that follow). Perhaps it is due to the visionary genius of the founders. They no doubt had their own notions of what it took to be successful in their particular fields, and their own personal values and belief systems reflected that notion. This in turn helped to shape their own basic blueprint for the kinds of people and the behavior that fit the nature of the business they wanted to create. Jim Casey, for example, who founded UPS in 1907, instilled the value of resourcefulness into the organization. Although UPS may appear conservative and old-fashioned to outsiders, this value has always been important to its culture. Resourcefulness has enabled UPS to continually evolve, grow, and remain sustainable beyond its original business foundation that involved delivering handwritten messages and telegrams, bail money for prisoners, and cocaine, morphine, and opium for Seattle's drug users.[15]

The values established by founders of firms remaining sustainable over the long term have a common theme: they are not constraining (e.g., "efficiency"). On the contrary, they are enabling (e.g., "innovation"). While long-held values continue to serve as guides to "the way we do things around here," the early struggles actually created a climate for collective learning that acted as a catalyst for each individual's continual development. In these organizations, it became possible for the original values to be revisited, and reinterpreted, in ways that remained not only true to the spirit of the founders but also relevant to the modern world. The core values did not change, and one value—*continual learning*—seems to be consistent across the sustained scalers.

The clarity of values stands out in these firms. These values serve, in effect, as permission statements—allowing people to act on their own for the good of the company. In my own consulting work I start with an assumption that employees want to do the right thing and all too often management refuses to let them do it.

The Burning Book. Gorden Bethune took over Continental Airlines in the mid-1990s as it gasped for last breaths on its deathbed. The firm had been managed by rules-bound managers for decades, a significant factor contributing to its severe *downward*-scaling condition. Prevalent throughout the organization was a nine-inch-thick manual that became known as the "Thou Shalt Not" book. Since it was so cumbersome, no one could be expected to know everything in it. The result? Employees played it safe by doing nothing at all. Shortly after joining Continental, the new leaders threw a copy of the book into a big drum, doused it with gasoline, and set it afire. It was a dramatic way to symbolize that people now had permission to think for themselves. The direction of Continental's scaling changed, and they not only stayed alive but grew consistently in revenue and profit.[16] (At the time of this writing, Continental was once again struggling, as were most airlines, in the wake of September 11, 2001.)

At The Container Store, the fast-growing seller of boxes, shelving, and closet supplies, the belief in granting permission to employees through its values is explicit in its "Permission Statement." That's one reason the company's turnover is less than half that of the average retailer. Any sales clerk, cashier—any employee—who gets a customer request or problem has the permission to solve it. While the notion of "permission" may help an organization avoid getting hung up on little things due to an overreliance on rules and bureaucracy, the real benefit is that it creates the opportunity to do big things. Scaling organizations must be nimble enough to continually conceive of and implement the big things.

Consistent, clear, and shared values affect personal and organizational effectiveness. For example, I and other researchers and consultants have found that when people are able to quickly understand the values behind their organization's culture, they adjust more quickly to their jobs. In turn, they tend to have higher levels of satisfaction and commitment. When the fit between individual and organizational values is a snug one, and when these values are made explicit, job satisfaction goes up and organizational turnover goes down.[17]

Visions need to reflect and be consistent with an organization's values and ideals, but they should go well beyond being philosophical statements. They must enable others to imagine easily what the values look like in action. By doing so, the link between values and the preferred behaviors required for the success of an organization is obvious from an employee's first day.

From an Idea to a $250 Million Business. In 1978, Kip Tindell and Garrett Boone founded The Container Store to help people streamline and simplify their lives by offering an extraordinary mix of storage and organization products. They wanted to help people save space, and ultimately, time. Since their beginning, the firm has continued to expand strategically from coast to coast; retail sales increased at a consistent average of 20 to 25 percent each year, from 1978 to 2000 and expected sales for 2001 should hit at least $265 million.[18]

For Boone and Tindell (now Chairman and CEO/President, respectively) the goal was never about growth for growth's sake. Rather, their focus was on adherence to a set of core values centered around deliberate merchandising, superior customer service, and constant employee input. They will both tell you that growth and success have been a natural and inevitable result.

Boone and Tindell are both fully immersed in the company's operations. It is not unusual to find them in stores interacting with employees and customers. And, while it may seem a waste of time for the CEO and Chairman of a burgeoning retail empire to be selling, dusting shelves, and helping customers with carryouts, leaders who walk the talk tend to have employees who reflect their passion.

Therefore, it's no surprise that The Container Store has been number 1 on *Fortune*'s "100 Best Companies to Work For" list in both 2000 and 2001.[19] Although the saying "employees are our greatest asset" has become hackneyed, eliciting cynicism and snickers from employees within most organizations, Tindell and Boone continue to say that employees are their greatest asset. And their actions say it even louder. One of The Container Store's core business values is that "three good people equal one great person." How does this value become transformed into policy and procedure? They stay focused on hiring only great people in an industry that struggles to find the acceptable—let alone good or great.

When it comes to selecting who will join their team, they go to great lengths to find the perfect person to fill the position. Most employees are college educated and became acquainted with the firm as customers first. While they come from varied backgrounds with significant depth and abilities, what they really have in common is their passion for the organization. It's no surprise. The values drive sophisticated employee development programs, succession systems that carefully match employees' strengths with the company's needs, and a focus on talent (identifying it; developing it) rather than titles.

Take, for example, the company's explicitly stated core value of customer service. This shows up on the radar of most organization's "nice to tell the world" tactical positions, but rarely is it woven into the organizational fabric as it is at The Container Store. It seems natural that customer service is also one of its core competencies. The company spends much time and energy ensuring that the people it hires are self-motivated and develops the kind of teams that result in a passion for service. How does this happen? Every first-year, full-time salesperson receives about 235 hours of training—in a retail industry where the annual average is about seven. After this, the training continues in other forms: all full-time employees are trained one on one on how to best serve and sell to their customers and are involved in training others on the features, advantages, and benefits of each product. At The Container Store, service equals selling; performance is measured by the quality of service and not by the volume of sales. Commissions on sales would be antithetical to the core value. (An approach for defining the principles covered in the previous sections, within the context of your own organization, is shown in box 2-1.)

From Concept to Communication to Implementation

When senior managers complete the development of a vision, they generally feel a sense of relief and accomplishment. On some level they believe that once it is announced to the organization, the job is finished. They expect that the vision will produce transformation. Often, the group responsible for its development becomes detached from the vision process once the initial work is done.

That's a mistake. Because in order for a vision to take hold in an organization, the rollout must be a lively process that reflects and in some sense mirrors the process that created it. In other words, rather than a "thing" that people are expected to mechanically buy into, vision implementation must be a *process* that involves learning what people most care about in a way that creates enthusiasm and shared commitment.[20]

It's not uncommon that the vision is unveiled and produces no tangible results. When this happens, management's knee-jerk reaction is to rationalize the breakdown or false starts by claiming that "people resist change." It's true that vision rollouts often are met with resistance, but this has become such a pervasive pretext for organizational change failures that it is typically accepted without challenge. Skirting the problem in that way won't get you anywhere.

Instead, you have to design a process for involving people so they can better understand and subscribe to a vision—a process that forces them to confront it and rationalize it as part of their daily work. This requires a rigorous communications process led by the executive group. While chapter 6 will more fully address the role of this group, vision deployment is best accomplished when managers articulate the current reality with clarity and honesty. Events are discussed as they really are, rather than as they are wished to be. Somewhere between current reality and the vision lies an "abyss" that must be traversed to reach the desired future.

An effective leader makes the abyss visible to everyone in the organization. The ability to recognize deficiencies in the current modus operandi, to present them in a way that most employees would find problematic, and to effectively communicate a more attractive alternative is the most important characteristic of the "charismatic" leader.[21] For example, if the firm consistently fails to exploit new technologies or new markets, this might be highlighted as a strategic opportunity. Similarly, a charismatic entrepreneur might more readily perceive marketplace needs and transform them into opportunities for new products or services *if* he or she convincingly communicates *why* the status quo is inadequate and *why* the vision will create a better scenario. The more idealized the future goal advocated by an organizational leader, and the more discrepancy people perceive between that vision and the status quo (the abyss), the more likely that employees will see the vision as appealing rather than as an ordinary goal. The abyss must be clear to everyone in the organization.

Whole Foods Market explicitly acknowledges the discrepancy between current reality and its vision. It ends its "Declaration of Interdependence" with the following:

> Our Vision Statement reflects the hopes and intentions of many people. We do not believe it always accurately portrays the way things currently are at Whole Foods Market so much as the way we would like things to be. It is our dissatisfaction with the current reality, when compared with what is possible, that spurs us toward excellence and toward creating a better person, company and world. When Whole Foods Market fails to measure up to its stated Vision, as it inevitably will at times, we should not despair. Rather let us take up the challenge together to bring our reality closer to our vision. The future we will experience tomorrow is created one step at a time today.[22]

Many well-developed visions fail during initial deployment because they do not strategically address ways to bridge the abyss. Bridging the gap between current reality and a desired future requires thinking and acting on multiple levels. The first step is confronting roadblocks. Many of these roadblocks are ones you set up for yourself. Chapter 3 will discuss roadblocks that trip up many of us and ways to counteract them.

Trigger Questions to Get at the Heart of the Three Vision Elements

Raison d'être

- What business(es) are we in?
- What unique value do we bring to our customers?
- What are our most important opportunities?
- What is the gap between our current or prospective customers' current and future needs?
- For whose benefit are all our efforts?
- Who cares about our success? What is our relationship to each of these groups? What can they expect from us?
- What is our own self-concept?
- What is our desired public image?
- What is happening in the world outside our organization that may impact our business?
- What external trends are occurring that may affect the needs, expectations, and desires of key stakeholders (employees, customers, suppliers, etc.)?
- What major contribution will we make to the communities we work in and serve?

Strategy

- What do we have to do extraordinarily well to compete or succeed?
- How do we bring unique value to our customers?
- How do we expect to serve the future needs of our customers?
- In what ways are we unique?
- What do employees want or deserve in exchange for their efforts?
- How do employees see one another?
- What do we believe about the importance of developing our people as opposed to hiring developed people?
- What is this organization good at?
- What is this organization's competitive advantage over others in the industry?

(continued)

- How will the nature and intensity of rivalry change in the industry?
- How will products/services be developed?
- How should we treat customers?
- What reputation(s) should the organization be known for?
- What should competitors respect and envy the most?
- What are the customers'/clients' experiences?
- Does the strategy drive growth?

Values

- What are some of the most important values we want all employees of this organization to bring to the work they do?
- What values lie at the heart of the most important promises we make to our customers/clients?
- What values serve as the hallmark of our service?
- What values might best capture our reputation and how we want to be seen by our customers in the marketplace?
- What are the core values or beliefs for how business should be conducted that will not be compromised?
- What will I see and hear that will characterize the values coming to life, day-to-day?
- What organizational achievements have meaning for me?
- What should be the hallmarks of all our managers?
- How will small problems be prevented from becoming big problems?
- How and where are employees performing work and serving customers/clients?
- What are employees saying to their closest friends and family about what it is like to work here?

Chapter Three

Dangers of Growing without a Vision

I N CHAPTER 1, I TALKED A BIT ABOUT WHAT CAN happen when a company doesn't have a coherent, effective vision. In this chapter, I dig deeper into that topic. The bulk of this book is devoted to creating a vision and implementing a process in preparation for growth. But I've found in my client work that before most managers can commit to growing an organization that is driven by vision, they need to recognize the characteristics of a company without vision. Why? Because in doing so, they often recognize mindsets of their own or practices that exist in their companies that are roadblocks to the vision process.

In other words, it's worth spending some time dwelling on the negative so that you'll be more aware of your own circumstances and context as you move forward.

The Strain of Scaling

Nowhere is a lack of vision more apparent than in a company that is trying to grow quickly. Just ask Seth Goldstein, a major player in New York's Internet development scene—and recognized as one of Silicon Alley's stars—when his name became linked to the carnage from the devastating collapse of the dot-com bubble. Several of the companies he had guided in his role as Entrepreneur in Residence at Flatiron Partners—one of the East Coast's most respected new venture capital (VC) firms—had tanked, abruptly. Among them was Internet Appliance Network (IAN), a technology service provider and branded hardware designer that Goldstein had himself conceived and founded. In the first days of 2001, Goldstein reflected on the roller coaster he had been riding for the past year:

> In so many cases, the failures didn't need to happen. IAN, particularly, should not have gone down. Sure, the capital markets were cratering around us. But money was in the bank for these companies. And, unlike many other VCs, Flatiron understood the need to provide intangible support systems. We believed in the business models; they were filling a recognized niche. Something less obvious was responsible for these failures.[1]

Internet Appliance Network went down as the dot-com bubble burst, but it was not just another dot-com with a solution in search of a market's problem. The needs for its products and services, recognized by independent market data, were emerging at warp speed. The company's business model was based on the increasing pervasiveness of the Internet, and IAN's hardware and software designers developed an appliance capable of surfing the Web and performing e-mail functions. One twist that made the model unique: IAN provided the appliance and ISP service for free as long as the user was willing to charge a minimum amount to a sponsor's credit card and see the sponsor's browser home page every time they logged on. The company had been strategically agile, continually transforming over its eighteen-month life to meet users' needs. IAN had drawn intense interest from Fortune 500 firms. Global behemoths wanted to partner with it. Very smart people were at the helm managing. And, despite rapid growth at its home base in New York and the acquisition of a software application business in California and a hardware development operation near Boston, its cash burn had been consistently below projections. There was money in the bank. What's more, the company had been partnering with its first famous brand, Richard Branson's Virgin Group, and even as IAN entered what was to be its final quarter, prospects for the next level of financing had looked promising.

IAN had been Goldstein's baby; he had assembled the initial group of managers to run it and had remained deeply involved as a board member. Failure weighed heavily on him. He was right when he said that "something less obvious" than the failed companies' business models were responsible for their downfall.[2] And, hindsight being 20/20, he later nailed the problem. Not one of the companies that failed had used a vision to hold it together as it attempted the kind of rapid growth that investors—and the market—demanded. Sure, each of the companies had a vague founding vision—but in most cases, that vision had never made it out of the founder's head and into the mindset of the organization as a whole. IAN was the strongest case in point.

Goldstein's vision for the future of pervasive computing had led to IAN's conception and its ultimate birth as Flatiron's first incubated firm. Once the founding executive group was hired, however, he began to relinquish his role as vision-bearer. The process had been difficult; backing away from developing and executing strategy tested his trust in others. But, when the management team was up and running, Goldstein's official role shifted to board director, and the job of further articulating the vision and communicating it to the ever-increasing employee base was now someone else's responsibility. The problem was that Goldstein and the new management team had never invested the time to solidify the vision to begin with. "Further" articulation wasn't possible because initial articulation had never happened.

You can't blame Goldstein for his inability to pinpoint the problem when he was immersed in the day-to-day business of funding and advising a whole string of new companies. As VCs go, Goldstein had abundant experience and seniority in the nascent industry of Web-related products and services. He had founded Site Specific, an Internet marketing agency that was ranked one of the top five interactive agencies by the time he sold it to the CKS Group in May 1998. (CKS was acquired in September of that year by USWeb and the new entity was renamed "Reinvent Companies.")

Goldstein knew the lay of the land as well as anyone, and better than most.

He was even a believer in vision. But he lacked the understanding of how to integrate "vision" into the daily demands of leading and then guiding a fast-growing business. The highs and lows of each day—the crises, the opportunities, the day-to-day management tasks—pushed vision to the back burner. Goldstein remembers,

> In IAN's case, senior managers quickly reached a point where they no longer agreed on a direction about the firm's future. They couldn't embrace a set of core values to create a healthy culture for IAN—and the culture was already becoming solidified organically on its own. The absence of focus on the "soft" stuff, things related to the vision, was worrying me more than the "harder" business issues. I could see IAN needed a clear vision to sail through the rough seas; I just didn't know how to influence executive management to focus on it. It was a race against time and I felt we were losing it.[3]

The VC markets began to crater just after IAN formally launched its product. Nerves among members of the executive group were becoming frayed as the impending collision of fewer pipelines of cash from outside investors was about to hit head-on with the need for greater funding. As tension mounted, the executive group agreed less and less on IAN's raison d'être. The question, "What business are we in?" elicited different answers each week from the executive group and, in short order, everyone in the company was wondering "What business *are* we in?"

The Illogical Nature of Organizational Growth

While Goldstein spent sleepless nights worrying about the crash course IAN seemed set on, many of his peers were similarly engaged and similarly frustrated at their inability to pinpoint—and solve—the problems in their organizations. Many of the organizations that were encountering insurmountable difficulties up and down New York's Silicon Alley in the early 1990s had the same problem: the lack of an effective, embedded vision at the crucial juncture where scaling meets speed.

Consider what drives a company to grow. David Packard, the cofounder of Hewlett-Packard (HP), wrote in his memoirs that over the years he and Bill Hewlett had "speculated many times about the optimum size of a company."[4] They "did not believe that growth was important for its own sake" but eventually concluded that "continuous growth was essential" for the company to remain competitive.[5] One reason growth was a matter of survival was because HP "depended on attracting high caliber people" who wanted to "align their careers only with a company that offered ample opportunity for personal growth and progress."[6] Growth for the sake of attracting and keeping great people would become a factor for virtually all firms in technology-driven fields. When the firm introduced *The HP Way* in 1957—essentially a manifesto for its future—it emphasized growth "as a measure of strength and a requirement for survival."[7]

Most companies understand that growth is essential for survival—for the very reasons Packard put so succinctly above. But few know how to reconcile the need for growth with the external and internal pressures to grow very quickly. Building any large and sustainable corporation requires a considerable organizational transformation rather than a predictable set of linear stages. Building it quickly diminishes the odds that it can weather the growing pains of that transformation.

"More businesses die from indigestion than from starvation," Packard said.[8] But *The HP Way* was more than a mandate for growth. It articulated such a comprehensive and enduring vision for the company that its principles and values have remained virtually unchanged and served as a beacon to guide the firm until Carly Fiorina took the reins in July 1999.

Start-ups are not just large businesses in miniature, and their trajectories do not necessarily point to either size or longevity. Rather than relying on opportunistic adaptation to exploit niche opportunities, their existence depends much more on formulating and implementing ambitious strategies that prepare the firm for the longer term. Put another way, the transition of a fledgling business into a large, well-established corporation requires nothing less than a series of fundamental yet relatively seamless transformations. Well-articulated visions guide these transformations so they are not experienced as traumatic surprises.

Unfortunately, there are relatively few exceptional entrepreneurs with the capacity to conceptualize, articulate, and relentlessly manage with a vision and survive the steep challenges wedded to accelerated growth. But a direct correlation exists between the entrepreneurial competency of vision management and the rate at which firms can successfully grow and sustain themselves. And fortunately, this competency can be learned.

Wrestling with the Enigma of Sustainability

We're at Amazon.com. It's December 2000. Gone are the days of "Get Big Fast" and firmly in place is the new Bezos motto: "Make some great cash, baby."[9] Instead of looking for ways to grow sales, employees look for ways to save money.

After losing a total of $1.74 billion and having borrowed $2 billion to "get big fast," by 2000 it was time to pay attention to process and a new set of values.[10] CEO Jeff Bezos put Amazon through a massive overhaul by slashing spending, revamping the culture, laying off people, and hiring brilliant executives from some of the world's best-run companies to teach Six Sigma (a system for measuring and creating continual quality enhancements) and inventory management. And in the space of barely one year, Amazon became a more effective retailer as the result of a transformation that created efficient processes and established core values to support these new processes. There is no guarantee this will lead to Amazon's long-term sustainability but Bezos continues to make the case that Amazon is fundamentally a different animal from other retailers, that it is a pioneer playing itself out in fashion that economist Joseph Schumpeter predicted in the 1930s: the incremental "morphing" of products and organizational processes due to innovation and competitive pressures.[11]

While Bezos crafted a founding vision that enabled the investment community and consumers to see clearly what Amazon was trying to do, it nonetheless had some critical pieces missing—such as elements of the strategy and articulation of values—that may have prevented some of the gross inefficiencies. What might have happened if Bezos's vision for Amazon was as comprehensive in 1998 as it is in 2002?

Now we're at PeopleSoft in 2000. Another turnaround story. PeopleSoft, the enterprise software maker founded in 1987 that scaled to extraordinary heights and became a Wall Street darling with founder Dave Duffield at the helm, nearly crashed in 1999. That was when the market for giant software packages handling everything from employee benefits to inventory management lost its luster. As CEO for eleven years, Duffield had a vision for the type of friendly culture he wanted for workers and customers. And that culture was enormously successful when measured against performance metrics such as revenue, profit, sales/employee, flow of new releases, and customer satisfaction. But that vision—limited to the cultural aspects of the organization—wasn't enough to help the company negotiate the market's downturn.

In early 1999, sales plummeted, the stock tanked, and the firm was on the edge of ruin. In June 1999, Craig Conway was brought in as the new CEO with the drive to instill new values and develop new processes. For example, customers were now asked—if not pushed—to pay their bills on time; product development strategy was recast; and salaries and option vesting schedules were overhauled to stem the flight of great talent.

The result: Revenue and profits have rebounded, attrition has been cut to 10 percent from 30 percent, and the stock zoomed 191 percent during 2000, the NASDAQ's worst year.[12] While much of the company's decline can be attributed to the depressed market for enterprise software systems, culture also played a role. Unless a significant mindset change happened within the firm, it would never have returned to health.

To bring PeopleSoft back, Conway walked a tightrope. He kept the parts of Duffield's warm and fuzzy culture that made sense to him, but drew the line at tolerating the sloppiness in process that had gone unnoticed eighteen months earlier. Has he created a vision that can lead to sustainability? The jury is still out, but the outlook for PeopleSoft is a lot better as I write this chapter than it has been in a long time.

Amazon and PeopleSoft have both wrestled with the enemies that conspire against scaling-up: Most pressing is the need to refine and execute a vision that will maximize process capabilities on a massive scale and in a narrow time frame.

Think back to Internet Appliance Network (IAN). The company was not taken down just because there was a market shift away from dot-coms. Along with other firms, IAN rode the Internet wave, looking for opportunities for its new technology and marketing acumen. The dynamics of the marketplace enabled the company to prosper at the outset because demand far outstripped available supply (and money was easy to buy). But waves crest, and as market imbalances disappear so too do new firms that have depended on their original resources to satisfy amorphous customer needs in the shadows of even-hungrier start-ups.

Without a growth vision to articulate the raison d'être and necessary organizational processes and values, firms are less able to stay ahead of the market's whims; their one great idea may become their last idea. Absent a growth vision, aggressive start-ups fade away as one-hit wonders.

The Related Causes of Failure

About 60 percent of start-ups fail in the first six years and more than 70 percent in the first eight.[13] Most of the survivors remain small, but smallness is acceptable only in the rare cases when an entrepreneur or parent organization has patient investors not demanding a significant return in a relatively short period of time.[14] For the overwhelming majority of firms capitalized by outsiders, however, staying small is a death knell; that is, these are ventures that have not yet failed but have slim prospects of providing the return originally expected by both the VCs and the entrepreneur. In industries such as e-commerce and most technology fields generally, being small is as good as being dead.

"There are a hundred reasons for success and a thousand reasons for failure," a VC sighed to me the day after he shuttered one of his portfolio companies. I disagree. There are likely a thousand variations of a far fewer number of reasons for failure. In fact, as I reflected on the firms that failed because of scaling, and outlined organizational obituaries from their histories, I realized that underlying the vast majority of these failures were five related causes. And that absent a comprehensive vision, there is no way to combat them.

The "I'm Right, the World's Wrong" Mind-Set

Entrepreneurs have a tendency to blame others for business problems rather than holding themselves accountable. This is an ironic twist, since decision makers like to project the sense of being in control.

They more frequently attribute failure of their own ventures to external factors, such as competitive market conditions and financing problems, in contrast to VCs who more frequently attribute failure to internal factors, particularly management inadequacies. Nonetheless, when entrepreneurs consider the failure of ventures other than their own, they more frequently attribute the poor performance to internal factors. Failed entrepreneurs attribute their troubles to external causes over 85 percent of the time.[15] Were they really responsible only for 15 percent of failures? This difference between the lack of accountability entrepreneurs take for failure and the actual rate of fault that belongs on their shoulders can profoundly affect which solutions are pursued when a venture starts to go down. If the assessment by entrepreneurs points to issues outside the organization, then why bother changing organizational components under management's control?

Entrepreneurs also seem to think that attributing their problems to external factors is the best strategy for negotiating with a VC. If they can convince the VC that their firm's problems come from the outside, then the VC will be more likely to help them ride out the storm. But VCs expect a decision maker—the person leading the growing firm—to be in control. The entrepreneur who displaces blame onto external factors is viewed as signaling an inability to realistically appraise the situation. VCs tend to view internal factors as causing failure, so requesting more capital to alleviate the problem results in the VC becoming uncomfortably skeptical about the leader's ability to fix the problem, and the ultimate survival of the venture itself.

This chain of displacement and perceptions can hasten the venture's demise and lead to an unfortunate self-fulfilling prophecy: When the entrepreneur wrongly blames external factors for the firm's problems, one crucial external factor—the VC—may become its ultimate problem if the cash spigot gets shut off.

The Liability of Newness

The most appealing and least daring explanation for failing to scale-up and remain sustainable is to attribute failure to a phenomenon known as the *liability of newness*. The risks of newness result from a wide variety of sources but we almost instinctively point to the invention itself—a new product or service. Although common sense would indicate that failure is higher for pioneers than for late followers (which is true), it would also let us believe that causes underlying the liability of newness would be attributed to competitive dynamics within the marketplace as it relates to the new product or service (which is false).

Actually, the risks arising from newness appear to result from a much wider variety of sources that are not weighted on product or market share issues as most believe. There are of course concerns about the level of refinement of the new product or service but factors *internal* to the organization take center stage when we analyze those who succumbed to the liability of newness.

Research again throws the spotlight on senior management as the key factor behind the liability of newness.[16] Management tends to pay little attention to the need for a consciously developed organizational culture, to create structures that support current but not future needs, and to ignore conflicts regarding evolving and new roles. Most important, management lacks clarity for how the organization's vision relates to peoples' roles and behaviors. In the overwhelming number of cases, no vision has ever been articulated. Executive management teams tend to have an outward focus, consumed with ensuring that the new product or service is accepted and gains increasing levels of market share. But the liability of newness blindsides them. They fail to pay sufficient attention to what's going on within the house.

This phenomenon further compounds entrepreneurs' "I'm Right, the World's Wrong" tendency to avoid accountability for acknowledging and managing strategic issues within the firm.

Uncoordinated Transformations

A new firm can maintain its desired rate of expansion only to the extent that it has seamless coordination of internal mechanisms. The problems of coordination, such as with the rapid addition of new locations and employees, are directly proportional to the rate of growth. An organization's capacity to digest new additions and activities depends on a complex set of organizational processes. It's difficult to add people and customers at an extremely fast rate without diminishing the quality of output or running out of cash. Unfortunately, many of the mechanisms chosen or allowed to evolve are grossly ill suited to the firm. Failure to define processes for recruitment, selection, motivation, control systems, and development of values within the organizational culture are some of the missteps that create chaos rather than provide relatively coordinated transformations. Ultimately, they crush any hope of sustainability.

A profound change in an organization that is growing quickly is the way in which each person who began with the firm must now change as the organization is changing. Days of seat-of-the-pants management are gone. Managers must learn how to work at a strategically higher and faster level and to define the principles that identify the people who should be hired and fired. They must learn, quickly, how to create structures so the company can spend serious money while taking bigger risks for bigger returns. Just as important, they must learn to let go of traditions and established practices in favor of more professional practices.

The Fantasy That There's a Map

In one analysis of the growth patterns of entrepreneurial ventures—the clearest example of a scaling organization—51 percent of the companies progressed sequentially, following a traditional linear pattern of development and growth. That means 49 percent of thc firms skipped the traditional stages of development one might assume to be necessary.[17] With nearly half the successfully scaled firms not following any model that explains or predicts growth stages, it stands to reason that models accepted and used in the past may be poor predictors of successfully scaled organizations overall. A slew of "growth stage models" exists but most are based on anecdotal observations rather than rigorous research.[18]

Blistering growth unfortunately does not follow a tidy linear progression. The stages or patterns vary when successfully scaled organizations are analyzed. No "stage" model has been shown to be sufficiently predictive. Executives who believe their firms will experience "predictable" challenges during the scale-up and who use these predictions as a guide for forecasting, planning, and decision making may end up focusing on an important challenge but at the wrong time.

There is no universal road map that guides scaling. Only the road map that results from managing a unique, comprehensive vision can predict whether a scaled firm will sustain itself.

The Struggle to Maintain the Family

Watching a start-up scale without an adequate vision is a familiar scene: As the need for processes and values takes center stage, old rules disappear, time runs out, work life and personal life at times become indistinguishable, and corporate gestures that used to mean one thing can mean the opposite. A warm family atmosphere where everyone knew each other and virtually everything seemed to be public knowledge becomes an environment where silence replaces the easy, informal communications. To compensate for that silence, which is unintentional yet inevitable, a plethora of ad hoc processes are set in place. Reporting systems, budgets, and performance reviews—which may be far from consistent—attempt to direct each person's behavior. Where the easy, informal communications channels begin to fade in place of more formal chains of command and departmental silos, people begin to feel overlooked if not abandoned by upper management.

As the firm launches, the environment feels intimate. Everyone knew who was getting married, having babies, caring for a sick parent. But the venture has to get bigger, add more systems, and implement more controls. What used to happen spontaneously now happens systematically. Through e-mail and voice mail, perhaps even with stringent reporting structures and weekly meetings, everyone may know everyone else's business—but they no longer know everyone else's name. The venture begins as a team or family and, as it scales, becomes an impersonal company. People within will likely remain strangers to one another in spite of the desire and hard work by some to keep the memory and spirit of the family alive. Often, the people who left a big corporation to become part of a start-up realize the firm is evolving into something all-too-familiar and distasteful.

Facing the Enemy

If we step back, consider these five causes of failure, and connect the thematic dots common among them, a picture emerges of the firm's biggest enemy to survival: its own executive management team. It may be a founding entrepreneur, a COO hired to "bring discipline" to the original vision, or the entire team. These hard-working people have enormous responsibilities for managing the liability of newness, coordinating organizational transformations, and determining which growing pains to address at different times. If correct and timely actions are not taken to address these issues, the team will probably fail at one or another goal. And when they do, there is the probability—however unintended and well meaning—to hold someone or something else accountable.

Leading a scale-up is difficult for even the most talented managers. The five causes of failure seem to conspire against these leaders to make their job even more complex. But if they incorporate the creation of a vision into the mix of their responsibilities early on, and are vigilant about its maintenance and relevance to evolving circumstances, they will find themselves working from a position of strength. They'll be better able to recognize and deal with the kinds of circumstances, mindsets, and tensions that otherwise could bring them down. Chapter 4 details the fundamentals of vision creation.

Chapter Four

The Vision Development Process

L UCY KELLAWAY, *FINANCIAL TIMES* JOURNALIST, aptly reflected what many managers feel about vision when she wrote "the very idea of visions—and missions and value statements and all the rest of it—has always made me feel uncomfortable. The jargon is repulsive and the idea of distilling a complex pragmatic world of business into a few sentences has always seemed a peculiar thing for anyone to want to do."[1]

A study by the strategy consulting firm Bain & Company in 1995 only seems to buttress her negative view. "Visioning," Bain found, was the most popular of all the strategic management tools used by companies, but despite its high utilization among a portfolio of similar tools, it ranked only fourth when it came to measures of satisfaction linked with its use.[2]

As we search continually for the Holy Grail of business success, the idea of corporate vision, in some corners, has assumed near-magical properties. The consequence has been a veritable worldwide vision *industry,* which has understandably left some people disillusioned and others questioning the fundamental validity of the concept.

Part of the problem, of course, is the hype. Any management tool, given its fifteen minutes of fame, inevitably suffers from misplaced expectations as to what it can do for your company and how fast. But another part of the problem is the natural tendency to expect immediate tangible results from the effort put into the vision development process. I mentioned this phenomenon in chapter 3 under "The Related Causes of Failure." Disillusionment with visioning is experienced by many senior teams when they realize that the ultimate "product" produced by the effort to create a vision is actually a dynamic, ongoing process. Invariably, "visioning exercises," although talked about as a process, end up as events that have as their goal the construction of a "vision statement," which is bounded and restrictive in its use. Understanding and accepting that *visions are not created so that they can be achieved precisely* is one of the most difficult hurdles to overcome in the vision-building process. Whole Foods Market, for example, considers its vision statement as a living document not as a binding contract.

The greatest roadblock on the way to creating an effective vision, though, is the negative part of the binary response, which stems from your own level of discomfort with the process. Your resistance (albeit sometimes subconscious) is the first and biggest hurdle you need to get over.

Prerequisites

One of two scenarios typically unfolds when a senior manager and his or her team set out to create a vision. The first (and most common) is that the managers rapidly become uncomfortable with the process, and, unable to rationalize their discomfort, succumb to their own resistance and quit before they ever feel the traction of real progress.

The second scenario (the one we're aiming to achieve) is that the managers rapidly become uncomfortable with the process, but, understanding that their own resistance is part of the process, persevere and ultimately create an effective vision.

I often compare the aptitude required for developing an effective organizational vision to that required for becoming an accomplished artist. Art requires innate talent—some are born with it and require relatively little formal training to express what is in their mind's eye. Others, by virtue of genetic misfortune, have little talent but persevere (through formal training, practice, sheer determination) to accommodate this natural deficiency. Perhaps, over time, they develop talent or seek ways to extract it.

Once in a while, a senior manager will "take to" the vision-creating process instinctively, but that's rare. I can't hammer home this point enough: Most of you are *not* going to like the process at all, but you will likely find it to be one of the most challenging, frustrating, yet insightful experiences of your career if you have the fortitude to stay with it and stay aware of the traps that can thwart your progress.

Often, I find that the most valuable point of departure for anyone poised to embark on defining their organization's vision is to first reflect on these four prerequisites to any successful vision development process:

1. Accept that the process is, by nature, imprecise, frustrating, and tedious.

2. Live in the past, the present, and the future—simultaneously.

3. Acknowledge the downside of having an entrepreneur at the helm of a growing organization (particularly if you are an entrepreneur/CEO).

4. Acknowledge emotion.

Accept That the Process Is, by Nature, Imprecise, Frustrating, and Tedious. Acknowledging that the process of developing a growth vision is an imprecise, frustrating, and tedious one represents a major step to overcoming resistance. The process involved is antithetical to the way most people in organizations, particularly senior managers, would prefer to communicate and make daily decisions. While some tomes on leadership acknowledge that the process should be soul-searching, they also imply that it be consensus-based and experienced as a relatively easy one. Once senior management is prepared to release the latest version of the vision, there is an expectation that everyone will sing "Kumbaya" and celebrate the emerging future. This hardly represents reality.

Conceptualizing a vision is rarely spiritual and pleasant, and those who have struggled through the required stages find that the process itself can be more enlightening and revealing about the organization's strategic future than the well-crafted verbiage they commit to writing. Be forewarned: The process is a creative and often chaotic one, requiring a series of iterations. It defies linear thinking and requires a mental capacity for synthesis and imagination, something that is unfortunately underdeveloped in too many managers. Anyone who claims to have sailed easily through the vision development process is either lying or has taken the wrong approach.

As one of the largest global consulting firms was scaling at breathtaking speed before the New Economy crash of 2000, a divisional head was concerned about his assessment of the firm's non-adaptive infrastructure and how it would ultimately torpedo any hope that the growth could be sustained. He, along with his five key deputies, became invested in developing a growth vision, at which point he became a client. He saw how the vision framework would enable his division, as a subset of the larger firm, to become more aligned for managing the torrid rate of growth. When they completed their final outline of the division's vision, the exec remarked to me:

> This was like putting together a tough puzzle, only more diffi-
> cult. You don't see all the pieces, know how many there are, or
> even where we go to find them. Then, we found that some of
> the pieces can change shape as a result of other pieces we were
> playing around with afterwards. God, I'm glad we went
> through this, but it was the most nerve wracking, soul search-
> ing, sobering thing I've ever done professionally.

Visioning cannot occur without confusion. A natural reaction when one's mental map is triggered by new, external, or unexpected inputs is to be confused; it's a sign that our brain is trying to process new data. Unfortunately, those in senior-most positions too often relate confusion to information not mastered, to not being professional, to something that one should avoid or hide from. Being—and appearing—consistently clear is seen as a virtue. It should come as no surprise then, to note that organizational leaders often display strong structuring and rationalizing behaviors during the visioning process to reduce their level of confusion. For example, if there's a problem within the organization, leaders develop a formal rule (a structure) that dictates how everyone must solve the problem the next time it comes around. Or they will rationalize the problem, by thinking about required actions that draw on past experiences, rather than the desired future outcome. At this point the process can become frozen. Confusion, in fact, is not only normal but an essential part of any learning or creative process. The vision development process can be enhanced by those leading it if they learn to accept confusion (their own and others) and use it as a vehicle for allowing new possibilities to emerge.

Think about the extent to which you or others may succumb to the discomfort inherent in the process and how willing you are to work outside of your comfort zone in this endeavor.

Live in the Past, the Present, and the Future—Simultaneously. Visions work—and fail—in part because those who develop them hold strong perspectives on time. A vision is about possibilities, desired futures, expressed optimism, and hope.

In a study of rapid-growth firms, researchers searched for key attributes that contributed to their viability for scaling.[3] "On first thought, it is hard to be very concerned about a company that is growing over 50% a year," one of the investigators reflected on the research questions before them. "But, on second thought, there are multiple reasons why such firms deserve some consideration in their own right."[4] Understanding the factors involved with very rapid growth, they believed, would contribute to our understanding of organizational success in general because we accept more than ever the belief that sustainability requires growth.

What did they find?

One of the most significant findings was that these firms held a particular perspective on *time*. They seemed to stay focused perennially on the state of their desired future. Rapid-growth firms focused on activities that continually reinforced the growth vision and the philosophy that guided the internal context (e.g., organizational processes like the structure, culture, and people processes) of the firm—the vision framework. With the vision as their beacon, they persistently modified or supplemented existing structures and processes rather than completely replacing old techniques that worked well in the past. The prominent theme characterizing the internal workings of these organizations was their ability to balance the firms' recent past with its intended future. From this perspective, one of the challenges of "instant size" seems to lie in establishing a dual perspective that acknowledges simultaneously an organization's past style and its future needs.

We could logically conclude from this evidence that executives in scaling organizations have, or create, a distinctive orientation to time that ultimately becomes critical to the way in which the firm functions. Not surprisingly, in these firms the "blueprint" for turning the present into the desired future was a plan that included extended goals for the future and the broad, sweeping strategies for achieving them. The exceptional people who lead scaling organizations have the capacity to stand in a future that does not exist and provide a detailed map that shows others how to get there. At the same time, they can lock their sights on the reality of the present moment. They have cultivated an ability to live in multiple time zones simultaneously: in the past, present, and future.

Most of us, though, are more comfortable in one time zone. We look unflinchingly at the nuts and bolts reality of the present. Or we see the opportunities on the horizon, but remain focused solely on the future without assessing the present and determining what gaps may prevent the future from being realized.

Ultimately, those of us who lead organizations successfully as they scale—even if we started out solidly in the present or were unable to reconcile the "here and now" with the "what could be," learn over the course of our careers to fuse the present with the desired future and to establish an ongoing comparison of "where are we now and where are we trying to be." As sailors tack an indirect course to capture the wind and ultimately arrive at their desired destination, so too do successful scalers: They keep their eyes fixed constantly on the long-term horizon but execute daily based on present reality, often in different and inconsistent ways, as a means to travel closer to that destination.

Whether the vision is conceptualized by an individual or a senior group, there must be an understanding of how one's time can be used—while the process itself may seem that it is being wasted. Minutes, hours, days spent on communication, checking out understanding, and discussion with others when elements of the vision are vetted, is time invested in the future. These are often the first steps toward an evolving common vision.

Only from a shared time perspective can a vision be developed and used to direct the vision framework. A growth vision should therefore create a vivid mental picture of what tomorrow will look like. It spans more years than we will probably be working for the organization, and it keeps us focused relentlessly on the future—always the long term. While substantial variations exist in the span of time it takes to embrace a vision, most research indicates that greater success and satisfaction is realized when the time frame is no less than ten years, with many extending to twenty years. At its minimum, a vision must describe the desired future five years out.

Think about the extent to which your orientation reaches out to the future. Is it far enough? Can you maintain that perspective while simultaneously staying focused executing on matters in the present?

Acknowledge the Downside of Having an Entrepreneur at the Helm of a Growing Organization (Particularly if You Are an Entrepreneur/CEO). When we recall the birth and nourishment of so many organizations that grew very fast, we can often attribute the early success to someone with a strong entrepreneurial character. But this factor, which may have been a key ingredient in the initial success of the enterprise, can lead to serious dysfunctional dynamics as it continues to grow. Entrepreneurial organizations risk creating structures and work environments that are completely dependent on, and dominated by, the entrepreneur. Such firms can easily become autocratic and top-down-oriented, with the decision-making processes centering around the entrepreneur. Such leaders tend to find it difficult to delegate, be impulsive, lack interest in conscious, analytical forms of planning, and initiate bold, proactive moves.

If that person is you, this prerequisite may be difficult to swallow. But it's essential if you're going to create a viable vision that can permeate your entire organization.

Your impulsive actions, for example, may have contributed to the initial successes, but now they can be deadly. Since planning has been more of a seat-of-the-pants rather than deliberative activity, the growing organization faces a greater risk. Entrepreneurs characteristically can have difficulty distinguishing between operating, day-to-day decision making, and more long-term strategic moves. They are often predisposed to impulsiveness—avoiding deliberation and judgment, while placing greater importance on hunches that span a rather limited time horizon. As the organization grows, such leaders may have difficulty establishing the right priorities. Too often, they inadvertently spend as much time on trivia as on major strategic decisions.

And with an entrepreneur flying the organization solo, growing pains accelerate dramatically. Why? The firm's overall structure is often poorly defined. Formal organization charts are outdated by the time they are drawn up—or are nonexistent. The organization resembles a spider web with the entrepreneur at the center. Control and information systems—particularly the sharing of information—may be poorly defined or ill used. Standard operating procedures and guidance for the daily routines of work life that could emanate from a vision are nonexistent or out of sync with the needs of a growing firm. A "spider web" structure almost guarantees that the number of people reporting to the CEO–entrepreneur will be large, adding to the general state of confusion.

As the organization grows, the situation only worsens. Often, subjective, personal criteria are used to measure and control. Job descriptions and job responsibilities are poorly defined or nonexistent. Ambiguity adds to the confusion, which, in turn, leads to stress. People stop communicating among themselves like they did in the past. Information is hoarded, day-to-day organizational policies are interpreted with increasing inconsistency, favorites are played, and a reluctance or refusal to let people know where they really stand pervades the organization.

What's more, while the leader may once have had the ability to inspire employees, doing so now is more complicated. As the firm scales, the lack of managerial slots with authority causes the capable people to leave while the yes-people, those who do not challenge the entrepreneur's authority, stay on. Eventually, few capable subordinates may remain with the organization. Those left will usually be mediocre and may spend too much time and energy on political infighting.

You may have heard the old saying, "A good mother ends up useless." By fostering her child's independence, she allows the child to experience mastery and grow into a responsible adult. The same idea plays out here. A leader of a scaling organization must loosen his or her grip on the reins of power and allow managers to come into their own. This is seldom easy for an entrepreneur. Try to resist the temptation to say, "that may be true of other entrepreneurs, but it isn't true of me." Acknowledging that some of your strengths as an entrepreneur are weaknesses in a scaling organization is a prerequisite to overcoming these limitations and creating an effective vision.

Acknowledge Emotion. Strategic *vision* depends on the ability to feel. It cannot be developed by looking coldly at words and numbers on pieces of paper or computer screens. In reaction to anxious calls for "some vision around here," detached managers tend to turn to more formal strategic planning processes, as if these mechanical systems will do what their brains, starved for a different type of information, cannot.

"What distinguishes the leader from the misleader are his goals," said Peter Drucker in a speech at the dedication of a graduate management center in his name at Claremont Graduate School.[5] "Management" he warned, "cannot be technique alone; it cannot be concerned solely with results and performance. Precisely because the object of management is a human community held together by the work bond for a common purpose, management always deals with the nature of man. . . . That means that there have to be values, commitment, convictions in management. Yes, even passion."[6]

I now realize that executives who truly desire to create adaptive organizations should begin the process by looking deep within themselves. They need to know who they are and what they want their organizations to be so that when they articulate a vision, it comes from a conviction that meets their personal need for action but is also part of a larger purpose. A deep, visceral commitment signals—to themselves and everyone around them—that they are open to changing the way they see, and think of, themselves. This is far from easy and, for most, it can be scary as hell. Top executives may resist change because they view their personal success—and that of the organization—as a function of the traits that got them to this point in the first place. The challenge is not to become someone different but to clarify who one really is. Only then does one have a basis for more easily and accurately defining what *forward* and *progress* really mean.

Elisabet Eklind took over the reins as executive director of HIPPY USA, a nonprofit organization committed to innovative strategies for helping disadvantaged families better prepare their children for educational success. Her self-imposed mandate as CEO was to stabilize a near-crumbling organizational infrastructure, prepare it for growth, then launch a series of initiatives to scale-up the breadth and depth of services offered across the country. While this was more of a turnaround than a scale-up, she nonetheless struggled with the same initial task for realigning her organization's internal context: to establish the vision so it could create a new vision framework. As Eklind was settling into her new role, she spoke to me about her frustration with various staff members and how their behavior was out of sync with the way she believed the constituency needed to be served. "It's really about the values [our clients] pick up in the existing culture here—and they are not the best values." There was a long pregnant pause in the conversation. "But I'll tell you what's really interesting, if not disturbing to me, though. When I consider the values that we must have, those that should drive the culture we need, I find it always leads me back to my own personal values. I'm examining my own values now more than ever. I think about how they influence me, those around me, and perhaps this entire organization. I've been managing for some time, but thinking so explicitly about my own values in the context of my organization's future is a new, weird experience."[7]

Executives like Eklind don't simply think about themselves in the context of the future they are defining. They allow themselves to *feel* enthusiasm, if not passion, for that future. When they feel this excitement, it leads in turn to higher levels of commitment and determination, which make it easier to overcome the often daunting challenges and roadblocks that can prevent the vision from becoming a living reality. *Commitment* is a heart-felt belief that the path chosen is the right one, and with it comes the strength to stay on the path despite the actions of others to take the firm down another road. *Determination* is the will to persevere, to resist any tempting diversions and stay on the future path that the vision leads toward. While many executives lack commitment and determination going into the vision development process, these traits often emerge once they begin the process. Developing a vision can be personally transformative.

If developing a vision can be so rewarding, why is it so difficult to embark upon this process? Executives are accustomed to setting goals and trying to achieve them, but conceptualizing a vision raises the process to a new level—one that may easily induce feelings of inadequacy. As Stuart Wells aptly notes,

> Vision is in the same terrain as dreams—dreams of the kind of life we want to live or the things we want to create. When we connect vision to dreams, we often relegate it to fantasy or useless daydreams; we talk about cold reality and being practical. We wind up with little expectation of dreams becoming real; they fade into the background, and we devote our attention to dealing with the problems and realities of the day.[8]

Yet another disorienting factor of the process is a requirement that those involved in developing the growth vision suspend disbelief. After all, executives have spent years of education and experience learning to be realistic and pragmatic. But suspending disbelief is necessary to enable the executive to think, from the start, that what he or she has envisioned can and will be achieved. While it represents the antithesis of practicality, it is nonetheless a necessary competency of executive leadership. Not only must there be a belief in the dream but also a belief in one's ability to make that dream come true.

George Bernard Shaw once said, "You see things; and you say, 'Why?' But I dream things that never were; and I say, 'Why not?'"[9] While dreaming about things that never existed may feel like a renegade organizational activity, it actually enables us to define a concrete possibility and to "experience" it before it exists. Rather than labeling this as foolish idealizing or fantasizing, it should be embraced as an effective method for stretching limits, boundaries, capabilities, and beliefs to get there. The "why not" question promotes the realization of opportunities that could be seized. Such thinking is the means for developing a vision that supports growth over the long haul.

When executives embark on the vision development process, they are often surprised by their reactions when they collectively discuss their personal perspectives on the state of the organization. A strong emotional catharsis often accompanies the richness of the dialogue. For most executives, this rich dialogue engages them in the vision development process once they begin to experience the sharing of these views.

Moving the Vision from Concept to Organizational Process

A criticism often cited of management education is that it represents a field rich in ideas that are poorly implemented in practice. For obvious reasons, this has led more than a few executives to question the value of academic concepts for effectively addressing problems they see in the real world. If a growth vision is to deliver on its potential rather than being just another faddish idea that fails in practice, then how the vision will be implemented must be considered from the start. In chapter 1, I discussed how strategic decisions were too frequently not implemented as originally planned; the same holds true for visions. Visions that are communicated, but never fully integrated into the fabric of organizational life engender cynicism. Should there be a desire to implement the vision later on, this cynicism makes it increasingly more difficult to do so and, more important, management can lose credibility since articulating and implementing a vision is seen as their number-one job. Remember, too, that the vision development process is generally iterative and messy. While the four phases of the process (1) form the planning group, (2) generate core elements of the vision, (3) debate the elements, and (4) articulate a "beta-test version" of the vision, which are iterated in the following sections, may create the appearance of a tidy, linear process, it will still feel iterative and messy.

Form the Planning Group

The evolution of a vision requires consensus building, listening, and provoking. The level at which participation occurs is an important decision in forming the planning group. If executives merely "tell" the vision, they may elicit compliance but lower the probability for commitment. An autocratically derived vision, developed in isolation and pushed from the top down, is doomed. While a vision should be born out of a process of collaboration that builds on diverse and perhaps conflicting visions from a myriad of levels, there are unfortunately limits to the extent of true top-down participation. I have found that broadly collaborative efforts invariably get bogged down by competing agendas and preferences. The struggle for consensus ends up watering down strongly held beliefs that belong in the vision. The agonizingly long time required for a broader collaboration not only delays the vision development but squanders more resources. Ultimately, the often-held belief that the vision for an established organization will accurately represent the hopes of all employees is just a dream. One must awaken from it.

An opposing view from some consultants argues that the creation of a vision does not come from group process techniques but starts with a single individual. Proponents of this view claim that the raw material of the effective vision is invariably the result of one man's or woman's soul-searching. While it is necessary that leaders soul-search to be committed to the vision, I do not think soul-searching by one individual is enough. Somewhere between a consensus-based approach and the outcome of a leader's soul-searching lies the most valid and meaningful material. The vision needs to be grounded in reality, in the values and needs of those who must subscribe to it. If executives are not sensitive to others' aspirations, fears, and beliefs, then they will never have the essential elements from which to fashion a growth vision that is shared.

So the process begins with communication, but not the one-way communication of speeches. Leaders have the talent to influence others, and listening—far more than speaking—appears to be at the core of this persuasive process. While certain leaders may be the first to openly advocate for a specific vision, the most successful visions are not perceived as the creation of one leader who suggested it. The most successful leaders of organizations in general—not just those enduring the scaling process—are great askers. They ask the right questions, and they pay attention to the responses they hear.

Those planning group members (who are invariably also executives) best at formulating a vision of what they want to see and hear in the organization are overwhelmingly the most careful observers of how their scaling operation worked. They scrutinize the current situation and the subtle ways in which behaviors affect performance. This provides the basis for the effort required to imagine what could change.

Invariably, the best starting point for developing a vision is a representative group with a leader who is typically the CEO. While many extraordinary growth visions were developed by groups without the CEO as a member, such as Whole Foods Market, it is unusual. What does "representative" mean? Along with the CEO, I generally recommend that the planning group include the members of his or her executive cabinet and perhaps three additional members plucked from lower levels and diverse functional areas. If no executive cabinet exists, this is the time to create it.

Regardless of whether the group is composed of the executive team or others, the group dynamics must be supportive enough to start and maintain the process. If working relationships are too inconsistent, if members hold contradictory values, if the individuals have no shared experience of what their scaling enterprise looks and feels like, and if people lack trust in others, then no sustainable or effective vision is likely to emerge. Under these conditions, we tend to see gamesmanship that ultimately leads to instability and a failed process.

In choosing members for the planning group, remember the nature of the vision development process. The process this group is about to embark on serves as an insightful exercise that allows each member to share and better understand the way others imagine or wish to see the future desired shape and state of the organization. Open-mindedness is important; all must listen and seek reactions to relatively primitive versions of the vision as they are developed and revised. If the group dynamics are well managed, the process is an intellectual, emotional, rational, behavioral, and existential one.

Generate Core Elements of the Vision

The sources of resistance noted in chapter 3 (e.g., binary response) attack the vision process full-bore during this phase. It is here that those responsible for the vision's development must acknowledge the discomfort, remain open, and maintain commitment. In this phase, initial ideas that will ultimately define the raison d'être, strategy, and values are surfaced and explored. Tactics for gaining traction during this phase will be discussed in the Appendix.

A first step typically involves asking each group member to express the way he or she sees the state of the organization. They should be encouraged to condense this view into one or a few sentences or loose phrases using "state" descriptive verbs ("Our customers are smart and discriminating consumers looking for service after sales") rather than "process" descriptive verbs ("We do a lousy job of following up after we close a sale"). Where is the organization now? What is it accomplishing?

The second step requires that each group member discuss his or her individual "visions." What is each member's ambition for him- or herself and for the organization? What are the expectations? What are the specific goals, values, or perspectives regarding both the group and the organization? This process facilitates a strong group development experience, as it enables the group to map strategic issues and perspectives. It is hoped that these discussions will also concretely illustrate the group's variety and richness. Individuals will be able to discuss common points of view about a desired future and to identify new potential areas of development. The questions addressing each of the three core elements of the vision (raison d'être, strategy, and values) are outlined in box 2-1 at the end of chapter 2. These should be placed in full view while the group works on this step. The process moves people from an individual sense of commitment to a shared group perspective.

During this exercise, individuals express their deeply held perspectives concerning their past experiences of the organization and the future meaning, shape, and culture they wish to see. This is the time when people start to address, share, and discuss issues that they had never or hardly ever broached together before. A feeling of confusion is normal as each member reconsiders certain aspects of their views according to how they are influenced by the discussion. Personal beliefs start to be reframed, new potential actions identified, and new meanings concerning the organization and its "constitution," or structure, take shape.

Another simple strategy for generating perspectives on the future involves asking group members to project themselves five years into the future. They are asked to imagine that, five years down the road, the organization has just been named by *Fortune* (the publication must fit the organization and be highly respected by participants) as one of the most admired companies in the world and will be featured as the cover story. Each group member must generate content for the cover story by addressing the questions listed in box 4-1.

Before individuals read their responses, I often have them complete an interim exercise. Each person is given a sheet of blank

---

BOX 4-1

Looking at the Future

- What is the organization's reputation? What is it known for?
- What is the customer's/client's experience?
- What do competitors respect and envy the most?
- How and where are employees performing their work and serving customers?
- What are employees saying to their closest friends and family about what it's like to work here?
- What new areas of business are being pursued?
- In what ways is the business making a difference to people? Who are these different groups of people?

---

newsprint and markers and asked to represent visually, through symbols and drawings, the essence of their answer to each of these questions. I noticed many years ago that when clients drew pictures that had no literal organizational representations but rather told a story through symbols, they were able to express more than if they had used words. The same held true for interpretation by others: When people post their drawings on the walls for others to view, new meanings—very relevant insights—emerge from observers when they describe what they see in others' sense of the organization.

A few years ago I was working with the senior executives of Oslo Energi of Norway, one of the first municipal electric utilities in Europe, to privatize and scale-up in order to sell wattage across the continent. The executives spent about twenty minutes working on their individual drawings to symbolize the state of the company just as it was about to go private. The head of engineering looked intently at a vice president's abstract collection of figures on the paper and described his analysis of what he saw. "My god," responded the VP, "You've described perfectly how I feel about some of the issues here, but that was not at all what I was thinking when I drew this thing [pointing to the collage of multicolored symbols on the newsprint in front of him]."

Often, as an additional or alternative exercise I give client groups a stack of pictures collected from magazines and ask them to think of an element of their organizational vision or an organizational problem and to choose a picture as a medium for describing their thoughts. Through the use of these images, their thoughts become expansive, vivid, and evocative. The ideas were there but not accessible through the customary methods by which managers solve organizational problems and make decisions. Since I began using this technique, the Center for Creative Leadership conducted research and found it to be a relatively simple yet powerful way to tap into a manager's subconscious thoughts.[10]

Too often, our thoughts and observations—of what is and what we dream may be possible—are so ephemeral that they slip out of mind as soon as they slip in. To counteract this tendency, I strongly suggest that each member of the group keep a journal close to them each day to jot down this fleeting "data." Journaling is a useful tool for formulating broader notions related to oneself and the vision as well as a memory device for the practical purpose of planning meetings.

Debate the Elements

After a list of possible elements is generated from the exercises in phase 2, group members brainstorm about which elements are essential to the vision, in what priority some may fall, how some may contradict each other, and whether those elements that surface as an intense discussion meet the criteria noted. In this phase, the elements that may contribute to vision definition are discussed with greater intensity. Mental models of the organization held by planning group members are explored. Operating at the level of mental models—our internal pictures of how the world works—entails understanding what our assumptions are, reflecting on them to test their relevancy, and changing them if necessary. Take the concept of "manufacturing." If Dell's mental model of manufacturing was one massive assembly line operation, they would not have been able to consider alternatives such as smaller independent manufacturing cells that are able to produce a higher mix of customized products at lower volumes.

Surfacing, reflecting on, and changing our mental models is often a difficult if not painful process. Why would anyone choose to go through this? Because a compelling vision of a new and different world that members are committed to creating may emerge. When our thoughts about vision are put into practice—even if they are not fully formed—our actions can be "generative," bringing something into being that did not exist before. A vision that provides a higher quality of work life and focuses on the learning and developmental needs of every employee in a large grocery store chain, for example, was probably the impetus behind the creation of Whole Foods Market. Someone took a good look at old mental models regarding how supermarket employees "should" be treated and not only created a vision for the current organizational structure, but a new organization all together.

The debate about what should constitute the vision's core elements may be limited to the planning group or widened further across the organization. Absent a formal debate, a more informal, covert debate will commence in its place as groups try to make sense of what has happened and work out what the implications for them may be if the vision becomes real. The more complex the activities of the organization and the more widely dispersed its activities, the more the debate may lead to some questioning of the vision. This often makes CEOs nervous because the questioning can be experienced as an attack on his or her beliefs for the future. But restricting conflict at this point—especially if there are genuine concerns—can be dangerous. Conflict should be welcomed; it invariably surfaces unforeseen issues and previously unrecognized elements that belong in the vision. When there is unresolved conflict over the vision's core elements, the potential for a far more incendiary disagreement increases significantly if it is left to be resolved at a later time.

Articulate a "Beta-Test Version" of the Vision

Once the core elements of the vision are decided and before the vision is rolled out, the vision should be beta-tested. An explicit testing of the vision should involve checking organizational behaviors and performance against predictions made (see box 4-2).

Some organizations identify a department or division and test the vision with them. Do the people respond to it positively? If there is resistance (which is important to identify and monitor) is it resistance due to:

- value conflicts,
- a belief that the raison d'être and strategy are not worth achieving,
- a lack of understanding of the vision,
- a view of the vision as an upset of the status quo (not bad by and of itself), or
- an inability to view the vision as a positive challenge?

BOX 4-2

Will the New Vision . . .

- Maximize our strengths—minimize our weaknesses?
- Challenge current culture? How?
- Respond to current and future opportunities and threats?
- "Fit" with the internal and external environments?
- Be right for everyone who will interact with it?
- Lead to improved performance?

Implicit assumptions about what constitutes a successful vision may initially feel more comfortable, but there is a danger that individual executives will prejudge based on their own unique perceptions of success rather than views shared across the executive group and/or vision development group. For example, the marketing VP may see improved performance only in terms of more sales leads and be blind to problems in quality.

When there is not a sufficiently robust set of assumptions that are shared and can be discussed, it will weaken the power of the growth vision. The group needs to discuss and agree on what will constitute "success" across the organization. The emotional strength of the executive group is critical here. When efforts to test a vision are met with resistance or produce no tangible results, the conclusion usually reached is that "people resist change." In many organizations, this has become the corporate maxim most often accepted without challenge. But rather than spending time formulating strategies to deal with these "unchangeable" people, it's generally a more effective use of time to step back and ask, "Do they really exist?" When people are invited to participate—if participation means fully understanding the vision process the organization is in the midst of—they are usually more than willing to change. I've noticed that they are sometimes actually impatient with the larger organization's inability to move fast enough toward the goal. Most people do not resist change; they resist being changed when it is imposed from the outside. Articulating a compelling vision and building commitment around it marks the beginning of the journey, not the end.

Launch the Vision Organization-Wide

Launching the vision across the organization will require the planning group to take the iterative process to one more level: review the feedback from the pilot launch and any other means to garner feedback about the core concepts, and then to determine whether anything requires modification. Once they reach agreement on key elements of the vision, and also agree that the means of communicating it are clear to those outside the planning group, the vision is then introduced.

Guidelines for Visions That Sustain Growth

A vision should describe a future world where the raison d'être is advanced and where the strategy is successfully applied simultaneously to the organization's guiding philosophy and values. It paints a picture of what success looks and feels like. It does not stop at declaring where the organization is headed or what its general aspirations are, but becomes so vivid by virtue of how it is communicated that it enables the listener to envision him- or herself in this desired future. The more detailed the description, the easier people understand how the future world is both similar to and different from the current one and what their potential role in it could be.

I analyzed the scholarly research on characteristics of effective visions and the vision development process. I then scrutinized the results of these meta-analyses from my perspective as a consultant, using the abundance of experiences helping organizational leaders articulate and implement the vision process across many industries and in many countries. From this synthesis of research and practice I recognized a number of universal guidelines for effective visions that sustain growth. Box 4-3 lists questions based on these guidelines to help you determine if you're making progress in developing an effective vision. Each of the points in box 4-3 is further discussed in the following sections.

Does the Vision Speak to the Entire Audience? The name of Whole Foods Market's vision, "Declaration of Interdependence,"

BOX 4-3

Questions for Developing an Effective Vision

- Does the vision speak to the entire audience?
- Does the vision include specific content points?
- Does the vision have specific stylistic attributes (brevity, clarity, abstractness, challenge, future orientation, stability, and desirability) to motivate follow-through?
- Does the vision tell a story?
- Does the vision look far enough ahead?
- Is the ideal future consistent enough with conditions in the present?
- Does the vision balance the abstract and the concrete?
- Does the vision convey a sense of urgency?

---

relays the profound insight that the company will grow or die to the extent that it identifies all the necessary stakeholders crucial to its success. *Inter*dependence mandates that the vision outlines how each stakeholder must be approached. Too often, a vision addresses the needs of only one or two stakeholders. Vital visions, however, consider every segment that has an impact on both success and failure. Stakeholders may include not only employees, vendors, communities, and customers, but the competition as well.

Speaking to the full audience implies more than just identifying who the stakeholders are and what one thinks they need. It requires seeing the organization through their lens, adopting their perspective of what an ideal future of the organization could be like—for them.

Does the Vision Include Specific Content Points? While each organization must articulate a vision that addresses its unique beliefs inherent in the three core themes (raison d'être, strategy, and values), I have found that the visions of many scaling organizations contain specific strategies related to the value of (1) learning, (2) positive challenges, and (3) growth.

The most fundamental characteristic of organizations where scaling has been sustained seems to be a commitment to the value of *learning*. Learning represents one value—operationalized as a strategy—that shapes the future. Both personal development and organizational learning involve setting new challenges continually and being held accountable for achieving them. These are important activities for a scaling organization. If people did not learn and develop themselves, growth and sustainability would cease. While every visionary firm has its share of failures, those that prevail seem to be in the habit of not just licking their wounds but dusting themselves off and pondering what they may have done wrong that led to a failure. They challenge their assumptions, devise new tactical maneuvers, and try again—and again. So it should not be surprising that organizations that unambiguously value learning also invest significantly in training and development for all their people and have other explicit values (e.g., openness to feedback, unencumbered communication up and down the hierarchy, the expectation of continuous improvement on the individual and departmental levels) that enhance learning on a broader organizational level. When desired characteristics of the culture such as these are clearly communicated and behaviors consistent with them are uniformly reinforced across the organization, learning is brought up to the broadest level.

Second, scaling organizations value *positive* challenges. When the value of positive challenges is explicitly stated, innovation and entrepreneurship are fostered within the organization. People grow professionally if they are able to take on new challenges or to revisit those they had with a renewed sense of stimulation. The desires to improve continually; to work more efficiently; to find more imaginative, better, and cheaper solutions; and to develop an improved product or service for the customer are aspirations shared by people in all types of organizations. When these desires are supported by underlying corporate values, people are not only given the freedom to engage in behaviors that best serve scaling organizations, they are also held accountable for engaging in them.

Third, organizations with a "growth vision" actually declare their desire for *growth* within the context of their vision. Organizations grow faster when their vision is focused on growth.[11]

Does the Vision Have Specific Stylistic Attributes to Motivate Follow-Through? Visions having the attributes in the following list have been found to be significantly related to subsequent venture growth.[12]

- *Brevity*—whatever is communicated in writing should be concise. Stories and anecdotes are best left for verbal communication.

- *Clarity*—there should be no ambiguity of the meaning by anyone who reads or hears elements of the vision. Organization-, industry-, or management-specific jargon must be "translated" so every stakeholder has a uniform understanding.

- *Abstractness*—while definitions should be uniform, they must also enable individuals to conceptualize how it will relate to them and how they can be a part of it. Visions do not articulate goals and objectives at the short-term, granular level but far into the future. When the vision also has the characteristic of abstractness, people can create their unique reality of how they will fit into it.

- *Challenge*—reaction to hearing and/or reading the vision must make one feel that it is achievable—but not easily.

- *Future orientation*—everything is focused on the future. While there may be historical references for context and to "anchor" the desired future, a vision is solely about the desired future.

- *Stability*—visions do not change year to year. The most effective have a profoundly enduring quality year-after-year, decade-after-decade (e.g., J&J, HP), visions can and should be reviewed every few years but if they were conceived according to the criteria noted here, then they will endure.

- *Desirability*—each person in the organization should (must?) be attracted to this view of the future. They want to strive with others to make it real. It resonates with their own values and beliefs.

While many visions may be explicit and thorough statements of the organization's core values and beliefs and may provide guidelines for how leaders and employees should act, they do not give a picture of the future. Guiding values and principles are important foundations for the vision, but they are not the vision. Visions go beyond this and describe those values and ideals in action. Missing from most visions is a description of *how* these ideals are practiced, what the experience is like for those affected, and the link between these preferred behaviors and successful performance.

Vision statements analyzed across many companies in diverse industries could be substituted with minimal editing for one another because they lack the richness of context and detail of a story. They are stuffed with recycled words and phrases like "we will be the employer of choice," and "the leader of our markets," or "the solution provider our customers turn to first." The assumption that these words and phrases will evoke the same meaning for everyone who must be affected by them is an erroneous one. Vision statements that are too general are more likely to generate multiple interpretations from organizational stakeholders. The stark weakness of bland visions that read like brief bumper sticker slogans mashed together with awkward grammar and syntax, therefore, is that they leave so much open to interpretation. They are so lofty that the people they are intended to impact cannot personally connect with them. For a vision to serve as a working basis for the vision framework, it must project people into the future so they can readily see it in action and imagine themselves as part of it.

Effective visions must therefore describe a future world where the raison d'être is advanced, where the strategy is in full play, and where everyone is operating in accord with the explicitly stated values and beliefs. Visions work remarkably well when they outline a rich, textural picture of what success looks and feels like. How is this accomplished? See the next point.

Does the Vision Tell a Story? Since it is not enough to simply state where an organization is headed or what its general aspirations are, the vision must be so vivid as to enable listeners or readers to transport themselves to the future. They must experience it as tangibly as possible. The more a vision can be experienced as a lucid story, which incorporates the three themes as its basis, the more people will understand how the future world is both similar to and different from the current one. They can see more clearly what their potential role in it could be.

This is another area in which I have been converted. In the past, I believed strongly that visions should be boiled down to a one-half or three-quarter page vision statement. I saw the vision as the organizational equivalent of The Constitution: The essentials were in black and white; anyone could point to an element of the vision on the statement and declare unambiguously what the organization stood for. The statement would serve not only as a starting point for discussion and further enlightenment, but a tightly worded vision statement could also be an effective mechanism for helping (or forcing) executives to define the essence of the three vision components.

In too many cases, however, such statements failed as a device to help people transport themselves to the ideal future the vision was trying to articulate and resembled another executive summary. Vision statements, as they are generally used, tend to be experienced as little more than hollow platitudes, slogans, or trendy phrases that just ask to be misinterpreted and misunderstood. Consequently, I have come to believe that the vision statement needs to tell a story about the desired future of the organization.

Visions do not work axiomatically through verbal and written communication alone. Leaders must nonverbally reinforce the values, through such actions as dramatic gestures, role modeling, and the way they select, train, and reward employees. But they cannot do this if everyone does not know the story.

Storytelling is effective for a number of reasons. Research has shown that it impacts our underlying psychological and cognitive processes, which in turn facilitate learning and behavior change.[13] Through storytelling and the use of metaphorical language, our habitual mind-sets, common everyday frames of reference, and belief systems are more or less interrupted and suspended for brief moments. This suspension evokes trancelike states in listeners during which we become more open to considering new possibilities and information.[14] This "vision story" shows people the future in such detail that it produces a virtual experience of it, providing vicarious learning. By hearing the vivid story told, employees gain an intuitive feel and visceral understanding of the desired future. Their increased understanding of, and appreciation for, what this future could be helps people personalize it and assimilate the learning of new behaviors and performance expectations.

Does the Vision Look Far Enough Ahead? Visions, as I've noted, must describe the desired long-term future of the organization. To develop such a vision requires imagination, a mental capacity for synthesis, and a trust in intuition. When a manager needs to be in control, fears mistakes, is uncomfortable with ambiguity, and tends to judge rather than facilitate the creation of ideas, then the result will probably be a vision constrained by a short time horizon. Taking risks in formulating the vision can mean the difference between wallowing in the comfort of the warm, safe swimming pool of formal planning processes and exploring (and yes, sometimes flailing in) the cold ocean of a future that is far less bounded by time.

Is the Ideal Future Consistent Enough with Conditions in the Present? While visions are not intended to mirror reality, they need to have an anchor in it. Between current reality and the vision lies the abyss referred to in chapter 2. People must understand it—and want to cross it—if the vision is to be a useful process. Employees have a healthy skepticism for putting faith in a vision that paints too rosy a picture of the future, fails to take into account the often hostile environment in which they must operate (e.g., fierce competition), or ignores inherent liabilities of the organization. While there appears to be no broad agreement as to how best to balance these conflicts, I have found that visions that *directly acknowledge* organizational issues as challenges that must be met head-on are more credible than those that do not. When a vision explicitly recognizes and addresses the relentless source or sources of adversity, it becomes believable and serves to unify and provide focus. Adversity may be addressed through an "us versus them" attitude in which "they" are competitors or by acknowledging a hostile environment or entrenched institutional liabilities that must be overcome together.

Although the vision should acknowledge and address adversity, it should not be overwhelmed by it. The process of defining the raison d'être, strategy, and values sometimes heightens leaders' awareness of their status as underdogs. If they become mired in the banal reality of survival, it saps enthusiasm and optimism from the vision development process. Visions should acknowledge adversity but simultaneously develop a perspective of success. Emphasizing the possible and the organization's strengths will help achieve this balance.

Does the Vision Balance the Abstract and the Concrete? Visions describe possibilities and ideal futures. Unlike goals and objectives with clearly defined, measurable ends, they take a broader perspective by implying that the vision may never be fully achieved. The inherent tension is between describing an ideal far out into the future that engages the imagination while simultaneously making it tangible enough that each member of the organization can identify with it, picture what it looks like when it is achieved, and see what is required to make it real. That is why stories can be so profound as a communication vehicle. As mentioned above, a story can paint a picture of what success looks and feels like, transporting the listener or reader to the future and allowing him to vicariously observe and experience it. While expansive, the vision should be detailed enough to help people understand how the future world is both similar to and different from the current one and what their potential role in it could be.

Does the Vision Convey a Sense of Urgency? When the vision is used as a platform to drive and influence the direction of the vision framework, there must be a visible sense of urgency to implement the vision. The vision establishes the desired future reality. Since most employees already understand the current reality, gaps between the two (the abyss) must be addressed through actions. The useful vision creates an organizational road map showing how the vision framework will direct and sustain actions. Immediate, measurable milestones help convey a sense of urgency.

Are Expectations of What the Vision Will Accomplish Reasonable?

Although the concept and use of vision is considered central to the process of building and refining an organization that can scale, too often managers see it as a magic bullet with the power to heal all their organizational maladies. Such unrealistic expectations become the kiss of death. The historical landscape of the management field is littered with the remains of beliefs and techniques that started as sound ideas but ended as religious dogma. While visions need to be embraced and followed if they are to be effective, the problem arises when they are seen as having terminal value as a stand-alone management tool. Rather than a tool, they are a *process* and work only to the extent that they continually inform elements of the Vision Framework and keep everyone focused on and challenged about the future.

You'll Know You're Making Progress When . . .

A company's vision should provide both movement and direction for the vision framework, and it should rally the energies, galvanize the aspirations and commitment from people in the organization, and mobilize them into determined action toward achieving a desired future that includes growth.

As you work through the vision development process, pause frequently and ask yourself if what you're creating will do the following:

- Will it motivate you to join this organization and continue to motivate you once you are there?
- Does it provide a beacon for guiding the kinds of adaptation and change required for continual growth?
- Does it describe a future that is more attractive than the present?
- Will it challenge you?
- Can it serve as the basis to formulate strategy that can be acted on?
- Will it serve as a framework to keep decision making in context?

Well-conceptualized visions accomplish all of these things.[15] While they also affect organizational-level performance as measured by growth in sales, profits, employment, and net worth, the operative word is "affect." Visions that accomplish what they are intended for do not declare what will happen to these variables because they are outcomes or returns an organization receives as the *result of* executing on its vision.

Tom Chappell, founder of Tom's of Maine, a company that has found innovative ways to grow continually within a notoriously competitive consumer goods industry, once remarked how the use of numbers alone provides nothing more than a treadmill. "Quantitative goals can't invest purpose in a process that has none. The quest for simply more of anything is inherently unsatisfying. If there is no point or joy in what you are doing, or if you lose sight of the point, then just measuring your progress can't make it worthwhile or fun. If I can organize people around purpose, that is the most powerful form of leadership."[16]

Part II

Making
Vision Work

Chapter 5

From Paper to Practice

I N PART II, I'LL EXAMINE IN DETAIL EACH COMPONENT of the vision framework. But before we move from paper to practice—from beliefs and aspirations to implementation and action—I'm going to step back and examine, once more, from a slightly different angle, the personal issues that can support, or impede, the vision process. Why? Because even though you may be committed to the notion of building a working vision, the negative side of the binary response nonetheless will continue to rear its ugly head as you work through implementation issues. It will lure you toward behaviors that undermine, rather than support, your goal. And although the articulation of a great vision can raise the aspirations of employees, those same hopes will be dashed if they see senior management and others they respect behaving in inconsistent ways. A vision absent substantive ideas and concrete actions, and personal passion becomes a joke, often backfiring on the leader responsible, as others turn to cynics. John Rock, once the general manager of General Motors' (GM) Oldsmobile division, put it most eloquently: "A bunch of guys take off their ties and coats, go into a motel room for three days, and put a bunch of friggen' words on a piece of paper—and then go back to business as usual."[1]

Believing is one thing. Following through with the right actions is another. The passion or drive that often results from a significant personal experience—or, as Elisabet Eklind says, becoming aware of "what water is"—are important factors when it comes to follow-through. In moving from paper to practice, the going gets harder, not easier. It's been my experience that you—the leader—need to sort through the challenges, worthiness of the pursuit, and the emotions that rise up at this stage and to harness your own personal passion.

Personal Passion: Building Momentum for the Vision Framework

In 1987, Elisabet Eklind got married and moved to the United States from Stockholm, Sweden, where she had lived all of her life. In March 1993, her husband died after a long battle with cancer. As she sat in her home after her husband's death, she told me, she realized that she could either "die" then and there as well—simply continue going through the motions of living—or she could rebuild herself. Start again, in other words, and work through the pain. She chose the latter and, as she says, has emerged "a stronger, better person for the effort."

> A fish doesn't know what water is until it's out of water. And before [those two experiences], I was like a fish. I didn't know what "water" was. I was not aware, in a truly meaningful sense, of how the nuances of my surroundings affected me and how I responded to it.
>
> Now I know what water is. I know when I'm out of it. I am much more aware of my needs, and I believe these experiences also helped me to understand the needs of others—and this includes people in my organization.[2]

Eklind's effort to find a new awareness—of her surroundings, of her values, of her own "raison d'être"—has shaped her life in ways she never imagined. It has also shaped the way she approaches her work as executive director of HIPPY USA, a nonprofit whose purpose is to enhance the potential for educational success of low-income children. I introduced you to Eklind in chapter 4, and talked about how she came to the realization, during the vision development process at HIPPY USA, that if she were truly going to realign the values of her organization, she would have to bring the effects of her own very personal journey to bear on the effort. "You carry significant experiences with you, and they shape the way you look at the world," she said. "And if you let them, they shape the way you approach your work and think about what your organization or company needs. My own personal experiences helped me see HIPPY with greater clarity than I ever could have before."[3]

This doesn't mean that Eklind's own values have to *align* with those of HIPPY or that she wears her past on her sleeve, but her effort as the chief executive for HIPPY is no less passionate and driven than her efforts on her own behalf *because* of her personal experiences. The success of a vision is *all* about passion. The reason the binary response does not catch some people unawares is that they have the passion to move through their own personal resistance to vision. The experience of dealing with her husband's illness and subsequent death, along with being an immigrant in a new land, helped Eklind to find that inner passion needed to identify the vision elements required of the precarious organization she was chosen to *lead*. Passion enabled Eklind, as it enables others to "work through" the implementation issues.

Taking a vision and using it to create an organization ready to endure growth starts from within. As Niall Fitzgerald, co-chairman of Unilever and co-creator of its vision-driven transformation process, reflected in the book *Primal Leadership,*

> We had all the organizational pieces in place—but it was like standing on the edge of the Grand Canyon. You know you have to get to the other side, but to do so you know you will have to take a big leap, then build a bridge. You feel anticipation, even deep uneasiness, but the excitement of the vision calls on you to build that bridge, take the leap. . . . At Unilever, the bridge we needed to build was all about people: we needed to tap into their passion; we needed them to see their business in entirely new ways; and we needed them to develop very different leadership behaviors.[4]

Antony Burgmans, Fitzgerald's counterpart as co-chairman, reflected in the same book: "As we launched into our growth strategy, I realized that I didn't feel right: something was missing. . . . What I saw was that even though we had an excellent change strategy, and an inspiring vision, what was really required to bring about change at Unilever was a new culture, a new leadership mindset, and new behaviors."[5]

"A new leadership mindset." In other words, as Burgmans was to find out, what Unilever needed was the passion at the top to fuel the change process throughout the organization. Innovation and the risk taking necessary for closing the abyss, and bringing the vision to life, require the same level of passion to overcome the binary response.

The philosopher Will Durant once noted, "Man is as old as his arteries, but as young as the risks he takes." Routine becomes the sclerosis that clogs the arteries of innovation in organizations, and it is up to senior management to ensure that these arteries do not harden. When the scrooge of overreliance on stability, rules, and procedures takes hold, peoples' eagerness to take risks and innovate is reduced. Growth stalls.

Are you passionate about your vision for your company? Can you articulate it to yourself and to others? And most important, are you willing to be true to your own values and refrain from placing blame for inaction on some institutional imperative? Are you willing to face that, if the vision process at your organization stalls, perhaps it's because *you* succumbed to a form of inertia?

To get at the answer to these questions, let's dig even deeper. Ask yourself, "Where does this appetite for vision, with all the risk inherent in its development and implementation, come from?"

The "appetite" comes from living. It comes from feeling the bumps and bangs and pain of life that create emotional jolts that stay with us consciously and unconsciously. It comes from living through life-changing events that trigger unique personal insights, and emerging with new resolve. It comes from finding the passion on a personal level, and harnessing it to hold onto, before the vision development process gets under way.

Twice Born

Some people have been forced to look inward for meaning in response to an emotionally charged event such as the death or serious illness of a loved one, a divorce, growing up poor or discriminated against, consequences from the September 11 terrorist attack, rejection by a role model—things that are beyond their control. They struggle to sort out the meaning of the experience, which may have left them with feelings of profound separateness, perhaps anger, and most likely disorientation. Often, what emerges is the need to examine goals, values, and norms of conduct. The question, "Why did this happen to me?" evokes emotional energy, which can either be turned on oneself in a counterproductive way or applied in a creative burst of productive energy.

When this happens, one becomes simultaneously an actor in the drama and a member of the audience, both acting in, and watching the events of the drama unfold. As events unfold, the actor–viewer searches for separateness as a way to gain perspective to sort through the confusion. Life becomes a journey with a sense of urgency to accomplish new goals. There is greater openness to risk, but not for the sake of risk taking; now, he or she wants to improve (or prove) something.

This concept of being "twice born" grew out of turn-of-the-century work by Harvard psychologist William James (the brother of author Henry). Nearly seventy years later, two psychoanalytically oriented management scholars, Abraham Zaleznik of Harvard Business School and Manfred Kets de Vries of INSEAD, independently adapted the notion to business leadership. "For a once-born personality, the sense of self, as a guide to conduct and attitude, derives from a feeling of being at home and in harmony with one's environment," Zaleznik observed.[6] By nature, the manager is a once-born personality. "Managers," he continued, "see themselves as conservators and regulators of an existing order of affairs with which they personally identify and from which they gain rewards."[7]

But those individuals who create a vision and make it come alive—some call them "leaders"—are twice-borns, often struggling with a feeling of separateness. They take nothing for granted. Self-reliance takes hold along with expectations of performance and achievement, even the need to do great works. They want to make a difference.

Consider the number of immigrants to the United States who have become not just good entrepreneurs, but great organizational leaders. Removed from their past, they reflect and question most of the new cultural norms as they deal with not only the words but also the complex meaning of a new language, new customs, and new social codes. Somehow they must integrate their past experience with the present environment to define a new world. Visionary leader Andy Grove, former CEO and chairman of Intel, for example, escaped Nazi Europe with his parents, learned new languages in order to survive, came to the United States with almost nothing, worked his way through college and a doctoral program, and waged a winning fight against prostate cancer.[8] Dave Thomas, founder of Wendy's, was an adopted orphan and high school dropout who ended up with six thousand restaurants. He had the audacity to believe that square hamburgers would taste better and a commitment to dedicate his life to helping abandoned children.

Theories and research that have tried to explain the success of organizational leaders express a similar theme: Leadership is less about sheer talent than about introspection forged from events that caused great discomfort, if not suffering. Most people who successfully build and run complex organizations have had this leadership-shaping experience. At one time or another they have had to let go of something they thought was important.

Now, *they seek to clarify for others the abyss*—the difference between a highly defined, desirable future matched by a dissatisfaction with the status quo—because they have had to do it for themselves. They have the capacity to speak to the depths of another person because they are in touch with their own deeper conflicts. They found support along the way through the intensity of their convictions and their awareness of the impressions they made on others.

Those who create and implement growth visions know who they are and what they want their organizations to be. Their articulated vision comes alive from a conviction that not only meets their personal need for action but is also part of a much larger purpose.

Alignment *and* Attunement

I'll address the need and process for alignment in the following chapters, but it's worth noting here, as a guiding thought, that alignment, on its own, is insufficient because it is a managerial artifact. While some people may change some behaviors by management fiat, change won't last unless they are emotionally integrated with the new direction.

Goleman, Boyatzis, and McKee noted forcefully in *Primal Leadership* that achieving alignment requires *attunement*—moving people *emotionally* as well as intellectually. The challenge, they found from their research, is in determining how to attune people to your vision and then to your business strategy in a way that arouses passion. It requires connecting directly with their emotional centers.[9] Warren Bennis, the leadership expert and University of Southern California professor, has referred to attunement as "managing attention through vision"—which he believes is the leader's fundamental responsibility.[10]

The organization's culture and its systems are what produce patterns and events that create its day-to-day reality. This is also where mental models and vision are translated into action. The point at which the vision becomes embedded into the routines and processes of the organization is the point at which execution has taken hold. Full execution happens when it informs the actions of everyone in the organization. It is "the way we do things around here," and people see, feel, and have a tangible sense of the vision to bring the abstractions to life. Where there is managerial alignment *and* emotional attunement, the vision framework comes alive.

Take, for example, Oakley's vision. It emphasizes the importance of "design" and "sculpture" in each product it creates. Oakley's most prominent product, eyewear, is the one produced completely in-house. This puts extraordinary demands on the manufacturing department to figure out how to manufacture something no one's ever tried before. But it's not just about making unique frames and lenses that seem to defy the laws of optical physics. It's also about making them to extraordinarily narrow market specifications, and doing so such that they end up with healthy profit margins, and being able to sell them at a price point that isn't in the stratosphere.

Oakley people feel an emotional attachment to this vision-driven strategy of design and sculpture, and it impacts the way they work and even how divisions are structured. It influenced Kent Lane, VP of manufacturing, to create a "cell" structure of manufacturing teams. Oakley's cells have been responsible for the continual flow of innovative ideas leading to manufacturing processes that address these concerns. And you will see in following chapters how people like Lane demonstrate what vision "feels" like on a day-to-day basis, and how people in the organization can live it. Lane and leaders like him are able to act consistently with their own values and with the values of the organization they are trying to create.

It was the same with Eklind. When she became executive director of HIPPY USA, the abyss she inherited was a struggling nonprofit organization with committed staff and a great deal of potential. But it was becoming weaker from a lack of vision and the absence of a vision framework. Her metaphor of a house was always a clear and powerful one to me:

> People were trying to put curtains on the windows, and I was trying to shore up the foundation. I needed people with me working down in the cellar, on the foundation.
>
> When I became Executive Director, I knew this was not a place for people who just wanted a job; we needed people who *believed* in what we were doing.[11]

Acting on Your Vision and Accomplishing the "Impossible"

In the 1830s, Western Railroad realized that success was based on executing a strategy of transporting people and commodities in a straight line from Boston to Albany and points west. The company wanted to be the first to accomplish this, but there was a problem. It was perplexed, if not overwhelmed, by a seemingly insurmountable obstacle in western Massachusetts—the Berkshire Hills. Indeed, a member of the Massachusetts legislature at the time declared a railroad through this area would be as "useless as a railroad on the moon."[12] But Western Railroad was committed to building a passageway because it was integral to its business plan. And it tapped Major George Washington Whistler to get it done. Whistler was given the task of finding the best passage and then doing what was necessary to ultimately drive a train through it. He started by surveying the route on horseback.

Most people thought Whistler was crazy for choosing this route; while it was relatively direct, it was steep, with tight curves, and required technology for economically blasting through rock-solid hillsides that did not yet exist. Surveyors for the Massachusetts Turnpike, who would reexamine the same landscape almost 125 years later, but this time by helicopter, claimed they could have found no better route for a highway that would traverse the state east to west than the one already claimed by Whistler. To this day, after almost 175 years, the route has only been adjusted on a two-mile section. The grades encountered in climbing the Berkshires (eighty feet per mile) in combination with the curvature (over 50 percent of the route) remain among the toughest in the world to traverse.

Whistler had a clear vision, at this tactical level (even if, as we will see in chapter 8, his employers lacked vision at a broader level) and through it he garnered excitement and enlisted support from his superiors, local townspeople, and the laborers who toiled for years. What started as a vision of his, and a curiosity to others, eventually became a physical reality.[13]

As the river twists and turns at the bottom of the mountain from where I live, it must be crossed no less than ten times by the ever-climbing railroad. Each complex bridge Whistler ultimately built is higher than the last, reaching seventy feet above the swirling waters. No photograph can do justice to the massive scale of these structures. His crew of hundreds, including stonemasons from Ireland, Italy, and Russia, took a decade to build the keystone arch bridges of two-thousand-pound blocks of granite. They stand in endurance, beauty, and simplicity.

Whistler proved his critics wrong. They said the bridges could not be built, but he delivered on his promise. They said the trains could not climb the terrain, so he set about designing the first engines capable of handling this task. Even today, multiple six-thousand-horsepower locomotives from GM strain as they chug up the mountain. The bridges they traverse support, without complaint, trains weighing well over one hundred times what they were designed for. Even those bridges left idle when the route was adjusted many years ago show no signs of sagging. These endure against the mountain elements despite being unattended for over eighty years.

What gave Whistler his persistence, sense of urgency, and will to be innovative over and above the wail of his critics? He had passion. He never lost sight of his dream to create these enduring structures that would enable people and goods to be carried far more efficiently and smoothly from Boston to Albany than ever before.

To connect the mountainsides and bring the rails safely over the river beneath, he chose the keystone arch as his preferred structure. This type of bridge is a Roman Arch—a semicircle of stone with an odd number of wedge-shaped segments called voussoirs. The keystone is the piece at the crown of the arch that locks all of the other pieces in place—it is literally the "key" to the Roman Arch. If one were to push down on the keystone, the stone could go nowhere due to the interlocking joint with the other segments. The keystone arch can withstand vast amounts of pressure, allowing these bridges to endure.

Concept to Action

Whistler is an example of someone who successfully made the leap from paper to practice. He brought his vision to life. What he produced can also serve as a powerful metaphor in our quest to understand the role of vision and how it can maintain the alignment of the vision framework.

It's not hard to see the symbolic links these magnificent keystone arch bridges evoke. Growth visions are the keystones for the vision framework. An organizational vision is not about "forcing" people to do things in a certain way, as the formal bureaucracy does. Vision is about getting everyone into alignment. Employees feel the "pull" of the culture, structure, and people processes and if that pull doesn't work, they ultimately cease being members of the organization. The "keystone" doesn't actually do much heavy lifting needed to keep the arch up—every other stone in the arch does that. The vision's effectiveness lies not in applying the "downward pressure" of formal authority but in enabling the rest of the system to stay in alignment. And with alignment comes the strength to accomplish extraordinary things. As long as the keystone remains nestled at the top and applies only the pressure of its own weight, no granite block can move out of alignment. So too can a vision keep the most important organizational characteristics—critical for guided growth—aligned, strong, and sustainable.

Whistler, like Fitzgerald and Burgmans of Unilever, had a vision and had to cross an abyss to make it real. Fitzgerald and Burgmans found the passion and drive for overcoming the binary response and used their own framework to translate their vision from a concept—perhaps on paper—into practice. They focused on the alignment of organizational elements necessary for continually moving closer and closer to realizing the vision.

Part II will delve into the organizational characteristics that must be in alignment with the vision: the executive group (chapter 6), culture (chapter 7), structure (chapter 8), and people processes (chapter 9). Once these elements—which together compose the vision framework—become aligned and integrated, the vision-as-keystone moves from a concept to a tool for action.

Chapter 6

Forming and Facilitating the Executive Group

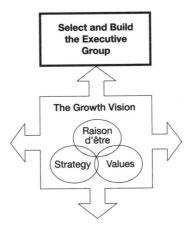

A S CHAPTER 5 ATTESTS, A CEO'S PERSONAL PASSION
and contribution to the vision process has enormous
importance. No one would argue this point. But as the size, complexity, and dynamics of growth increase, so too does the requirement that a *group* of senior executive-level managers work together
in ways that keep the forward momentum constant. A collective
effort at the top maintains the focus that keeps elements of the
organization aligned with the vision.

This is why VCs, when scoping potential projects, so closely scrutinize the composition of the top management team and how that team is set up to work. How do the players relate to one another? What processes are in place to ensure that these people get the most out of one another and give the most possible to their organization? More than a few VCs note specifically to perspective clients that they are "more attracted to outstanding management groups" than to specific industries.[1] Folk wisdom in the investment banking community over the past two decades has also hammered home the point that a great founder cannot compensate for a mediocre team at the top. And if we think back to chapter 4 and the dangers of having an entrepreneur at the helm of a growing business, the importance of the senior management team becomes all the more obvious.

Indeed, the characteristics of the individuals at the very top and their interpersonal chemistry have a far more critical role than I imagined when I started my research. When Laurence Weinzimmer and his colleagues tested the simultaneous impact of market factors, top-management-team factors, and strategy factors, the combined impact of top management teams had significantly more influence in predicting growth than markets *and* strategies.[2] This rings true with my observations, and I believe it's the reason why some firms find ways to grow consistently even when their markets are retrenching.

The role of senior managers in organizations is changing. First, they must go beyond strategy formulation to continually reaffirm the organization's sense of purpose. Second, they must go beyond dependence on mere formal structures to advance the organization's ability to solve problems and provide better service to its customers. And finally, they must go beyond the formal systems and stress the development of people who work in the organization. In other words, top managers must perform on all three of the following essential dimensions:

1. The *executive dimension*—the ability to solve problems

2. The *strategic dimension*—the ability to think about the organization and its relationships with customers, suppliers, and competitors in the long term

3. The *leadership dimension*—the ability to address the organization's institutional structure through both formal and informal
mechanisms

As we begin to realize the extent to which a growth vision
guides each element of the vision framework, and in turn impacts
the achievement of sustainable growth, we also realize how these
organizations must orchestrate their activities at the highest level.
That is why the executive group is the first element of the vision
framework I'm addressing.

The Mandate

An effective executive group uses the basic philosophy of the
organization—the vision—to lend consistency to the organization's
actions and to help employees think and act responsibly, without
requiring a complicated set of rules that direct what should be
done. As developers and guardians of these ground rules, which set
out the ways people should be managed and treated, they become
the creators and arbiters of the culture. In other words, the members of the executive group should be able—individually and collectively—to identify and diagnose the need for alignment and
realignment of elements within the vision framework and to execute the necessary changes.

Each element of the vision must be communicated accurately
and passionately throughout the organization by members of this
group. While the executive group serves multiple purposes on a
short-term basis, its most important role strategically is to delineate
other elements of the vision framework and ensure that it remains
aligned over time.

Indeed, executive managers can not only change the formal
control systems and the organization's culture, but, through these
changes, they can also enhance or diminish the role of the organization's vision. Top managers, therefore, have a very special responsibility for both the final decisions—those with greatest impact—
made by an organization and for shaping the framework within

which these decisions emerge. They also define the climate for innovation and improvement existing in the organization.

Members of an effective group also behave in ways that encourage actions by others to support the organization's purpose; they don't just pontificate, they walk the talk. They are willing to set limits and make difficult decisions about resource allocation that are in keeping with the vision. While this may not appear different from any other executive role, the distinction here is that many of the allocation decisions made collectively may not involve the unit or division that a particular individual manages.

The executive group, therefore, serves for the collective good rather than protecting the individual silos of interest that lead to vision-drift. They are accessible and in contact with people inside the organization. They remove roadblocks and stay out of the way of employees who are trying to achieve short- and long-term objectives. While they are confident in and trusting of employees throughout the organization, they also are able to admit they do not have all the answers and to seek them from others when and wherever it may be necessary. They are willing to admit to mistakes and learn from them.

Lacking an effective executive group, organizations can grow and remain sustainable to the extent that they adapt to shortened product and technology cycles, fuzzy industry boundaries, increasing competitive intensity, shifting economic conditions, and an incessant need to balance employer–employee relations. But changes conceived as piecemeal and isolated within silos of organizational divisions have proved to be insufficient. Changes that are too little, too late and not aligned with a larger organization-wide vision typically yield insufficient results. Even organizations that are widely diversified and whose businesses would seem to institutionalize various paces and directions of change at the decentralized level have discovered the advantage of a collective body that ensures each unit conforms to the vision.

For most companies, this mandate makes intuitive sense. But what happens when an organization's business units have little in common and only nominal interdependencies exist among them?

Top executives then may feel justified to operate more as a federation of management talent rather than as independent free agents. And I would agree. There are some existing corporate structures that do not lend themselves to the mandate that I'm advocating here. One could force greater collaboration in such organizations, but why? These organizations, rather than forcing interdependence, should ask themselves the kinds of questions that are being posed increasingly by Wall Street and other financial intermediaries: "If these business units have nothing in common, then why are they part of the same organization? What's the point of having an extra layer above the unit leaders to second-guess and slow them down?" If an organization lacks a collaborative membership at the senior-most level, focused on deploying a unified vision, then it may be a not-so-subtle sign that the organization has a fundamental strategic weakness.

Johnson & Johnson (J&J) is an excellent example of an organization that manages seemingly far-flung units interdependently through something like a vision framework. The company's scaling strategy is to create subsidiaries that grow out of its nourished entrepreneurial culture. While it was founded to provide surgical supplies to physicians, the firm grew by expanding into related markets and beyond the needs of doctors, hospitals, and consumers. As it scaled, the firm developed separate companies for each distinct market and allowed them a fair degree of independence—to the extent that their framework was aligned with J&J's nearly fifty-year-old vision ("The Credo"). The separate companies collaborate and coordinate their activities when it serves them well. J&J had 195 subsidiaries by 2000, with over 100,000 employees, operations in fifty-one countries, and approximately $24 billion in sales.[3] Despite the sheer size and diverse operations, this is an organization for which the mandate is clearly a "fit."

Johnson & Johnson remains one of the fastest-growing large organizations in the world. The group there that takes the lead—and responsibility—for executing the vision and ensuring that it is aligned with the vision framework is the twelve-person Executive Committee, the principle management group.

Thinking about Executive *Groups*
Rather than *Teams*

Why do I refer to the executives responsible for implementing the vision as a *group* rather than a *team?* It's not to be argumentative or nitpicky. Rather, I'm hoping that raising the issue will lead to consideration of a different way of thinking about how a CEO can best manage his or her senior-most people. If one of the group's most important roles is to communicate and reinforce the vision, and keep far-flung units consistently aligned with it, then the dynamics and composition of a diverse yet tight-knit executive group will vary from the conventional way a "team" is ideally managed.

Most CEOs now recognize the importance of a strategic and organizational mindset, but far fewer have taken this awareness and acted on it to design and orchestrate their senior executive groups. I have found the widely used expression "top management team" a misnomer for the groups that exist at the very top of many firms.[4] These groups more accurately represent a constellation of individuals who rarely operate in the organizational definition of a team. While groups may come together and truly collaborate for the greater enterprise—it is rare to *not* find them focusing exclusively on their own piece of the enterprise. That is the difference.

Senior executives sing the praises of teamwork at the lower levels, and the notion of having a team at the top is appealing. We see it relentlessly perpetuated by the business press when it discusses a CEO and his or her "teams" leading great initiatives. But I believe too many CEOs have an honest misconception of what it takes to be a "team" and, more important, I have reservations—perhaps heretical in this era—of whether there should actually *be* executive "teams." Is a "team" really in the best interest of most organizations?

My guess is that many CEOs, in their hearts, understand that the executives they surround themselves with do not really behave as a team. The performance of this group may be adequate, but it doesn't feel like a team at meetings or in the way people talk about each other between meetings. CEOs are probably aware that the rest of the organization does not experience this group as a team, either. But before exploring the role of the executive group and how the most effective ones roll out and maintain their vision framework, the issue of "team" versus "group" needs to be clarified.

One definition of a work *team* suggests that it consists of a small number of people with complementary skills, who are committed to a common purpose and have performance goals and an approach for achieving the goals to which they hold themselves mutually accountable. Given this definition, I could argue strenuously that the senior group of executives defining and implementing a vision framework cannot meet these criteria.

Teams at all levels within an organization have the opportunity to stay focused on a common purpose but only those at *middle* and *lower* levels have the luxury of having a purpose that can be measured relatively easily in the short run. While teams at the top are certainly the caretakers of a purpose (the raison d'être), it is one that is difficult to measure and easy to ignore. It is intended to reach far into the future, not to be easily achieved. The goals of lower-level teams are concrete, measurable, and often persistent. They embrace the daily work required to produce the product or deliver the service. But at the senior-most level, "team" goals get fuzzier. Even below the vision they are linked to business unit plans, share of market, and perhaps individual-level performance.

Attempts to set goals for executive teams—and here's where the real acid-test surfaces—result in indistinct targets that may frustrate those in senior positions.

Ideally, teams are formed based on a complementary mix of skills. But at the executive level, people are brought together because of the position they hold, rather than the competencies they bring to a working group. Their formal responsibilities are why they were hired, what they get rewarded for, and typically where their priorities lie.

The definition of a team also implies mutual accountability, which contradicts the reality that senior executives are wedded to goals, performance, and rewards based on *individual* accountability.

Finally, working with a collection of individuals in a group is simply much more efficient than trying to manage a team. At this level, the CEO can—and typically prefers to—make assignments quickly and keep people tightly on track. Ironically, while the dynamics of most executive "teams" may look collaborative and egalitarian, the processes underlying group behaviors at the top are actually quite autocratic in nature.

So, let's call it what it really is—or what it should be: a highly functional vision-focused group of the senior-most executives, who are conscious of—and adept at—the roles and behaviors required of such a group and are accountable to the CEO. High-performing executive groups are in relatively short supply for a number of reasons. Many CEOs fear that such a group represents an abdication of their leadership role or that it is at odds with the existing culture that demands individual initiative and accountability. Sadly, these executives miss the point that an effective top management group not only expands their power and influence but also enhances the growth of individual business units.[5] Fragmented executive groups lead to organizations' having great difficulty in creating and exploiting their core competencies and in achieving global strength. These organizations act in slow, piecemeal, maladaptive ways to changes. Hard-charging executives who are not vision focused, and find their comfort zone in individualism and being able to control all the levers of change, are a liability not only to the executive group, but to the organization as a whole. Coordination is limited in organizations with people like this at the top because relations among senior management is limited to bilateral exchanges between the CEO and individual executives. Real collaboration is nearly nonexistent and coordinated organization-wide change becomes nearly impossible.

How Executive Groups Work

The most enduring executive model since the early 1960s distinguished the roles of a CEO and a COO. The Chief Executive Officer handled primarily strategic issues, external relations, and broad governance issues. The Chief Operation Officer was charged with running the operation. Typically, the executives responsible for running major functional units reported to the COO. Increasingly over the past two decades, a different structural form of executive governance emerged in the United States (it had already taken greater hold in Europe): A team of executives reported to the CEO, and this executive group collectively assumed the role of COO in managing internal operations and helping the CEO formulate strategy and deal with external relations. Members of such groups began to realize that their effectiveness was the result of being more than a set of individuals working together; they were interacting and *inter*dependent.

The executive group model configuration began to gain considerable momentum in the 1980s and was fueled further when three resulting benefits were realized. First, it enabled firms (they were overwhelmingly limited to the private, for-profit sector) to respond to the complex and ever-changing external environments in which they found themselves. Second, it provided a more systematic process for managing diverse yet interdependent units inside the organization. Third, it was a nifty way for the CEO to test the competencies and potential of candidates for CEO succession.

While these three functions are becoming increasingly important on their own, my experience in the bowels of scaling organizations working with well-oiled executive groups showed me another critical benefit: These groups were far more capable of developing and implementing their organizations' vision than any other configuration of power and control at the top.

Executive groups enable each member to determine how the growth vision will be implemented in their strategic sector of the organization. Here, the executive group is differentiated from the more traditional CEO/COO model by the significant involvement of each member in broad policy and strategy discussions and in implementation of the vision framework across the organization. These discussions and organizational interventions lead to a far greater sense of "ownership" for vision implementation.

A defining characteristic of a true executive group is its ability to collectively provide strategic, operational, and institutional leadership. Each member is responsible for not only a unit or function; he or she also wears the "hat" of corporate leadership.[6]

As I consider the most effective executive groups, particularly in scaling organizations, I find that they manage a five-point agenda that includes the following:

- Build a shared vision.

- Assess the organization to determine its alignment with the vision or the gap that must be closed.

- Formulate strategy consistent with the vision.

- Develop and manage a growth-enabling culture.

- Continually modify the organization structure to ensure that it can support the implications of growth.

This agenda necessitates that the executive group first embrace the growth vision. In addition, the group requires core skills that any good group needs to master: developing the ability to facilitate meetings well, holding truthful discussions, setting clear goals, clarifying roles and accountabilities, and capturing and accessing collective knowledge.

To maintain effective *inter*dependence and avoid overreliance on the CEO, the executive group's members work at holding each other accountable. Perhaps this is the one "team" trait that exists across these groups—accountability is shared far more than in other configurations of senior executives.

Shared accountability also provokes a shift in leadership roles. Typically, lines of authority are very clear at the top; while the CEO may delegate responsibility for a particular assignment, the CEO is still accountable—and everyone knows it. This process has worked well through the annals of organizational history because it was a rational, effective means for maintaining order and accountability as firms grew in size. But the new stresses and strains on scaling organizations demand a variation. Leadership capacity can be enhanced if the CEO's role shifts back and forth somewhat among group members depending on the task. Ideally, leadership is targeted to the executive who has the knowledge or experience most relevant to the particular problem.

The natural response of CEOs to feel that they must "take charge" is magnified by the frustrations of working in groups— particularly when the stakes are high. Jean-Paul Sartre was close when he wrote that "hell is other people."[7] Hell actually is organizational group-work. What makes it hell is the tyranny of tradition that invariably defeats the spirit of change in groups and the inability of group members to manage their differences. The strategies below can help overcome these limitations and maximize the effectiveness of the executive group.

Strategies for Selecting the Executive Group

The dynamics in high-performing executive groups seem almost paradoxical. They create an environment that continually rattles the status quo and motivates people to be comfortable with change. But rather than create chaos, these dynamics enable the leadership to stay focused on creating opportunities that contribute to the long-term viability of the organization. Effective executive groups keep their eyes not only on the vision but also on the peripheral environment, keep an open mind, and embrace change.

What makes these groups so open to constant examination of their organization and industry? How do groups continue to scan the broader environment that may have a direct bearing on the business and allow all of this information to lead ultimately to possible regeneration of the organization itself? What can you do to ensure that your group meets those criteria? Figure 6-1 outlines some of the dynamics and basic steps in maximizing the effectiveness of the executive group.

Seek Out Differences. Who should be in the executive group? This is a crucial, albeit difficult, question to answer. One characteristic to strive for is diversity. While *diversity* in organizations is defined in a number of ways, in this context it has three dimensions: (1) functional diversity, (2) diversity in industry experience, and (3) diverse corporate backgrounds.

First, diversity in the functional background of members requires a variety of functional areas of expertise. In a study of two hundred firms, one characteristic of the executive group—functional diversity—had more of an impact on top-line growth and bottom-line profit than a company's market characteristics.[8]

FIGURE 6 - 1

Maximizing Effectiveness of the Executive Group

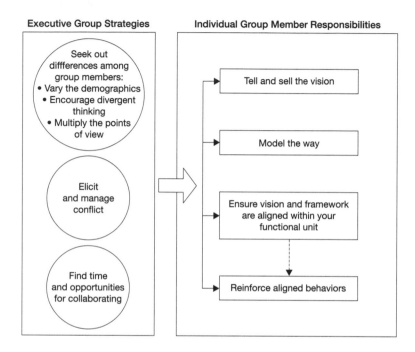

Executive Group Strategies

Individual Group Member Responsibilities

Seek out diffferences among group members:
- Vary the demographics
- Encourage divergent thinking
- Multiply the points of view

Elicit and manage conflict

Find time and opportunities for collaborating

Tell and sell the vision

Model the way

Ensure vision and framework are aligned within your functional unit

Reinforce aligned behaviors

Members should represent a cross-section of the business units and central activities of the organization, including marketing, operations, accounting and finance, research and development, and human resources. Functional diversity can evoke constructive conflict when team members with different functional backgrounds provide a system of checks and balances in decision making. For example, those with research and development experience will be tempered from influencing a disproportionate allocation of capital resources to research if they are competing with marketing for the same resources. Those with extensive accounting backgrounds may influence the group to stay within the budget.

Second, diversity in industry experience results in better decisions because members can offer greater insights based on broad experience through business cycles and over time. Members who have been with the organization a long time and a short time are complemented by newcomers with limited experience who often find it easier to offer fresh ideas generated without the weight and bias of a legacy within the organization. Those with limited professional experiences can provide an outside perspective that a well-seasoned executive may overlook. Their legitimate naivete may enable them to see interrelationships or opportunities that are missed by the more experienced.

Third, diverse corporate backgrounds also yield multiple perspectives based on different organizational experiences. These varying perspectives can be brought to bear on issues before the group. If well managed, the conflict generated by diverse perspectives has the potential to have positive results, enabling the executives involved to make better, more informed, and often more innovative choices.

Nike's struggles in the late 1990s attest to the importance of fresh blood in the executive group. Nike's growth trajectory began to flatten in 1997 when annual sales became stuck at about $9 billion through 2000. Its share of the U.S. athletic shoe market slipped from 48 percent in 1997 to 42 percent in 2000, and earnings fell from a 1997 high of $796 million to about $590 million for fiscal 2001.[9] The problem? Wall Street analysts, industry rivals, and former Nike executives say the company was starving for fresh blood and new ideas. They believed Nike's insular mind-set and inward focus was a significant reason for the troubles. "Nike's corporate culture will make [innovation that comes from fresh blood] hard to do," a Sanford Bernstein analyst commented in 2001. "The feeling is 'what we do is so special, no outsider can ever understand it.'"[10] That is flawed thinking.

In March 2001, Phil Knight, Nike's mercurial CEO, realigned his top management by stacking the corporate suite with a number of twenty-year Nike veterans. Few newcomers advanced in the shuffle. "This was a decision to get the old warriors back in place," commented Nike board member John E. Jaqua. While Knight had, in fact, hired outsiders to top posts representing the senior governing group, many ended up cutting their tenures short, often after an inability to survive the unproductive conflict with Knight and other long-term Nike executives. They commented after their departures that the short tenures were prompted by "an inability to adapt to the company's notoriously tight-knit jock mentality."[11] Newcomers were encouraged to "lay low and keep your head down" and to spend much more time with "old-timers who know our brand."[12]

Building diversity into the executive group helps overcome the tendency of executives to "reproduce" in their own image. In a study I conducted two decades ago, this dynamic helped explain why executives in a particular organization may have gone to the same (or similar type of) university, found interest in the same sports, and looked the same (white and male).[13] As far back as the 1950s, Wilbert Moore observed this organizational phenomenon and labeled it with the now oddly descriptive moniker, "Homosocial Reproduction"—men procreating themselves in their own image.[14] There is a strong pull among virtually all members of organizational groups to attract and select members that possess attributes similar to themselves. Such similarity may increase the comfort level of group members, but it dampens the fire of creative conflict necessary for an effective executive group.

While leaders need loyal followers, what distinguishes great from merely competent leaders is the ability not just to tolerate but to seek out and encourage dissenting ideas from a diverse group of people. Jim Burke was such a leader. As CEO of Johnson & Johnson, he led his company through the Tylenol tampering crisis of 1982 by being an open-minded leader.

After several people died from poison that had been inserted into Tylenol capsules, Burke realized the brand and the entire company were at risk. At first, authorities were clueless about who had poisoned the Tylenol and why, and how many packages had been compromised. Burke immediately sought out advice from senior people inside and outside the firm. And, once the crisis broke, he let the debate rage among his senior group.

For example, he listened to conflicting advice about what to say to the public. When asked to appear on *60 Minutes* to talk about how he was handling the crisis, some colleagues said that if he was straightforward and honest, consumers wouldn't blame the company. But the director of public relations disagreed and told him that appearing on the show would be the worst decision anyone at J&J had ever made. He listened to his colleagues and agreed to be interviewed. A poll conducted days after the show indicated that people who had watched were five times more likely to buy Johnson & Johnson products than those who didn't see it. But a different test of Burke's leadership came afterward: He did not turn against his PR director. He was strong enough to accept conflict and to use it to shape his decision making because he knew what he and the organization stood for.[15]

Many past political leaders had to reach outside themselves and beyond a friendly circle of senior advisors for answers. Franklin Delano Roosevelt assembled a diverse team of scientists for scaling up the Manhattan Project during World War II. John F. Kennedy conferred with hawks and doves during the 1962 Cuban missile crisis.[16]

Abraham Lincoln included in his first cabinet his chief rivals from the opposition party. The group was neither harmonious nor loyal to Lincoln. But he knew that to hold the Union together he needed a truly national team. He made significant attempts to learn from and understand those who opposed him. Secure leaders will be able to hear other opinions; they tolerate not only others' weaknesses but are also not threatened by their strengths.

How do scaling firms avoid the trap of self-reproduction that serves only to limit dissent and, in turn, innovation? How do they step out of their artificial "comfort zone" of the like-minded? They stay conscious of the characteristics inherent in executive groups that create the kind of conflict that leads to creative ideas and betters ways to implement them.

Vary the demographics. Diversity in the age of members represents a potent source of conflict for executive groups. The most effective groups often include individuals with age differences of twenty or more years. Typically, older executives rely on expertise drawn from many years in the industry and often from many organizations. Younger executives bring fresh, albeit often naïve, ideas about new ways to compete.

While demographically dissimilar people may have different worldviews, lending multiple perspectives, their diversity also elicits an *expectation* of conflict within the top management team. Kathleen Eisenhardt and her colleagues explored this need for conflict at the top through their academic research. One of the insights they gleaned from these studies helps us better understand the connection:

> When decision makers look across the table and see visibly different people, they expect and come to listen for contrasting viewpoints. So a diverse team is more attuned to picking up on disagreement. In contrast, when executives gaze around the group and see people similar to themselves, they are likely to assume agreement and so to be less cued into the possibility of conflict.[17]

Multiply the points of view. Divergent viewpoints and out-of-the-box interpretations to events and organizational performance issues are needed to spur people to see, think, and act in new ways. New ideas spring from the encouragement of nontraditional points of view and taking advantage of divergent information to fully explain and understand the current state of a problem or opportunity facing the group.

When different ideas are brought into an organization or new information is presented, there could be as many different ways of viewing it as there are individuals looking at it. But in many organizations, there is just one way—the company way, the way these ideas and information have always been viewed and a way not likely to reveal new directions or new processes required for keeping the organization innovative. When multiple points of view are heard within the executive group, the greater the likelihood that the group will arrive at the best interpretation for people to act in positive new ways.

Multiple points of view are critical because innovation depends on making sense of new and different information. By its nature, new information is incomplete and ambiguous.

Scaling organizations seek out individuals with different thinking styles when forming a senior management group. Often, this plays itself out in the different roles members assume in the group as a result of how they act out their preferences for decision making and problem solving. Eisenhardt and her colleagues found that members of high-conflict senior groups take on one of five archetypal roles.[18] While the roles may come naturally or be artificially imposed, what is important is that the group realizes the need for them and that members step up to the plate and assume them if they do not already exist.

Ms. Action is the doer, go-getter, impatient member who operates in the here-and-now. She pushes for quick action and decisions and hates things and people getting in her way. She creates conflict by continually raising opportunities and reminding the group to act.

Mr. Steady is the anchor, serving as a moderating influence by keeping things close to the status quo. While he may be experienced as resistant to change, his role serves to temper runaway enthusiasm if initiatives catch fire and are launched too quickly without consideration for collateral damage. Mr. Steady likes structure and planning and often serves to throttle back the unbridled enthusiasm of Ms. Action.

The *Futurist* looks to the future. She may be seen as relatively ineffectual because, rather than focusing on getting things done, she prefers to hover thirty thousand feet above the action and consider long-term future implications and the ways in which strategies may or may not be aligned. Her focus is often three to five years out, and she often exhibits characteristics associated with organizational visionaries.

The *Counselor* tends to be an older member of the senior team, and he serves as sounding board and advisor to others on an individual basis. Often in the early stages of a scaling initiative, or when problems emerge that have not been experienced before, he provides advice, feedback, and his education from The School of Hard Knocks. Since he may perceive himself as off the fast track and secure in his position, he is not wary of being candid or motivated by political expediency.

Finally, the *Devil's Advocate* induces conflict by challenging ideas or being a dissenting voice when none other is heard. Research found that rather than experienced curmudgeons filling this role, the incumbents were typically more junior-level members of the executive group.[19] While they may have lacked the confidence to advocate their own ideas, they felt confident enough to voice objections and alternatives to others' ideas.[20]

Why do roles such as these promote the kind of conflict so invaluable to the senior management group and, by extension, to the successful scaling enterprise? They seem to highlight the essential tensions in competitive, turbulent, stressful organizations: tensions between short- and long-term thinking, between status quo and change, and between the need for flexibility and structure. They force the executive group to confront head-on the incessantly competing facets of organizational life at the top. While all managers face—or should face—these tensions, we fall prey to the preferences rooted in our personalities. On an individual level, the more enlightened managers develop their own system for stepping out of their comfort zone to explore alternative ways of viewing a problem or decision.

It becomes easy to maintain a mindset marked by homogeneity in groups of managers. In contrast to the complex set of role dynamics in senior groups that serve to evoke productive conflict, low-conflict groups lack many—and in some cases all—of these roles. The result is a group of people who do little more than serve as advocates for their own products, geography, or functional responsibility.

Elicit and Manage the Conflict

Encourage Divergent Thinking. Accepting, if not welcoming, divergent information is central to helping an organization develop a new focus, create new products and services, and reach further in pursuit of its vision. The executive group recognizes the need to bring new information and ideas from the periphery into the organization (e.g., due to diverse group members, open-mindedness, built into the group process, allows others in organization to be heard?). Whether those ideas are accepted or rejected depends largely on just how different they are and whether they are consistent with the vision. If the new information is subtle, it will probably go unnoticed. If there is not enough of a difference, the normal surroundings will moderate the importance and the possibilities for innovation will be submerged into the background.

The consequences of introducing difference are not always positive. The secret of dealing with difference successfully is to be aware of the impact it is having, whether in individual or organizational terms, and being prepared to take corrective measures.

Members of the executive group invariably face high-stakes conditions that involve ambiguity and uncertainty. When they come together, conflict can be more the rule than the exception. It is only natural that bright, achieving individuals see the world in different ways, make contradictory assessments about what might happen in the future, and therefore prefer different alternatives. Given the high-stakes consequences of their decisions, they are even more likely to be passionate and vocal about their beliefs. The probability of conflict is further exacerbated when each member of the executive group manages his or her own significant sector of the organization. Because of this role, they are constant recipients of information and pressure from their constituencies. Inevitably, they develop a frame of reference that reflects their respective, yet diverse, set of responsibilities.

As mentioned already, conflict is not something to be avoided. On the contrary, it is essential for effective strategic decisions. When well managed, conflict leads to the consideration of more alternatives, better understanding of the possible choices, and, overall, significantly more effective decision making.[21] Given the likelihood of conflict in the kinds of situations that top management teams face and the importance of conflict to successful organizational performance, it is striking how little conflict is openly expressed in these venues and, when it is, how poorly it is managed. Agreement—or the façade of agreement—is amazingly common.

The evidence showing low conflict levels being associated with poor decision making is significant. Without conflict, groups lose their effectiveness. Members become apathetic, disengaged, and only superficially harmonious without conflict. Significantly different alternatives are not offered and opportunities to question falsely limited assumptions are missed.

"Tough" CEOs may actually be uncomfortable with conflict and fear that it could spiral their executive group downward into personal animosity and broken working relationships. They may avoid it because they see it as too time-consuming, leading to endless debate that stalls decision making and diverts attention from more important issues. These CEOs especially need to better understand the value of conflict and the ways in which it can be constructively harnessed.

Find the Time and Opportunities for Collaborating. Executive "teams" fail to generate sufficient healthy conflict because members have been unable to hone in on their own positions or they fail to understand those of other members. In part because the scaling process generates so much information flow and requires such rapt attention at the local level, it exacerbates the inability to share and understand vast amounts of data among the group. A relentless tension exists between the need for each member to maximize their learning about the broader organization and the amount of time they have to devote to this learning. While the degree of resistance to meetings seems to correlate with the level one has in the organization (i.e., the higher up one is, the more resistance), meetings are nonetheless an effective means to increase the quantity and quality of interaction and a vehicle to enable members to understand their own position and those of others. Through discussion, preferences surface and become shaped further. Meeting frequently is at the heart of the learning process of executive teams.

Less conflict is also related to low interaction. Executives often profess to be too busy for meetings. They do not schedule common meeting times, or they communicate almost exclusively through mechanisms such as e-mail. E-mail communication is not as productive as a meeting because it is asynchronous and usually between two people (typically the CEO and another executive). Missing is a robust level of interaction among the full group.

Face-to-face interaction elicits conflict simply because it increases the *opportunities* for conflict. More issues arise when executive group members talk with each other more often. But more important, the quantity of interaction also helps focus one's preferences. We formulate our opinions about complex issues in debate and discussion with others; the more we engage in it, the more effectively and clearly we understand where we stand on an issue.

Finally, meetings help executive group members get to know each other. While on the surface it may seem paradoxical, familiarity and friendship can enable people to feel less constrained by expectations of politeness and therefore more comfortable to argue if conflicting positions are raised. Familiarity breeds a sense of security that enables us to express opposing points of view.[22]

If these dynamics are not well managed when the group is together, an outside facilitator can model the way in which meetings with the potential for high conflict can and should be run productively. Alternatively, the CEO can consider working on a short-term basis with a personal coach, who can focus on strategies and techniques for facilitating executive groups diverse in their functions, industry experience, and corporate backgrounds.

Shaking Up the Leadership at EDS

When Dick Brown took over the reins of EDS in 1999, it was a scaling has-been. Although it pioneered the information technology (IT) services industry—the fastest growing industry in the world—it had become a slowpoke among its more aggressive and nimble peers by the time it split off from GM in 1996. The culture that Ross Perot had ingrained into EDS during its formative years now contributed to slow growth and a declining market cap in a rapidly growing industry.

Brown's first order of business was to deal with top leadership that had grown aloof and distant from people on the front lines. Recalls Jeff Heller, EDS vice chairman: "We'd have meetings, meetings, meetings, but nothing would ever get decided. It would all end up warm spit."[23] The company's culture was hard-wired to encourage those at the top to compete, rather than collaborate, with each other. But competition at the executive level is a far different concept from conflict.

Brown fully understood that *urgency* was a critical cultural value for any scaling enterprise, and he needed a litmus test to see how much it was a factor among the senior leadership group. In one of his first meetings, he asked thirty top managers to e-mail him the three most important things that they could do to improve the company and the three most important things that he could do. He made his request on a Monday and asked the mangers to e-mail him their action items by the end of the week. "I was interested in what they would send but I was more interested in when they would send it."[24] Ninety percent of the managers waited until Friday afternoon to reply. "It never crossed their minds that they could e-mail me within the hour," Brown recalls. "They just did it at the last minute. And that's the message they send to their people: Do it at the last minute. In the end, almost all of them loaded up on what *I* needed to do. They were pretty light on what *they* needed to do."[25] Most of those managers are now gone.

Brown implemented a number of mechanisms to maximize the amount and quality of interactions among his group of senior executives. Two or three times a year he brings them together for a three-day off-site meeting. Each month, the top 125 global leaders participate in an intense conference call that fosters instant feedback and direct, unfiltered communications.[26]

Tell and Sell the Vision

A hallmark of executive groups in sustainable scaling organizations is the active leadership role they take in implementing the growth vision. Starting with each executive group member, and ultimately cascading down to other managers, we consistently find three core requirements necessary for bringing the organization into alignment to sustain the rigor of scaling.

First, each member must be sure that every action they take is consistent with the growth vision. Rather than simply telling others to provide outstanding customer service, innovate through risk taking, and continually learn on the job, each member must be seen and heard *doing* these things. This is walking the talk. Senior management behavior that is out of sync with the vision is one of the most pervasive reasons why organizational visions fail to "take hold."

Second, each member determines how to help others within his or her division understand the growth vision and the ways in which the vision framework supports it. Scaling-up can feel chaotic to people in the midst of it, and the potential for mixed messages, confusion, frustration, and anxiety is insidious. During the torrid rate of growth, people ask themselves questions like the following:

- What does all this mean to me?
- How do I fit in?
- What do you want from me?

They need answers. They need to know how they should act, what they are supposed to do, and what will happen if they do and do not behave consistently with the vision.

Third, the executive group must determine how behavior will be reinforced, and each member must set a strong example. Reinforcement—whether it is used to promote desired behaviors or to douse those that are inconsistent with the vision—guides the individual through the various organizational processes that the Framework defines. It also sends clear signals to others about how to succeed in this environment.

These three guidelines sound fine. But on a day-to-day basis, how does an executive group member demonstrate consistent behavior, help others understand their roles, and reinforce the behavior of others?

One Group = One Voice

To demonstrate consistency and support for the vision process, it is crucial that one voice emanate from the executive group and that members work out their conflicts within the group rather than behind the backs of their colleagues. Those who are viewed as grudgingly carrying out the will of others will ultimately lose the confidence of their peers and weaken their subordinates' perception of them. Members should do everything possible to identify themselves with the coalition of executive group members since they champion the vision and determine the resulting vision framework.

When managers cannot "own" the growth vision and define the implications of what it requires of everyone, this is more frequently the result of an inability to understand the vision rather than an incapacity to embrace it. To help others understand the vision requires each executive group member to see how the vision and the framework impact their unit, how deviation can compromise the scaling process, and how it all remains consistent with each person's value system. Owning therefore requires a commitment on both an intellectual and emotional level and often represents the moment of truth when each must decide whether he or she can get on board and if they are willing to make the necessary commitment. Once a member demonstrates hesitation or skepticism, his or her ability to lead others becomes seriously compromised in this environment.

Executive group members must reflect on the ways they express and demonstrate personal ownership for the growth vision, their belief in it as a means for the organization's growth strategy, and what it will require of everyone in their unit.

Follow the Golden Thread

As details of the vision framework begin wending their way down through the organization, individuals from the executive group must ensure alignment between decisions from the group and activities of people in their division. The "golden thread," a concept borrowed from the quality movement, is appropriate in this context. Managers at each level take the set of guidelines from above and make them specific to their own unit's work. As they cascade down to each successive level, they are adapted to the unit's diverse roles and responsibilities. In large organizations this may require a significant amount of trickle-down, but ultimately there will be a direct link—the golden thread—from the organizational vision to each employee so that everyone identifies with the executive group's understanding of the vision.

Visibility at the top is like a lightning rod. The higher one is in an organization, the more one's behavior is watched, if not analyzed and scrutinized. This is why walking the talk is taken quite seriously and why executive group members have to consistently model to others the behavior necessary for their personal success and that of the organization. Each component of the growth vision will require behaviors that are either implicit or explicit to making it come alive. Values, for example, are converted to action when organizational members see executives acting in ways that directly support the values espoused.

Communicate through Multiple Channels

The scaling process can be experienced as chaotic, ambiguous, frustrating, and anxiety-provoking. People need information; when they consider themselves deprived of it, they will fill that vacuum with rumors, abusive gossip, and embellished stories plucked off the grapevine that misrepresents reality. While none of these communication channels will ever disappear from the organizational landscape, dependence on them as a primary source for disseminating information can nonetheless be catastrophic. Information needs to be multidimensional as well as multidirectional to ensure that people hear the status and news of scaling activities and that management can verify that they understand what they hear.

Organizations continually growing are also continually changing, so what we have learned about the critical role of communications during transformations is equally relevant to scaling organizations. In successful change efforts, a continual information loop flows from senior managers in the executive group to their direct reports. In turn, lower-level managers and supervisors communicate for both accuracy and understanding to their immediate colleagues. As nonmanagerial employees stay in the loop of information, the receptivity and reactions to what is communicated flows back up the loop to the executive levels. If more elaboration is requested, it is provided. If resistance is encountered, the executive group discusses how best to address it.

The loop provides for more than information dissemination; it is a powerful strategy to engage people throughout the organization in shaping their own environment and implementing modifications in their work to support the scaling initiatives. When managers think of "empowerment" it often becomes constrained by the assumption that people require more authority or resources to feel it. Often, what they need most is information. We have learned over the past decades that—at least in organizational contexts—information is the most valued resource for enabling others to experience power.

Reinforce Behaviors to Keep Them Aligned

When individuals understand the vision, know how its strategy impacts their work directly, and are rewarded for contributions, it's an organization designed for growth. Rewards are tied not only to organizational performance but also to behaviors consistent with the vision and the vision framework. While these organizations believe that profit is essential, the real focus is on getting everyone to contribute to the growth vision. The term "reinforce" rather than "reward" in the heading above was chosen with care. Some individuals may be effective at what they do in their own way, but act inconsistently with the guidelines implicit in the vision. Moments of truth in organizations arise when an individual's behavior gets results, but in ways that contradict what is considered acceptable.

When John Reed was CEO of Citibank in the 1990s (before it merged with Travelers to become Citigroup), he revised the banking giant's vision. A key element of the new focus was "Global Relationship Banking," and this required not only a new structure but more importantly a new set of underlying values in the culture. Rather than operating as independent silos, business units now needed to cross-sell and collaborate extensively. Reed expected his executives to walk the talk—to show others what a culture of collaboration and joint problem solving could look like. He also knew that he had to put his money where his mouth was: Those working in the old Citibank style—arrogant and highly competitive within the system—now had to change or live with the consequences. Some senior execs, regardless of their status as rainmakers, found themselves with smaller bonuses if their behavior was not consistent with the new values. And for those who did not change after getting this message, a few found themselves without a job.

The executive group demands consistency across all units and people; when the behavior is inappropriate, but gets results anyway, that behavior should be negatively reinforced (e.g., with verbal or written feedback) in the hope of motivating the individual to change.

For too long, business leaders at EDS knew that success meant competing—and too often that involved competing with each other. Operating units refused to communicate or cooperate. The company lacked a vision and therefore lacked a single overarching strategy. They were rolling out duplicate offerings, duplicate capabilities, and diametrically opposed strategies. Executives at the top hoarded information and acted as though their division had an independent silo. When Dick Brown became CEO and made it clear he would not put up with this from his senior group, things changed.

The company that was wired to compete has learned to collaborate at the top. In the old EDS, senior executives in the same division would fight head-to-head to grab new business. Now, they are still competitors, but their focus is directed against EDS's competition. How did Brown change this behavior? "People are motivated by how they get paid," says one of the division directors.

> I'm compensated on how my organization [division] performs against its financial goals. I'm also compensated according to how we do in the wider [organizational] arena. If my counterpart is having a problem, now I need to help him solve it. The point is, we've made everything open and transparent. I have an incentive to make sure he doesn't have people on the bench and not billing out to clients. I have an incentive to help him get those people off the bench. I trust that man with my career, and I know he feels the same way about me. That's a different peer relationship than I've ever had at this company.[27]

Architects of the Framework

In their book *Hidden Value,* Jeff Pfeffer and Charles O'Reilly refer in their preface to what they call the "Anna Karenina principle of management."[28] The first sentence of Tolstoy's novel begins, "Happy families are all alike; every unhappy family is unhappy in its own way."[29] Tolstoy was trying to say that in order to be happy, a marriage must succeed in all basic respects—such as compatibility, sexual attraction, dealing with money matters, raising the children. Failure in any one of these areas can destroy a marriage even if it has all the other pieces in place for a great relationship.

The same holds true for organizations rocketing through extended periods of growth. To succeed, they need a combination of all the right ingredients and they must be in near-perfect alignment. If one element is missing or out of alignment, then the potential for failure rockets as well. While all organizations are profoundly different, they share the same need to have the right ingredients in place and to ensure they are aligned. And that is what the executive group accomplishes through the vision framework.

Chapter 7

Putting the Cult in Culture

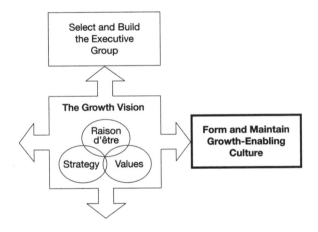

WHEN GORDON BETHUNE TOOK OVER CONTINENTAL Airlines in 1994, it was a crippled organization limping down a trail destined for failure. The airline was one of the least respected in the developed world: It ranked on the bottom rung compared with other major airlines in every category; it had been through ten presidents in eleven years; it had suffered through two Chapter 11 bankruptcies; and that year, just as Bethune was stepping in, it had posted a $200 million loss.[1] Continental was far from a scaling operation; as Bethune quickly realized, any initiative that would have promoted scaling was typically squelched before it saw the light of day.

As mentioned in chapter 2, the company's former management team had stifled risk taking and innovation in part with a nine-inch-thick book of rules known throughout the organization as the "Thou Shalt Not" book or just "The Book."

Bethune had his work cut out for him. He knew at the outset that he had to do nothing less than change the entire culture at Continental, and he had to do it fast. Why? He believed that the key to Continental's survival was to earn employee involvement. In order to do that, employees had to understand the company's new vision and to *see their role in achieving it.* The current culture wouldn't allow either. The Book was the most visible symbol of that culture; it had contributed to dragging the airline down by establishing a punitive environment that stripped from employees most of the freedom to make decisions and take initiative. In 1995, when Bethune ceremoniously set afire a copy of The Book, it symbolized to employees that they were now going to have permission to think for themselves.[2]

Between 1994 and 2001, Bethune led one of the most impressive turnarounds in U.S. corporate history and created an organization that, after many long years, began to scale again.

Why "Culture" in a Vision Framework?

In the business world, practice tends to lead research, with scholars focusing mainly on documenting, explaining, and building models of organizational phenomena already being tried by management. Culture, however, has been one of the few areas in which organizational researchers have led practicing managers in identifying a crucial factor affecting organizational growth and performance. Culture has been an area in which the research has provided guidance for managers as they searched for ways to improve an organization's agility and capacity for growth.

Yet organizational scholars didn't begin paying serious attention to the concept of culture until the beginning of the 1980s, in large part, I think, because culture is undetectable most of the time. *Culture* refers to the taken-for-granted values, underlying assumptions, expectations, collective memories, and definitions of the present in an organization. Since it represents "how things are done around here," it reflects the prevailing ideology that people carry around in their heads. It conveys a sense of identity to employees and provides unwritten and, often, unspoken guidelines for how to get along and get the work done. Unfortunately, people are unaware of the culture until it is challenged, until they experience a new culture, or until it is made explicit through a model or a framework such as this one.

The real culture of a company is usually invisible—no matter how many visible attributes, such as "casual Friday" or "open offices," there are that seem to suggest otherwise.

But culture has now been universally acknowledged as a critical variable in determining the success or failure of growth.[3] It can and should be actively created, managed, changed as needed to move a company forward. That's why it is an explicit central element, in these pages, of both vision itself and the vision framework. Culture is key.

This chapter not only explains why a well-conceived and explicit culture is critical to growth, but it also provides guidelines and examples for conceptualizing and creating a culture that permeates the organization. My research and the consulting experiences that brought these issues to life for me were sobering in a particular respect: I found a glaring omission in organizations that claimed to have "a vision" but were not using that vision as a management process. Typically, the "disconnect" was that the desired culture was never articulated. Even if it was (perhaps in a nicely worded vision statement), the executive group rarely held each other or their divisions accountable for ensuring that "the way things are done around here" was consistent with what was stated.

But culture, like nature, abhors a vacuum. Cultures emerge and become solidified whether or not we manage them to be consistent with our strategies. Since culture is undetectable most of the time, it must be managed to ensure that it is what it should be. And managing it takes vigilance, which sometimes needs accountability as a prod. Cultures need to be monitored and continually fine-tuned if the growth vision is to come alive.

Weak and Strong Cultures

We often hear about "strong" and "weak" cultures but either descriptor can have positive or negative implications, depending on the context. So, for our purposes, *strong cultures* are those that support the organizational vision, where everyone agrees about the importance of specific, high-performance values tied to the vision. In these organizations, you can feel the human energy that flows from this alignment. *Weak cultures,* then, are those in which little agreement exists. In weak cultures, like the old one at Continental, effort toward the vision is fragmented and often dissipated through conflicting agendas, blaming, unclear communications, and other messages communicated (like through The Book) that tell people not to be innovative.

In the broadest sense, culture is the personality of the organization, the shared beliefs and the written—and unwritten—policies and procedures that determine how the organization and its people behave and solve business problems. Culture provides meaning, direction, and clarity; it is the human glue that mobilizes people to aim for the vision.

To understand an organization's culture is to remain focused on the five elements that create it and their attendant questions:

- *Shared values:* What do we think is important?

- *Beliefs:* How do we think things should be done here?

- *Norms:* What are the unwritten rules: the do's and the don'ts?

- *Heroes:* Who are the people who personify our culture and serve as role models for others?

- *Systems:* What do we do to influence people through our written and unwritten policies?

In the end, it all comes down to behaviors—as I said earlier, "the way we do things around here." The answers to these questions need to be put into action as a living, breathing part of the organization's day-to-day functioning.

The "Hardness" of Culture

The gap between the plan and reality of organizational performance—and the scrooge of scaling—is often significant and has been the subject of countless articles and books on motivation, leadership, management skills, and other elements heaped onto the "soft side" pile of organizational performance variables. But what is "soft"? At its most rudimentary, a strategy may look concrete with its definitive goals, data, and spreadsheets, but it's actually an abstraction. It is an idea for the future and has no real existence in the organization or in the marketplace. The organization's culture, however, is a living, breathing, dynamic force that has a life of its own, operating independently of all plans and projections yet determining the success or failure of those plans.

In 1992, a Harvard Business School study measured the impact that culture had on organizational growth and performance. The results, after observing over two hundred organizations for twelve years, were sobering and dispelled the myth that culture was not a "hard" business issue.[4] Cultures with values, beliefs, norms, heroes, and systems that supported high performance significantly impacted the financial metrics that matter to most executives (and their shareholders/investors) as outlined in table 7-1.

TABLE 7 - 1

Impact of Culture on Growth and Performance

Performance Indicator	With Performance-Enhancing Cultures (%)	Without Performance-Enhancing Cultures (%)
Revenue Growth	682	166
Employment Growth	282	36
Stock Price Growth	901	74
Net Income Growth	756	1

Source: Data from John P. Kotter and James L. Heskett, *Corporate Culture and Performance* (New York: The Free Press, 1992), 78.

The notion that organizational performance is dependent on a set of often subjective and intangible "organizational behaviors" is not a new one. But its importance cannot be minimized because a growth vision will fail unless the culture directs and sustains individuals' behaviors, on a daily basis, in pursuit of strategy. While these intangibles may be far harder to measure than sales volume or return on equity, they are often the key factors in one organization's competitive advantage over another. The difference between success and failure can often be attributed to a limited set of organizational characteristics. When they are combined, they create "culture."

Many organizations emphasize values such as quality, customer service, teamwork, respect for the individual, and innovation—themes with broad appeal that can help people feel they are reaching higher goals for themselves. But all too often these values are communicated merely as organizational spin control in the form of annual reports, recruitment sections of the corporate Web site, and token discussion at management retreats. They fail to become alive, to be fully infused in the fabric of their culture.

The Container Store was rated the number 1 company to work for in the United States by *Fortune* for 2000 and 2001; a more relevant achievement is the firm's ability to grow 20 to 25 percent annually since 1978 in the hotly competitive home furnishings business.[5] But for cofounders Kip Tindell and Garrett Boone, the goal has never been growth for growth's sake. Rather, they are obsessed with adhering to a set of core values that has established a culture aligned with creative merchandising, outstanding customer service, and unyielding employee input. Growth and an impressive income statement, they believe, are the natural and inevitable consequences of these business practices.

"Soft" Control?

I have found that people with a somewhat detached, rational approach to management have particular difficulty with the concept of culture because of its supposed lack of "hard" measurements and the indirect, though significant, causal impact it has on performance. If you are so inclined, this might help: An alternative way of thinking about how culture can be leveraged as a tool for scaling, and a way in which many managers can understand its value, is to see it as a highly effective control mechanism.

One of management's primary roles is to control or influence behavior—the way in which work is completed. There may be many levers available to managers for exerting control over others, but the perennial struggle has been determining which levers to pull for different people in different circumstances to yield all the desired results. At the same time, the trick is to avoid the negative consequences that too many attempts at managerial control can evoke. Prior to Gordon Bethune, Continental Airlines saw The Book as its means of controlling people. Organizational culture provides more control through the social system of the organization rather than through fabricated devices like rulebooks.

The research on influence and power illuminates a dynamic we often take for granted: behavior based on mutual regard. Most of us, for example, genuinely like and care about some other people, and, in turn, we want them to like us, so we behave in ways that will promote this liking. If we have a mutual understanding about what is important to us collectively, however implicit it may seem, we are positively influenced by this regard for each other. In other words, if I care about my colleague Susan, and we agree about what is important and how we should act, then whenever we are together we exert control on each other's behavior.

The "Cult" of Culture?

It's the same deal in an organizational arena. While senior managers may be explicit about certain things that are important, most people figure out what really matters on their own. We learn how to behave relative to what is real, what people really pay attention to and comment on, and we react as a consequence of these signals. An ever-present danger exists for a chasm to open between the values that may be espoused by management as part of a formally communicated vision and the *real* values that underlie and actually determine the culture. Talking about the values, printing them on desk trinkets, and espousing them in annual reports and formal gatherings does not guarantee they are the ones actually shared. Too often in our real organizational worlds, we come face-to-face with cultures that are antithetical to the values espoused.

In scaling organizations, there's an intense focus on norms, rather than formal rules, that act as the social control mechanism. Since norms are the unwritten "do's and don'ts" that are far more powerful than any rulebook, continually communicating and reinforcing them ensures that they remain ever present and visible. But if norms are to operate as an active social control mechanism, then a strong, shared agreement about what values, beliefs, and behaviors are desired must exist. Trying to reach consensus around these issues doesn't cut it. Many organizations have compelling internal public relations functions that can broadcast the importance of nice-to-have values like quality or innovation but making them real and practiced requires more. This notion of "intensity" is critical. People who share a norm must feel strongly enough about it so they are willing to tell others when it is being violated.

At Oakley, for example, the norms about creativity, design, and performance create a culture that strongly motivates people to think differently—if not thoroughly unconventionally—about style.

Strong cultures in vision-driven organizations are anything but "soft." These firms are not necessarily great places to work—for everyone. Visionary firms do not need to create comfortable environments. In fact, they tend to be more demanding of their people than nonvisionary firms, both in terms of performance and congruence with the ideology. The culture dictates how everyone thinks, acts, and behaves. It determines choices and actions, how people communicate with and treat each other, who gets rewarded and promoted—and perhaps fired—and who gets brought in from the outside.

Becoming part of an organization strongly guided by a vision often feels like joining a very tight-knit society. If you don't fit, it may be best not to join. If you are prepared to buy into the raison d'être and values that so strongly influence the culture and to dedicate yourself to helping the organization achieve, then you may be quite happy and satisfied. But if the fit isn't there, you will feel miserable and out-of-place. These vision-driven cultures have a way of pushing the misfits out quickly. We're talking almost cult-like here.

In their book *Built to Last,* Collins and Porras compared characteristics of the vision-driven firms in their study with those attributed to cults.[6] Vision-driven firms that grew successfully were more cult-like than the comparison firms that did not grow so successfully. "Cult" and "cult-like" evoke some negative connotations. But *cult* can also have a positive connotation in the sense of the great devotion that cult members feel toward a person, idea, or work. The people at vision-driven firms feel this shared devotion and it shows in how they do their jobs.

To say that visionary companies have a culture doesn't tell us anything that we didn't already know. Every organization has a culture. But the firms that grow year after year, decade after decade, share common characteristics that distinguish them from their more sclerotic brethren. These characteristics are discussed below under "Ingredients in a Scaling Culture"; first, let's see how Oakley brings these to life.

The Scaling Culture at Oakley

From the time Oakley was founded in 1975, the people working there have been obsessed with the design and manufacture of inventions that "defy convention." They drive themselves to continually innovate, to reject any product idea that has even a faint sniff of mediocrity, to move fast, and to foster a belief they can accomplish anything they set their minds to. Yes, there is a level of confidence at Oakley that some may consider close to arrogance. It hits you the moment you talk with anyone in the organization.

At Oakley's huge headquarters, design, marketing, and manufacturing center in Southern California, I got a first taste of the culture before walking in the door. While other tenants in the sprawling corporate park had directional signs guiding guests to their location, if you were looking for Oakley, you had better be prepared with a map (which I wasn't). After driving around for a while, I finally asked some teenagers at a local gas station. "Oakley?

Oh, they're in the cool, weird building at the top of the mountain. Just look for the big flag and you won't miss it." The big flag?

I drove back to where they pointed me, looked up, and saw a menacing, dark gray building sitting high above all the others. Futuristic-looking stainless steel cones with sharp tips jutted out from each support bay. The daunting place atop the hill looked like a fortress. And the flag? An enormous skull and crossbones was flapping for all to see in that corner of Orange County (where it remains a violation of zoning ordinances to fly any flag other than the American flag from a building).

I drove up the mountain, keeping my eyes on the building. Still no signs telling me Oakley existed anywhere in the neighborhood. A driveway looked like it might get me to the main parking lot—which it did—and then I saw the business end of the building.

The main entrance loomed before me, far out of scale in relation to the typical main entrance to a building of this size. It was an ominous mixture of darkened, industrial-strength metal plate—huge bolt and rivet heads protruding from beams and cross braces—all with a patina of rust. It looked mean. It looked like the entrance to a sinister Darth Vader headquarters.

Opening the door and looking in could not prepare me for what I was about to experience. After passing through a short, angled hallway, I was transfixed and overwhelmed by the outsized lobby stretching the length of a football field and rising a hundred or so feet into space. But it wasn't just the sheer space. The heavy industrial symbols—even larger bolt and rivet heads, steel plate gears, and flywheels—confused this visitor into wondering whether he had entered some scary image of the future (think underground bunker from the movie *The Matrix*) or had gone back in time to the dawn of the industrial revolution.

Employees are scurrying around in the cavernous lobby area wearing Oakley gear—the eyewear, footwear, shorts, shirts, watches, and backpacks. Are they doing it because it's expected as the corporate uniform? Do they just get the stuff so cheap that it isn't worth buying other peoples' product?

President Colin Baden explained the uniform of Oakley's "close knit army": "People wear Oakley products because it's only one of the ways to identify with, and show our commitment to, what we do here. If you don't believe in the way we do things here, you just don't last very long—you leave. And we rarely have to ask people to leave."[7] What does it take to succeed? "We look for people with enthusiasm squirting out of their ears. We have emotion, we feel passion about what we do . . . and we expect that of everyone."[8]

People want to feel part of the "army." They wear the Oakley uniform, and they cannot avoid the constant flow of communication that tells them how the company is performing and, to the extent possible, what the top-secret design and development groups are up to. The whole place oozes entrepreneurial spirit when you give folks the opportunity to talk about what they do and how they do it. Management takes careful steps to reinforce this culture. They wear the same uniform—down to the branded skateboarding shorts, shirts, socks, footwear, eyewear, and watches. While earlier in this chapter I mentioned how visual clues like "casual Friday" can be meaningless for interpreting the culture, the choice of apparel at Oakley is quite meaningful.

"If you work here, you understand the vision and culture implicitly. We just don't do a great job communicating [them] out to the rest of the world," Baden (co-designer of the building) told me.[9]

> The world sees our products, the people who choose to use our products in their sports, and the images we choose as metaphors for who we are. They either get it or they don't. We create things where there is opportunity. We've never done a market test or a focus group. We're a design and technology company; not a marketing machine, not an eyewear maker, not anything pegged to any particular product we design and make. The thrill here is not about money, it's about creating coolness.[10]

There are several reasons Oakley should have flamed-out years ago. The company has a product mix that seems to lack coherence, resists hiring highly qualified managers from the outside, and is obsessed with manufacturing as much as possible in-house rather than contracting out. Most employees are arrogant about the greatness of their products, and they abhor job titles.

But none of these factors has a negative impact because the Oakley culture, under the close watch of founding CEO Jim Jannard and his executive group, is a very strong one. Everyone understands what the company's raison d'être, strategy, and values are and why the culture that exists does—and must—support these components of the Oakley vision.

While athletes will always be Oakley's center of gravity for the type and style of products it develops, they are only a fraction of its market. In the mid-1970s Oakley designed what was considered the most technologically advanced ski goggle. The company proceeded to develop other types of sports-related eyewear, all the while perfecting optical technology to not only exceed all standards for safety and clarity, but to provide prescription lenses "wrapped in sculpture."[11] In 1997 Oakley expanded into apparel, including gear bags, and later into footwear. But its creative outlets continued to expand. In 1998 Oakley introduced a wristwatch that utilizes a subminiature inertial generator to convert human motion into electricity, once again defying convention and setting the bar for competition.

Oakley has no vision statement posted on its walls or in its annual report; it's hard-wired into the culture. "We have three purposes," Bill Daily, vice president of consumer marketing, told me.

First, to make wicked cool products. Second, to have fun. And third, to make enough money to do the first two. We don't go out looking for opportunities; we create them.

So, inherent in our culture is the need to be fast, fluid, and flexible, which dictates why we do a lot of things the way we do. We bring virtually everything possible inside (design, development, manufacturing, distribution, marketing, advertising). We can correct mistakes quickly . . . and we do make mistakes. We're very gutsy; we take chances on very bold designs that are not driven by what we think the market wants. Our culture is also about passion—and passion overcomes process. We're constantly worried about process around here as we grow. If there's too much process, then we destroy the culture that made us who we are. The culture keeps us honest by staying close to two key values that keep the amount of process to a minimum. We always ask two questions: Will more process improve communications? Will more process get us better efficiency without sacrificing who we are? If the answer is yes to both, then we carefully explore a little more process. Otherwise, the culture is the process.[12]

Jim Jannard, who also holds the working title of "Chief Mad Scientist," remains at the helm and has resisted hiring an army of "professional managers." The company has 1,500 employees, and revenue was about half a billion dollars in 2001.

When you ask any of the senior managers at Oakley about how the firm deals with people who take risks and fail, they look surprised, as though you're suggesting there's some other way to handle the risk–failure conundrum that may not have occurred to them. At Oakley, risk always seems to include the possibility of failure. "People have to make mistakes here, if they aren't making them, then they're not being creative enough," Baden retorts.[13]

> Everyone here is given the freedom to do great work on their own. We're like professional athletes, we have to collaborate and work as a team, but in the end if someone can't get the ball in the fucking basket, we've all got a problem. There's a strong spirit here that's supportive and that demands open communication. So, failure is sniffed at because we know it comes from trying to do really, really great work.[14]

When they design, develop, manufacture, and launch a product that fails in the market, they blame it on being "too far in front of the marketplace."[15] Arrogant? Probably. But that's what builds the cult-like Oakley culture. The employees at Oakley are smart, competitive, talented, self-sufficient—and they know it.

Kent Lane, VP of manufacturing, told me

> I have people who never finished high school designing highly complex manufacturing processes that leave well-trained engineers in the dust. People know they have to be innovative, push the envelope, and keep learning. They have to know that there are no limits, no obstacles, just expectations to succeed. And you know, when we keep this expectation on them through the way we lead and the culture itself, they execute with passion.[16]

Darlene Kennedy, director of human resources, is one of the relatively few professionals—along with Lane—brought in from the outside to create some process within the firm.

We have very, very strong values here. We're competitive. We don't just like to win; we *have* to win. But the values also tell us that winning is not about any one individual. If one wins, we all win. If the organization wins, every individual feels like a winner. I've been doing senior-level HR work at many big companies, firms that started small and grew big. But they got stale after a while; they lost the magic. At Oakley, we do things different and we're just committed to being different, seeing ourselves as different, and realizing that to continue growing and having fun requires that we approach this differently. That may look unconventional to the outsider. We have a sense of urgency that I haven't experienced in other places, a way to break through barriers that get in peoples' way. It's an attitude, but it comes out of the culture.[17]

"Management is expected to be respectful, supportive to all their people," Baden says.

The higher you rise in management, the greater the expectation that you are approachable to everyone. It's almost the opposite of what you find in most companies. That's why the offices of senior managers are cubicles out there with everyone else, being out in the open sends a strong message: We're out here with you, let's keep talking about the issues we face. Why do you think the execs wear all the stuff we design and sell? It's to communicate approachability, to send the message that those of us at the top have the same enthusiasm squirting out of our ears. The only way you can move up at Oakley is to become more and more approachable for people to want to connect with you. The challenge for us as managers is to continually balance the tension of getting serious about what we do while still trying to operate like a garage company. How do we deliver and still keep the magic? That's the scariest part, for me at least. The vision never changes. The issues change every day.[18]

What do they do at Oakley to manage this tenuous culture? How do they maintain the key principles of innovation, a healthy attitude toward change, confidence (bordering on arrogance), urgency, and collaboration?

While Oakley is deeply influenced by its charismatic and visionary founder, Jannard, the company's passion does not stem from devotion to a person but rather from devotion to its ideology. The cult-like religiosity builds a reverence for its values that, in turn, creates the tangible culture. Oakley, and organizations like it, converts its ideology into mechanisms designed to send a consistent set of reinforcing signals to everyone. The mechanisms indoctrinate people, impose a tightness of fit, and create a sense of belonging through concrete actions. Oakley reinforces its culture through:

- Orientation and ongoing coaching from managers with content that is both practical and ideological. It teaches people the values, norms, history, and tradition of the firm.
- Real-time, on-the-job socialization of new employees by peers and immediate managers.
- Tendency to promote from within and shape employees' mindsets early.
- Exposure to mythology of "heroic deeds"—people going out of their way to support the vision—and corporate exemplars.
- Development of language and terminology specific to the organization that reinforces a unique perspective and creates a sense of belonging to a special group.
- Recruiting systems that have a rigorous filtering process to screen out those who may not be comfortable with the values and norms supporting the culture.
- Incentive and advancement criteria linked explicitly to fit with the culture.
- Awards and other forms of public recognition that acknowledge those who display significant effort consistent with the message espoused by the culture.
- Tolerance for reasonable mistakes that are not in conflict with the vision, but severe penalties for breaching values held dear to the firm.
- Relentless reinforcement, through a myriad of media, of organizational values, beliefs, history, and the sense of being a part of something special.

- Physical design that facilitates and reinforces the culture. Oakley's building communicates timelessness, creativity, and being different from everyone else.

Ingredients in a Scaling Culture

While all organizations must create their own unique culture, current research, corroborated by my observations over the past two decades, has concluded that specific culture characteristics support sustainable growth.

Innovation, Which Equals Creativity + Execution

We know that scaling requires innovation. But innovative organizations must cope exceedingly well with unpredictability, risk taking, and finding nonroutine solutions to the new problems that can stall growth. Formal control systems have never been able to manage these conditions well. Managing a growth-oriented culture, driven by the vision, therefore lies at the heart of a successful scaling enterprise.[19]

Innovation results from a set of prevailing norms that promotes two linked processes: creativity and execution. Creativity is wonderful, but if the ideas are not implemented, they will fail and further creativity will be squelched. Why bother taking risks and trying to be creative if the ideas only get talked about? But when execution is considered an important norm, in tandem with creativity, people not only talk about new ideas but also consider ways to make them real—and they become increasingly skilled at it. Innovation embodies an attitude that drives the organization's actions and people's activities. It is at the heart of the development of new products, new technologies, new delivery systems, and new business concepts. It is one of the engines of growth and, while shaped by the firm's organizational structure, systems, and values, it also influences them. Innovation can constantly activate and renovate the raison d'être.

An essential challenge of the scaling organization, therefore, is creation of a culture that embodies *innovation, diversity,* and *trust.*

Since people approach innovation and change in their lives in a variety of ways, the culture must be able to support the diversity of these approaches. As already mentioned, innovation requires the organization to value and allow for both creativity and execution. Since creativity involves risk taking, people in the organization need to trust that the organization does indeed value such risk taking—even when it is not successful.

Being innovative and responding to change and uncertainty requires a willingness to accept that all decisions and actions will not necessarily be the right ones. Punishing decisions that turn out to be mistaken discourages the creativity critical to deal with new situations in which uncertainty is the norm.

Mistakes and imperfection play an important part in creating long-term sustainability and keeping organizations moving forward. Unfortunately, in too many companies, especially those that place a premium on staying "lean and mean" as a way of dealing with uncertainty of the modern world, making mistakes is regarded as something to be avoided. While it may save precious resources in the short run, in the long term it is far more costly. By not allowing for mistakes and the learning that comes from them, creativity is stifled. Results from a number of academic studies suggest that innovation requires a readiness to:

- think the otherwise unthinkable;
- be enterprising and inquisitive;
- be nonconformist and flexible;
- be open-minded to the irrational and off-beat;
- take a chance on being wrong and failing;
- shun cynical, know-all, and perfectionist attitudes; and
- stand up for cranky ideas.[20]

A Healthy Attitude toward Change

If the culture embodies the notions of creativity and execution, then it stands a good chance of being innovative. But innovation is predicated on the existence of yet another set of norms. For employees to become innovative, the climate must support risk taking, which involves comfort with change and tolerance for well-intentioned mistakes. Managers hoping to stimulate creativity must be prepared to encourage risk taking and accept failures.

Giving license to make mistakes—as a prerequisite to creating an innovate culture and an adaptable organization—is easy to say and hard to do. Many level-headed employees have learned the hard way to be cynical when bosses say that it's okay to make mistakes, having seen careers career off-track when people took these comments at face value.

In many scaling organizations, seemingly insignificant programs become a means for institutionalizing norms and reinforcing the value of risk taking—even when it does not lead to a successful outcome. For example, one manager at Hershey Foods instituted the "Exalted Order of the Extended Neck" for employees showing entrepreneurial behavior. A number of my clients offer "The Best Idea That Failed" award on a monthly basis. At FedEx, many organizational heroes are those who tried their mightiest to satisfy customers whether or not they succeeded. What makes them a hero in this culture is showing commitment to the value (customer service) and the norm that gets it realized (innovation). Ultimate success or failure may be a minor factor in the bigger scheme.

Managers can erode employees' natural resistance in part by being clear about what types of risk taking and mistakes are acceptable and encouraged; for example, those that are based on analysis, foster learning, and are modest in impact. There must be continual support for those who try and do not succeed. Under these circumstances, innovation and openness to change cannot help but be fostered as employees see innovation modeled by managers, watch coworkers get rewarded, hear it talked about by peers, and see that good-faith mistakes are not only tolerated but may even be approved of.

Underneath seemingly odd behaviors at some companies is a serious message: It is okay to think out of the box. Managers who want to inspire employees to be open to change must be creative in how they convey the consistent message that challenging the status quo is expected. And managers have to be prepared for the consequences of succeeding at this. Some organizations depend on managers informally communicating the need for openness to change at both the individual and organizational levels.

Other firms go further by institutionalizing a culture of openness to change. Proctor & Gamble, for example, builds it into its performance appraisal process. When subordinates set their annual goals, they are expected to show how they will change their job during the coming year.

Confidence, Bordering on Hubris

Viewed from the outside, visionary companies seem audacious in the risks they take. They look more audacious to outsiders than insiders, who believe that they can do what they set out to do. This tends to evoke what some call "The Hubris Factor," self-confidence inspired by a certain level of unreasonable arrogance. Oakley does well on this count. Its self-perception as the most talented designers, manufacturers, and marketers enables it to step back from the occasional product failures and conclude that "we were just way ahead of what the customer wants . . . maybe we'll reintroduce it in the future."[21]

Internet Appliance Network (IAN), the firm described in chapter 3, had this element of their culture down pat from day one. The employees knew that innovation was the key to their success—if not survival—and that confidence in what they were doing was critical to bulldozing through the competitive landscape closing in on them at the time. They were smart and creative people—and they knew it. While they were realistic about the Goliaths moving into their market space, they were also confident that they offered the best technology to fit the consumer's needs. This kept spirits high and momentum consistent, but just as important it gave everyone the wherewithal to weather the storms. Every month, a threat to their survival surfaced and, scary as that was, they rallied together in the belief that they were the best of the best. Without this confidence oozing out of the culture, and reinforced almost daily by CEO Audrey Parma, IAN would never have existed as long as it did.

Speed and Urgency

Scaling organizations are very conscious of time. Speed, the completion of tasks with urgency, is part of their DNA. One element of speed is the rapid cycle required for decision making. FedEx's policy that every employee or customer inquiry be answered that day, even if the answer is only that the issue is being worked on, sets the norm that decisions require timely action. In bloated hierarchies where decisions must go through levels of approval, this is impossible. People must be given the authority and trust to take action, as they are in The Container Store where autonomy reigns.

Individual employees not only need the latitude to take action but they must feel the obligation do so. A core value at Johnson & Johnson, for example, is decentralization. The parent firm stresses autonomy of the subsidiary companies. This enables them to act quickly and seize opportunities or solve problems fast. Managers are expected to run their own companies and undertake their own strategic planning without interference from corporate headquarters. Hewlett-Packard has historically made a core element of its culture the belief that managers give their direct reports a well-defined objective and then turn them free to work toward the objective.

When speed and urgency become part of the culture, it means that certain norms have taken hold. First, people understand that decisions should be made quickly. In some organizations, this is reflected in a rapid pace of work and/or the expectation that people work long hours. Second, there are expectations that encourage flexibility and adaptability. This translates to control at the local level, which can push decisions down to teams, for example. When those closest to the problem have control, decisions and actions are accelerated. Finally, the cultural norms promote a sense of personal autonomy. This provides individual employees with the latitude to take action and promotes the obligation for them to do so. When Gordon Bethune torched Continental Airlines' rulebook, he was sending a clear signal that autonomy was not only allowed but expected.

Valuing speed means a shift from relying on prediction, foresight, and formal planning to building a culture of flexibility, courage, and faster reflexes. At Oakley, speed and urgency are promoted through the way they minimize rules and design jobs. At Continental, rewards are tied to getting the planes in and out on time (as well as doing what's necessary to satisfy the customer). While organizational structure issues also impact speed (these will be discussed in chapter 8), it is important to emphasize here that *autonomy*—and the norms, values, and beliefs that support it in the culture—has a direct link to creating an organization that moves fast and is quick to adapt.

Collaboration

When new products, processes, or technology disrupt the way people work, they need to be flexible. This flexibility often requires working as part of a group. Group members need to like and respect each other and understand others' perspectives and preferred styles of operating. They resolve their conflicts and communicate effectively. In a word, they collaborate.

Chapter 8 will discuss ways to maximize collaboration through the organization's structure, but structure alone will never solve what is essentially a process challenge. Collaboration is like the yeast that enables the other ingredients of the scaling culture discussed earlier to bake and rise. The prior four can exist on their own, but without collaboration, neither the culture nor the structure ever reach their full potential.

We know collaboration is embedded in the culture when information and ideas are shared widely throughout the organization. When employees have a common sense of the vision, and a wider swath of information about the organizational issues and challenges in implementing it, they will be more accepting and willing to focus on addressing them. What else will we see? Competition is directed externally, rather than internally. Various groups within the organization cooperate to advance a shared agenda rather than vie to protect turf. And people are not rewarded for creating fiefdoms.

Seven Lessons for Managing a Culture Ready for Scaling

Visionary growth companies impose tight ideological control while simultaneously providing wide operating freedom that encourages individual initiative. The practical implications of this statement are enormous. It means that organizations seeking an "empowered" or decentralized work environment must first impose a tight ideology through its culture, screen and indoctrinate people into that ideology, ensure that those who do not fit are removed, and provide those who remain the tremendous sense of responsibility that comes with belonging to an elite organization.

It also means understanding the seeming paradox that organizations driven by visions to a cult-like intensity are also those that turn people loose to experiment, change, adapt, and act.

Most discussions on the management of culture ultimately center around pocketbook issues, ascribing to the theory that people's behavior is influenced predominantly by economics. If the formal reward system is designed to reinforce those behaviors consistent with the culture, then people will be motivated to engage in them. In reality, this is an expensive and largely ineffective strategy. Greater impact is felt when managers have the foresight and imagination to understand how small rewards and informal recognition have the power to motivate and sustain creativity.

Many organizations work on changing their culture, and most fail miserably at it. From all my experiences trying to change cultures and get them realigned with a vision, what lessons have I learned?

1. Organizational Leaders Cast a Long Shadow

Few organizational cultures support scaling efforts when the "real work" of managing the culture begins below the executive level. Assuming the norms, values, beliefs, and systems are in place to support growth, it then becomes essential that the executive group stays mindful of the direct and subtle messages sent through their behavior. This group owns the culture, and it is their responsibility to ensure it aligns with the values of the vision. The executives at Oakley, The Container Store, Whole Foods Market, and other organizations with a functional vision framework know that if the culture starts feeling out of whack, it's their responsibility to fix it.

Most executives know that people pay close attention to their processes, habits and activities, the ways they respond to critical incidents, and the rituals they perform. What they are often in the dark about, however, is how they are actually perceived by others. They may think they are acting consistently with the values they espouse, but others know better. I think everyone can name a senior manager who stands for certain elements of a culture and proclaims the importance of these elements at ceremonial events, yet acts at times in contradiction to these proclamations. Not walking-the-talk is one thing. Walking in a direction that disagrees with the talk is a dangerous road to go down. Not only does this send a clear message since everyone is watching, but it is precisely the wrong message. Executives must be committed to making what they do match what they say. They need to be attuned to those events and people that push the buttons for behavior that veers from that required by the vision, which casts an unintended shadow.

Although James O. McKinsey provided the vision that drove the prestigious consulting firm bearing his name, it was Marvin Bower, McKinsey's managing partner from 1950 to 1967, who articulated its values and embedded them into the culture. He believed the firm needed to become a collaboration of professionals with standards of personal integrity, technical excellence, and professional ethics equal to those of the most elite law firms. This would serve to raise to a profession a group that had been known merely as "efficiency experts."

At the heart of these values was the "one firm" principle that required all consultants to be recruited and advanced on a firmwide basis, with the responsibility of all clients resting on the firm itself and all profits to be shared from a single pool. Bower believed that this was the key to ensuring professional standards, commitment to clients, and a spirit of collaboration.

And if Bower's commitment to these values rested on a series of well-chosen moments for speeches, his partners would never have converted the good thoughts into action. Over the years, each of McKinsey's leaders has worked diligently to ensure that each member of the firm understood that his or her association with McKinsey required a commitment to making a positive and lasting impact on their clients' performance and to helping uphold and maintain a great firm able to attract and retain extraordinary talent.

Executives need to *demonstrate* what the culture looks like, what it feels like, and how people can live it today as well as in the future. They use themselves as vehicles of change. In each interaction, each decision, a manager acts consistently with his or her own values and with those of the organization he or she is trying to create.

2. You Cannot Realign What You Cannot Define

Specific definitions of norms, values, beliefs, and guiding behaviors are the foundation of these efforts. No organization would
operate without an income statement, balance sheet, or budgeting
process. These define the quantitative goals and enable everyone to
see the extent to which the goals are being met. But when an organization embarks on a drive to realign its culture, more often than
not a clear definition of the culture is lacking and there is no means
for measuring the cultural ingredients.

Making the values that create the desired culture requires quan-
tifying when and how they will be achieved. In the absence of
such measures, the company's strategic goals and operational
targets—inevitably qualified and carefully monitored—eventually
overwhelm the soft statements of value-laden aspirations. McKinsey
& Company, for example, developed client impact measures that
made tangible the firm's commitment to client service. Over time,
the firm found that the best way of articulating this value, and
keeping it strong and executable within the culture, was to reorganize around firmwide client-service teams and away from office-
based, project-driven engagement teams. The need to manage values
within the culture requires a process for actively ensuring that the
values are converted to action. In McKinsey's case, the emphasis on
measuring client impact has served to reemphasize the value of "one
firm" collaboration as a means of providing superior client service.

One method for defining your organization's culture is offered
in the appendix at the end of the book.

3. Behavioral Change Starts at the Emotional, Rather than Intellectual, Level

In organizations stuck with maintaining the status quo, where
growth is more of a chimera than a distinct possibility, cultures
influence people quite differently. Discussions are mostly inward
looking, dealing with matters like inventory reduction, allocation
of overhead, and how to increase penetration rates of existing
products. In general, the focus is on things people can control. Peo-

ple don't want to take risks. New ideas are seen as aberrant and dangerous to careers. Employees wait for marching orders rather than jump up and take initiative. There's a safe rationality to conversations and decisions. There is the belief that change is bad.

Cultures are changed more often than not as the result of a crisis, after people have faced emotional events that reduce their resistance to change. But how does an organization reshape a culture ill-suited to scaling without a looming crisis? People can be drawn to a compelling vision when they experience it as having attractive emotional rewards. This makes sense, considering that deep-seated values and beliefs live in the heart, not in the head. And that is part of the reason why statements of values and beliefs hanging as proclamations on walls but not living in hearts have no impact. Unless the desired values and beliefs are internalized by the executive group, there is no way for the rest of the organization to understand them or develop a commitment deep enough to act consistently with them. Culture, and the habits people get into as a result of a strong culture, can only be changed through an insightful personal experience, not an intellectual seminar or lecture.

For the values of a vision to be compelling and the subsequent culture it creates to become real, leaders need to touch peoples' hearts. People need to see and feel the values to ensure they are not relegated to intellectual abstractions. That is one reason I emphasize the use of stories over a tersely worded vision statement (as discussed in chapter 4).

4. There's Value in Keeping It Local

Not too many years ago I was asked to review the culture change initiative of a medium-sized organization growing quickly. It spent a fortune in training and education, but nothing made a dent in the existing culture that encouraged avoidance of risk, not taking responsibility, and working without collaboration. The organization held elaborate in-house workshops on leadership, team building, and culture, and sent its senior managers off to fine executive development programs at Harvard Business School and the Center for Creative Leadership.

The first thing I noticed was that people who worked together never went to these workshops and programs together. The folks who worked closely day-to-day couldn't develop a common language or help each other reinforce what they were learning. There's a flaw in the "cascade" strategy of training and development when it comes to culture change. When an organization starts a program with the senior-most levels, then rolls out the same program or variations of the theme to successively lower horizontal levels, it results in the people working together having a much more difficult time applying the concepts and behaviors inherent in values, norms, and beliefs of the desired culture *in their group*. As intact groups, they lost the opportunity to share a potentially powerful bonding experience and did not feel the permission to coach one another in the new ways of working together. All the resources thrown at this well-intentioned change initiative served to create an interesting intellectual experience—but this type of experience does not change or reinforce a culture.

Find examples of success within the current culture. As we already know, there is no such thing as an ideal culture that fits every organization. But if you look hard enough, you will generally find existing examples of cultural characteristics that can serve as models of the cultural change you need. When people see that models already exist in the organization, the changes implied may not seem so overwhelming. Which departments and employees should be models? Some firms promote hybridization. Who are the people who could serve as positive examples within the current culture and should these people be promoted and put in charge of something?

Changing culture requires getting people to think differently and to consider new ways of operating. What can be done locally (or in the short term) to initiate alignment of the culture without having to change strategy, structure, or people? The following approaches may be useful:

- *Set up pilot projects.* Try "experiments" that enable employees to change behaviors. If "thoughtful risk taking" is a value desired for the culture, it will be hard to expect people to engage in behaviors related to this if, in the past, they were punished for making mistakes. A pilot would be to assure that managers understand what the value of "thoughtful risk taking" actually could look like and the consequent behaviors resulting from it. Then, as employees are encouraged to be innovative, and take a risk, and perhaps fail, then the manager provides feedback as a learning/coaching tool rather than beats the crap out of them for making a mistake. Design the experiments to ensure that successful impact on the culture comes early, tie them to business needs, require people to model new behavior, and provide developmental and political support if indicated.

- *Rethink the way performance is measured for a localized activity.* If a higher value is placed on teamwork, then create rewards that measure if and when it's happening and provide incentives to reinforce when objective data shows that behavior is moving in the right direction. Start by creating a few new metrics that can be locally controlled and focus on them intensely.

- *Find and promote the pockets of distinctio*n. These pockets may be hidden clusters of innovative people or groups that have been restricted in their range of activities, or moribund projects that have been left to die for lack of resources but are critical to illustrating the culture you are trying to create. Find the pockets, shape their objectives, channel resources to them, and increase the visibility they have to the rest of the organization.

5. Honoring Your Past and Rewarding the Future Strengthens Culture

I find it so fascinating how those firms with consistent growth maintain a strong sense of pride and appreciation in their capabilities. They simultaneously reassure those devoted to tradition while creating a readiness to change when necessary.

How does a firm honor the past? It learns from the stories about the history of the organization, however short that history may be. Who were the heroes and legends that led the firm to greatness? What did they do? What did they stand for?

One way of honoring the past is to let people mourn the loss of what must be left behind. I see many managers who are frightened to allow people to express their sadness at the termination of a division or a change in organizational orientation. They worry that expression of emotion will get out of hand or that people will hold out hopes for the revival of a division or the old ways. Paradoxically, until employees are able to mourn for and "bury" the past, the past seems to linger and haunt them. In many subtle ways, people continue to live in the past, reminiscing through stories about the "good old days."

Symbolic gestures like burning an eight-hundred-page book of rules are powerful, but they don't last over time to inculcate new behaviors. Concrete actions are necessary. Knowing that gestures only go so far, the executive group at Continental Airlines knew that to reach all the way down into the organization they would need to put money where their mouths were. They decided to tie incentives to the U.S. Department of Transportation's measures that include on-time performance. Employees were offered a flat $65 for each month the airline ranked in the top five for on-time performance. The first month it finished fourth. The second month it was first. Change had been motivated that quickly. In 1995 Continental was in the top five rankings nine times—putting $585 in the pocket of each field employee. The next year it paid $100 for a top ranking, $65 for a second or third, and nothing for placing after that. Continental remains the only airline to identify performance indicators, actively manage a culture to support these indicators, and then tie rewards to the indicators. To ensure the reward money was firmly linked to these accomplishments, all bonus money was sent in separate checks and not with the weekly payroll. Even those with direct deposit were sent hard copies of the checks. Similar incentives were put in place for the sales and reservations divisions.[22]

6. Growing in New Ways Keeps a Culture Relevant

Changing an organizational culture is more like pruning trees than remodeling machines or buildings. The arborist doesn't engineer a tree, but instead shapes and redirects existing energy, which manifests itself in shoots that go in many directions. Essentially, the arborist's role is to decide what should be allowed to grow.

Realigning the culture to support the vision, too, involves allowing existing branches to grow toward the light and removing the obstacles in the way. This is more effective than hacking off limbs, grafting on new branches, or forcing growth toward the darker side.

How can you help the growth vision thrive? Find those groups and people who exhibit behaviors aligned with the desired culture. Nurture and reward them. Influence others to grow in the right direction by explaining why the culture shift is in their interests and demonstrating your belief in it through your own actions. "Prune" those who cannot change.

7. Revolutions Rarely Succeed

Often, executives who feel they don't have much time to engage in a cultural realignment process decide that revolution—that is, abrupt and drastic changes—is the answer. In organizations, as in countries, revolutions may result in changes very different from the ends originally sought. Organizational revolutions too often successfully destroy particular aspects of the past without holding on to the "usable past." It is more effective to build on the past than to throw it away.

Revolution is usually a sign of impoverished leadership. When an organization feels the necessity to engage in revolution, there may be an executive asleep at the controls. If they had allowed the firm to grow in new ways, rewarded efforts in the right direction, and encouraged continuous innovation—which requires experimentation and learning as well as creativity and execution—they would have been much more responsive and able to adjust and apply their history to new situations. The need for a revolution, therefore, is an indictment against current management, and it almost always involves the pruning of executive group members who were sleeping at the controls. Organizations that have chosen this option would probably have changed more effectively if they tried building on their past.

While the culture change at Continental Airlines may have seemed revolutionary, it was not. Values, beliefs, norms, heroes, and systems were carefully identified and linked with the performance metrics that led to satisfied customers. Each year, the airline made consistent progress and won an increasing number of awards from such arbiters as J.D. Powers, OAG, *Fortune,* and *BusinessWeek* magazines for the things that matter most to flyers. Change was a measured process that did not yield everything that the company envisioned overnight. But over a relatively short period, it achieved its hopes. It has been on *Fortune's* "100 Best Companies to Work For" list for the past four years. In 2000, it awarded employees $39 million for on-time performance bonuses and that year (the sixth since Bethune took the reins as CEO) represented the sixth year of an average 18 percent in diluted earnings per share.[23]

Is Your Culture Ready for Scaling?

While many methodologies exist to assess cultures, one that I have used with many organizations works particularly well because it minimizes or eliminates the need for external consultants. I include an outline of this process in the appendix at the end of the book.

Let's return to Oakley. Jim Jannard founded the firm with a belief that you design products that you like, and avoid being taken over by speculation of what you think the market is looking for. The company creates a set of products that happen to be successful and happen to make a lot of money. He and his managers attract and retain others who come to believe the same thing (that one must not be focused outwardly on what the market wants now but on what the market doesn't even know that it may want). As Oakley continues to be successful in creating products the market likes, these beliefs and values have gradually come to be *shared and taken for granted*—they're part of the culture. They've become unspoken assumptions about the nature of this organizational world and how to succeed in it. To understand any culture, therefore, you must unearth these taken-for-granted assumptions that are prevalent yet outside peoples' awareness.

"Culture" is an amorphous concept to grasp and to see how it dramatically impacts organizational performance. Even more difficult is the task of assessing a culture and determining whether it represents a close enough fit to support the vision.

We are all culture diagnosticians. Think back when you began working for any organization. There was always a strong inherent need to create a mental map of how things worked, how we were expected to behave, what things were permissible, and what was verboten. We needed to understand the culture, whether we were conscious of that need or not. We may have asked ourselves: What do I have to do to fit in? What gets rewarded and admonished around here? What do I need to do to be accepted by the group? What are the good and bad things I do that gets my boss's attention? What does it take to get ahead? We watched closely to see what behaviors were rewarded formally by the organization and, more frequently, we watched and heard what was approved or disapproved immediately in a more informal way by our coworkers and boss.

Based on the increasingly compelling data linking culture to organizational scaling in general, and performance in particular, the essential question then shifts to whether culture can be changed. And if so, how? Reshaping culture, and bringing it in alignment to support the vision, is not unlike the challenge required to stop smoking or permanently lose weight. It is not easy, but people accomplish it. While it may not be easy for organizations to tear down the invisible yet impermeable boundaries between departments, for example, organizations do become more boundaryless.

In a scaling organization, senior executives are responsible for growing the organizations, and employees for continually expanding their capabilities to shape the future of the firm as well as their own. In turn, executives need to understand themselves, their people, and potential sources of conflict, all of which require reflection, listening, and giving people the freedom and power they need for innovation and reality testing. To achieve this, organizations adopt what many refer to as "lavish communication," which occurs only in organizational cultures that promote truth and do not suppress or limit the distribution of information.

Chapter 8

Building a Structure That Will Withstand Growth

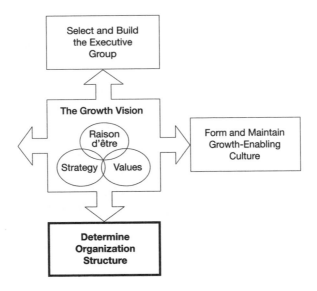

I N 1841, TWO PASSENGER TRAINS COLLIDED HEAD-ON in Westfield, Massachusetts, about twenty miles from my farm. Public outcry was loud and severe, demanding that the railroads have better management and control.

In response to the catastrophe—and the outcry—the directors of the Western Railroad took steps to "define responsibilities for each phase of the company's business, drawing solid lines of authority and command for the railroad's administration, maintenance, and operation."[1] The directive resulted in the Western becoming the first U.S. business enterprise to operate through a formal structure staffed by full-time salaried managers. Other railroads took the cue and, by the mid-nineteenth century and near the time of the Civil War, the vertical organizational chart was serving as the predominant design model for one of the first industries in the United States to experience massive growth. Many U.S. businesses followed suit; the era of the vertical hierarchy had arrived. And for many companies, the structure opened new avenues to profitability and to accountability.

In chapter 5, I relayed the story of one of the heroes of the Western Railroad—Major George Washington Whistler. Whistler had a vision; unfortunately, the railroad industry as a whole did not. This new vertical structure did not follow a vision; it was a structure in response to a mistake. Too often, organizational structures are taken too far as a means of control and then result in unintended consequences: suffocated innovation, reduced quality of communication and decision making, and ultimately, throttled growth.

Fast-forward to the mid-1990s and Site Specific, one of the first online network marketers to understand the power and payoff in getting people to see ads targeted specifically for them and motivating them to click to the sponsor's Web site. Site Specific's proprietary technology was first-rate. The senior team was bright, creative, and focused. Fortune 100 firms were willing clients, and, in the company's nascent days, Harte Hanks, an "old economy" mainstay in the direct-mail marketing business, became a major investor. (The *Wall Street Journal* carried a front-page article on the awkward, but functional coexistence between the relatively young and rakish Site Specific leadership and its more conservative investors.[2]) Not that Site Specific had tens of millions in VC money to burn; it was just a small business getting bigger very quickly through real revenue growth and relatively modest equity investment from the outside.

The outlook was rosy. The company had what looked to be a good vision which, in part, was to provide online advertisers with the richest information available about the use and effectiveness of their ad placements, coupled with the inherent advantages of being first to market. But it soon found itself in trouble. Employee satisfaction dropped, communication foul-ups jeopardized client relations, and hand-offs between people became sloppy. Why? Site Specific had just about as vertical a structure as one could imagine, and that structure was choking the firm. (With fewer than one hundred employees, Site Specific had more hierarchical levels than FedEx with 215,000 people, and almost as much as the old Western Railroad.)

The problem might have become apparent if Seth Goldstein, the founder and the CEO (yes, the same Seth Goldstein of IAN fame—his trials provide good fodder for learning), had bothered to draw an organizational chart. But Goldstein thought that the company's structure was "organic" and adapting to the ever-changing and growing firm, so he never stopped to analyze it. As a result, he didn't realize that Site Specific's structure was actually *operating in direct contradiction* to his vision. Boundaries between designers, producers, marketing people, and customers were becoming impermeable, and customers were starting to feel the slippage wrought by breakdowns in communication and slow decision making.

The Connection between Vision and Structure

Even with a well-defined vision, an organization's growth may stall if its structure is out of alignment with and cannot support, the vision. The Western Railroad initially had no formal structure; as a result, the incident described above was (excuse the cliché) an accident waiting to happen. Then its managers created a structure, but since railroad executives saw a world where dependency on rail transportation was immutable, there was no vision in place for that structure to serve.

Site Specific had Goldstein's vision, but a structure that couldn't support it. Neither scenario allowed for sustainable growth. Site Specific went through a rough period (detailed later in this chapter). And we all know the sorry state of the railroad industry in the United States.

To appreciate the connection between vision and structure, and to fully understand the need for structure to be aligned with vision, it's useful to return to a few concepts noted in past chapters.

When we consider modern business organizations, it should be easy now to accept the basic idea that underpins the rhetoric of vision and values: Modern business organizations need a vision to guide growth. On its own, the goal of profitability—or its more recent surrogate, shareholder value—provides little in the way of strategic direction for an organization and even less as a concept to inspire the wholehearted commitment of its members. For both reasons, companies need to harness a vision; a more precise idea of their raison d'être, strategy, and values unites people with disparate personal motivations and ultimately gives meaning to the existence of the organization.

Over the past two decades, the business world has become an infinitely more complex, fluid, and unpredictable place, even for long-established organizations. As I was in the midst of my early research on vision, Lou Gerstner had just taken the helm of a wounded IBM, and the press was hounding him from Day One for his vision. (Lucky for him and IBM he resisted talking about it until a year later, after he had time to conceptualize the vision's main points.) IBM has come back stronger than ever, but other companies have been transformed beyond recognition or have failed to survive.

Ambiguity and uncertainty, and the internal dissent that accompany these, are pervasive parts of this new landscape.

There are two schools of thought about how organizations should operate in this environment. One school argues that uncertainty, ambiguity, and internal dissent are not only uncomfortable but probably dysfunctional. The remedy? Strong management (based of course on a clear vision), conformity to rulebooks, written policies, and a structure that "protects" people from the uncertainty, ambiguity, and dissent.

The other school of thought suggests something quite different. It proposes that because the future is unknowable and because human beings are, well, human, organizations have to figure out a way to not only tolerate uncertainty but to positively exploit it. They do this by shaping a way to allow, even to positively encourage, ambiguity in the interpretation of meaning and diversity of thought and behavior. This requires exercising what might be considered, in the conventional, old school sense, "weak leadership."

Fast-growing organizations find ways to foster organization-wide innovation, flexibility, and speed of response. The role of top management shifts from one of control to one of constructing channels to manage this seeming chaos so people can innovate, stay flexible, and move fast over the longer haul.

When organizational structure is aligned with other elements of the vision framework, it becomes a principal means for managing the discomforting consequences of an uncertain world. Instead of falling back on the natural tendency to allow a sclerotic-inducing hierarchy to grow (as Goldstein did)—a liability for moving closer to the vision—consider structural alternatives that allow the vision to become an organizational process.

Isn't It All Just Boxes and Lines?

Whether the discussion is about the appropriate structure for a small upstart firm or a global corporation, the fundamentals remain the same. Designing the best structure requires thinking long and hard about the optimal way to group and link people so that the organization has the best possible capacity to coordinate interdependent work that crosses formal boundaries.

Look beneath the veneer of the boxes and lines on an organizational chart and one realizes that the primary work of today's organizations is to *gather, channel,* and *process* appropriate information. The increasing complexity of competitive demands and strategies has been matched by a growing number of *inter*dependencies within organizations. Throughout the entire value chain, each cluster of people working away on one or another part of the business is more reliant on others for information about technology, suppliers, customers, and competitors. Concurrently, as mind-numbing routinization of jobs gives way to more complex responsibilities requiring people to think and make judgments, we are seeing an infinitely greater need for information to flow directly to people at the front line. Few companies, however, have mastered the ability to get that information where it needs to go, in the form it needs to be in.

Many organizations possess a strong entrepreneurial drive to grow yet find themselves shackled with a structure that inevitably retards their growth. A survey in mid-2000 by Pricewaterhouse-Coopers of the 441 fastest growing U.S. businesses found that 32 percent of the CEOs believed their inability to manage or reorganize their business could be "an impediment to growth" during the coming year. Only 10 percent of the CEOs felt that way in a similar survey conducted in 1993.[3] More than ever, we see the need for dynamic, "reconfigurable" organizations that recognize and respond to rapid changes. Firms that focus *only* on growth and ignore their structure tend to fall into cycles of rapid expansion followed by retrenchment, cost cutting, and sometimes failure.

In the early stages of a firm's development, the creation of traditions plays a significant role in organizational dynamics. But these dynamics are paradoxical: While the relatively small, growing firm may have more "freedom" because it is not bound by tradition, the very lack of timeworn traditions causes inefficiency and a poor use of resources as executives try to develop routines that "work" and are effective. Entrepreneurial executives tend to be impulsive, relatively emotional, and desire control. They also tend to be visionaries who have the ability to generate excitement and commitment among their followers. They prefer informal ways of working because they disdained the bureaucracy when they were in large organizations. Something odd begins to happen when they're at the helm of a scaling organization, however. While they strive to maintain disproportionate amounts of control over facets of the organization, they often begin to distrust others. In response, a new organizational structure begins to evolve, one based on an authoritarian model.[4]

This model often resembles a form of paternalism. The founder or senior executives "take care" of employees in return for their loyalty. They make all the key decisions, supervise employees closely, and carefully control the information circulated to employees. The implications can be devastating: Innovation and creativity are often stifled. Little employee development takes place. Employees remain in the dark regarding organizational goals and objectives, let alone progress toward the vision. Insufficient information is shared regarding employee performance. People don't know or understand where the organization is going or how it's performing. While the intent of this culture and structure may be to ensure that people are "cared for" and stay loyal, the effect is the opposite:

People feel cut off and their commitment to the organization wanes. The counterintuitive consequence of these dynamics is a dangerously high probability that the organization's structure will become too centralized, with accompanying authoritarian systems thoroughly ill-suited to growth.

Thomas Jefferson, intrigued by the inability of European countries to adapt their laws and constitutions in response to the changing world of the early nineteenth century, said, "We might as well require a man to wear still the coat which fitted him as a boy."[5] That same resistance to change exists in growing organizations when they become mired in a structure perhaps appropriate when they were young and small, but ill fitting their increased size.

Breaking Free of the Traditional Hierarchy

An organization's management practices are typically reflected in its structure. Organization charts provide some insight into the relationship of people to the firm and the degree of authority each exercises. Authority, decision making, individual responsibility, personal status—all relate to a large degree to the organizational structure.

As I already mentioned, entrepreneurial executives have a way of sacrificing potential organizational performance in order to feel in control. The traditional, vertical hierarchy provides that control. It is therefore the most commonly leveraged organizational form in use today, despite market and technological forces pressing for greater delegation and less direct supervision. Let's start with a definition. When I speak of the "traditional" hierarchy, I am referring to an organizational structure with the following characteristics:

- *High specialization.* Peoples' jobs are quite narrow and broken down into tasks and perhaps subtasks.
- *Small spans of control.* This creates the "tall" rather than flat pyramid shape on the organizational chart. With this vertical hierarchy, relatively few people report to each manager.
- *Centralization of power.* The real decision-making authority resides at or near the top.

The preference for hierarchy is not only paradoxical but also ironic. When we examine structures distinct from the hierarchy, and perhaps considered nontraditional, such as "Front-Back Hybrids," we realize that control does not have to be sacrificed. With vision, leadership, employee development, and properly aligned compensation systems (which I address in chapter 9), independent organizational units can be collectively aligned so that the results wished for in the hierarchy are actually achieved through a different structure.

I am not suggesting that one new, relatively nontraditional organizational structure will work for every growing organization. That would be foolish. I am suggesting, however, that organizational leaders largely abandon the traditional hierarchy as the structural path to growth because its inherent characteristics make it unsuitable for today's environment. First, it is internally focused on functional goals rather than outwardly focused on delivering value and pleasing customers. Second, too much information is lost as knowledge travels up and down multiple levels and across functional specialties. Third, it costs more to operate. Coordinating overly fragmented work and departments requires people who essentially do little more than "manage." Finally, it stifles innovation and motivation in those at "the bottom" as a result of how they respond to their narrow, limited roles and decision-making capacity.

The business literature has been replete over the past decade with many innovative ways to structure the "new organization," and most authors suggest that their form will replace the traditional hierarchical form.[6] The emergence of the fields of complexity and chaos theory into the business world introduced concepts of organic growth and change into the management of organization structure. The virtual organization, front/back organization, cluster organization, horizontal organization, empowered organization, and high-performance work team organization are only some of the most notable new models. While I think highly of them and have implemented many in organizations, I cannot help but question claims of their universal effectiveness when I return to the corporate examples their authors used to convince us of their worthiness. Not too many years ago, the likes of Digital Equipment Corporation (DEC), Xerox, Sears, and AT&T were touted as the paragons of "new" organizational structures, destined to ensure continued health and sustained growth. Now those claims serve to put a chink in the credibility of those doing the touting as well as the structures themselves. DEC is dead, while Xerox and Sears are still in the intensive care ward. AT&T in early 2002 was still trying to figure out what business it was in, while stemming the blood loss from ill-conceived acquisitions.

Organization structures with the capacity to become self-renewing and adaptive are appealing to more tradition-bound managers once they understand the underlying mechanics of why they work so well: They are more responsive to a rapidly changing external environment. Many managers have used these forms to create more open, flexible organizations that achieved the organizational equivalent of perestroika from the hierarchy.

Where a person resides in the organizational structure affects what he or she sees as important. The traditional hierarchy provides disheartening examples of what happens when one's vision becomes increasingly narrow as a result of the squeeze that an ill-fitting structure can apply. Resources allocated to executing on the narrow strategy become limited. Fighting seems to be a rational response as a way to protect one's turf or special interests. In the end, traditional hierarchies subvert visions by forcing those within the organization to accept a vision that becomes more limited and compartmentalized across organizational units. The notion of a shared vision mind-set stays that way—an unrealistic notion in people's heads that neither gives direction nor promotes action. The principles enumerated in the following section, however, encourage people to broaden their line of sight as a means to understand how their work benefits the entire organization.

Finally, with all my ranting about hierarchies, one might presume the remainder of this chapter will provide radical alternatives to this organizational scrooge to scaling. In my heart I wish we could figure out a way to replace the hierarchy, but I am ever mindful of the cold fact that, as an important part of our social fabric, some form of hierarchy will be present. The search is not for a fantasy-driven new radical structure but instead for a way to create a *vital* hierarchy. The concept of the "vital hierarchy" is not an oxymoron. It still acknowledges the need for some vertical layers, but its resemblance to the traditional hierarchy—with its impermeable boundaries, inward focus, and slow adaptiveness—makes it a distant cousin.

From Strategy to Structural Characteristics of Vital Hierarchies

How do we create a vital hierarchy so that growth is not constrained by structure? Given the advantages and disadvantages attributed to the myriad of organizational forms, how should an executive group decide which form to use at various levels of the organization? The golden rule, at each and every level, is the same: *Strategy determines structure.* Whether it is at the broader organizational level or within particular work units, structural decisions must always flow directly from larger strategy. Perhaps that is why newer forms of organizing people and their work have evolved over the past two decades. New strategies have emerged that are nearly impossible to execute in traditional hierarchies.

While new organizational structures may look different from their historical brethren because of equally new strategies, the design solution still remains wedded to the way in which labor is divided into tasks and the tasks are coordinated to deliver the organization's strategy quickly and efficiently. As I noted in Part I strategy is not a one- or three-year plan for accomplishing equally short-term goals, but a way to articulate the operational logic for what the organization hopes to accomplish. If, for example, the raison d'être is to change the way people make decisions about how they manage their inventories, then the strategy must explain the principles that will make this possible. Strategy defines the distinctive competencies or competitive advantages the organization currently has or plans to develop. It articulates those benefits that an organization offers to influence customers and to differentiate it from anyone else. Structure, in turn, enables the organization to execute on its strategy.

Most of the same structure-related questions organizations struggled with for nearly a century continue today: Who goes where? What do they do? What elements of a process have to get accomplished and how do we group them? How is the reporting structure sequenced? What is each person accountable for? In sum, these questions still go to the question of authority—who has it and how does it flow? But now, the questions also go straight to the vision: What does the organization claim to do really well? How does it accomplish that work and deliver on its distinctive competency?

The necessary first step in determining the structural design, therefore, requires assurance that a linkage exists between what the organization has to do to realize its strategy and the means by which it is supposed to deliver that performance.[7] Strategy must always precede structure. Everything in the organization is focused on executing the strategy. While in most organizations strategy from the vision determines the *value propositions*—the set of benefits the organization offers—in others, strategy is the value proposition. Value propositions are important because they define the nature of the performance challenges inherent in moving the organization forward. They also identify the core processes of an organization and what they are expected to achieve.

For example, if markets are uncertain, competition is stiff, and customers have various needs, then customer-focused work groups make the most sense. But if innovation in particular product niches is necessary for growth, then it may be most effective to organize around output. From each value proposition flow the elements required to achieve the desired performance.

First, the executive group helps identify the value propositions. Second, the competencies and processes needed to execute the strategy are identified. Finally, superior value to customers is delivered, and a competitive advantage is maintained.

Oakley's case provides a glimpse into how a company might take action along these lines. Oakley's huge headquarters in Orange County, CA, described in chapter 7, also houses the plant where virtually all its eyewear is made. Kent Lane, the VP of manufacturing, has created an extraordinary team-based "cell" structure that follows the three steps above and has laid out a separate "Manufacturing Mission." For example, two of the manufacturing division's value propositions are: "Exceed Customer Expectations" and "Attack Non-Value-Added Activities (anything the customer is not willing to pay for)." Some of the competencies and processes they have identified? "Annihilate lengthy flow times, distances, queues & change-over times! Do not tolerate unexpected break-downs & production interruptions! Track down and eliminate all variations at their origin! Make killer decisions based on killer data! Synchronize to internal & external demands!" And what else is stated in their mission that informs the devised cell structure to make these highly stylized products to such exacting tolerances? "Involve agile kick-butt teams to strategize, execute, & improve process! Frontline teams record and own process metrics! Fanatical dedication to the training of every team member!"[8]

Oakley may seem unorthodox or extreme, but the point is clear: its structure has evolved as a result of a strategy tied to the vision, and this structure fully supports the strategy.

Rather than attempt to sell an instant elixir of the perfect structure (which we all know would be a fantasy like other management fads), I'll offer structural-related criteria that CEOs and executive groups should consider in planning for the way their organization will accomplish its strategy.

Cluster People as Business Units around Customers and Products, Not by Function

Break away from the traditional organizing principle of function to which we seem to be naturally drawn. Functional structures are fine if the organization has a single line of business, stays relatively small, requires common standards, has a core capability that requires deep expertise in one or more functional areas, maintains a narrow product/service line, and doesn't compete in the market-place based on speed of product development cycle times. (Are there any scaling organizations that meet these criteria?)

Grouping people based on the core process in which they are engaged allows employees from diverse disciplines to know and understand one another. It encourages tighter social relation-ships, joint decision-making styles, and collaborative approaches. Together, these serve to melt away the boundaries inherent in functional silos that have stifled communication. Cross-functional responsibilities also broaden an employee's scope, skills, and decision-making acumen.

The vital hierarchy places an emphasis on grouping individuals around products, customers, and services. The result is a reduced need for hierarchical coordination or for managers and artificial control mechanisms to hypothesize what might be best for the customer. The focus shifts from bosses to customers by making people responsible for satisfying customers. The only way this will work, however, is to embrace the notion of a structure based more on teams than individuals.

Teams essentially create a substitute for levels in the hierarchy, and they assume many of the responsibilities usually placed on managers. D. Quinn Mills of Harvard favors the term "clusters" because he believes "team" has been overused and abused in the context of traditional hierarchies.[9] I agree. I have used the term and concept of clusters to restructure scaling organizations, and, while I am not advocating it as a universal solution, it has proved effective when other organizational elements suggest it is appropriate.

A cluster is a group of people arranged as if they were growing on a vine, like grapes. The common vine in the organization is the vision, and the vine and clusters together produce the results ("wine of the business?"). Clusters are groups of people drawn from many disciplines who work together on a semipermanent basis. The cluster itself handles many administrative functions, develops its own expertise, expresses a strong customer or client orientation, pushes decision making toward the point of action, shares information broadly, and accepts accountability for its results.

While I like the term "cluster," the broader concept is similar to the structural alternative of "high performance team-based organizations" proposed by Sue Mohrman, Monty Mohrman, and Susan Cohen.[10]

When I have employed this structural design, up to six types of clusters were used. Figure 8-1 illustrates what a cluster organization "chart" might look like.

- *The Core unit.* This is the executive group.
- *Business units.* Clusters that have customers external to the organization. The units conduct their own business and deal directly with customers in a relatively semiautonomous style. In the ideal, they are profit centers, and their effectiveness and

FIGURE 8 - 1

Cluster Organization

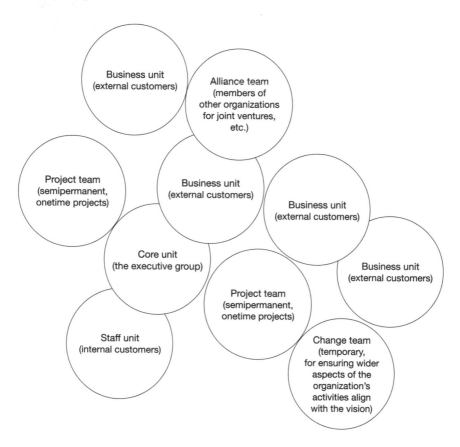

efficiency can be measured continually and accurately. Business units are the primary organizing principle for the cluster structure. Because of their flexibility, focus on the customer, and relative autonomy, they can respond with the speed of organizations much smaller in size.

- *Staff units.* Clusters that have customers internal to the organization. Whenever possible, these units create internal profit centers by pricing their services to those who use it. Typically, human resources, marketing, accounting, and legal organize themselves as one or more clusters. The training unit of IBM, for example, was established as a staff cluster and found that its products and services satisfied their internal customers so well that they began to develop external customers. It then spun-off a business unit.

- *Project teams.* These groups are assembled for a particular project, but lack the ongoing business orientation of business or staff units. They are semipermanent and terminate when the project is completed.

- *Alliance teams.* These groups handle joint ventures with external organizations and include representatives from these organizations. Such groups are increasingly used in technology-driven industries where product development is fast, complex, and dependent on leveraging diverse competencies across firms. Alliance teams differ from project teams by virtue of their external membership. They may be permanent or temporary.

- *Change teams.* Cluster groups created for the purpose of analyzing and improving aspects of the organization's activities. In days of yore, they may have been the quality circles, a group of employees drawn from many points of a production process that came together regularly to critique process flow and find ways to refine it for a higher quality product, but here they are envisioned as clusters representing the broader organization. They take on larger mandates and have a life limited by a particular objective.

A cluster structure is not the de rigueur replacement for the matrix form, which was in vogue during the 1970s and 1980s. Manufacturing companies used matrixes to solve the conundrum of creating depth in technical expertise while focusing on new product development. A number of multinationals used it to sell a wide range of specialized products to highly diversified customer bases. Matrix structures fell out of favor because they were seen as a solution to complex organizational problems rather than a tool that must be used in concert with other structures, mechanisms, and processes to integrate peoples' work. Their dual reporting relationships, need for complex communications systems, and most important, the propensity to make people who were part of the matrix feel "lost" and without a home in the organization require high maintenance from talented managers.

Traditional hierarchies filter their customers' needs through a managerial structure, losing accuracy in the process. Employees respond first and foremost to what their managers want, next to what managers say the customers want, and finally to what the customers say they want (if they ever get to hear it). In the cluster model, the business units are in direct contact with their customers or clients. The cluster responds directly to what customers want, to what members of the team want done, and to what the executive group wants.

But many attempts to shift from a traditional hierarchy to more cluster-like forms fail. Not because it is a flawed model but because managerial thinking was too often stifled by the mindset of "traditional hierarchies." The traditional mindset fears delegation would erode managers' power in the hierarchy and openness would undermine their authority. If the hierarchy was made more flexible, then managers would feel a lack of control. If there was full employee involvement, then differences in status and reward structures based on the formal position in which one resides would be undermined. While those who created this structure may honestly believe these phenomena to be true, the irony is that a vertical hierarchy brings unintended negative consequences to those who maintain it.

Create Permeable Boundaries

In the traditional hierarchy, the relative impermeability of boundaries blocks critical information. Boundaries are rarely eliminated, but they can be made more permeable. Ed Lawler, Michael Tushman, and David Nadler, noted authorities on organizational structure, have separately used the metaphor of architecture to describe principles of structure.[11] The growing organization can be thought of, in many respects, as the metaphorical equivalent of an office building with movable walls and lots of open space. Boundaries within every organization can be envisioned as *vertical* (the floors and ceilings), *horizontal* (the walls between the rooms), *external* (the thick walls that separate the building from the outside world), and *geographic* (distance between the "outbuildings" related to the central building). But the notion of boundaries is more than a theoretical construct; boundaries create tangible problems that fly in the face of the growing organization's needs to keep information flowing, make decisions quickly, and take timely action.[12]

Vertical boundaries are created by the hierarchical layers of the organization that distinguish people's status, authority, and power. Rather than focusing on authority and rank, the relatively boundaryless organization emphasizes and rewards those who have useful ideas and skills to implement them. We see vertical boundarylessness when managers jump in to help when they are needed at lower levels, when decisions are made quickly by those closest to the work and action on decisions is taken quickly, when big problems are tackled by groups representing a number of organizational levels without people pulling rank, when new ideas are evaluated and decided on without the need for long formal meetings with fancy presentations.

Horizontal boundaries exist between functions, product lines, or disciplines. This boundary is reduced as people emphasize the critical processes shared across functional lines. Work and ideas are transferred more quickly as the boundary becomes more permeable. New products or services move out to the consumer at increasingly faster rates, quality is monitored and controlled more efficiently, and the impact of silos created by the traditional hierarchy is minimized.

External boundaries are the barriers between the organization and anyone in the outside world—potential employees, customers, suppliers, government agencies, or other organizations with whom an alliance would be beneficial. When external boundaries are up and impermeable, much is made of the distinction between "insiders" and "outsiders," and each is in competition with the other. As this boundary becomes lower, people and organizations become more fully aware of how they can help each other become more efficient. Since the early 1990s, an increased number of organizations have realized the need to build alliances with other organizations. These "partnerships" require communication and a deeper understanding of how they can complement each other. As communications open, boundaries drop.

Geographic boundaries exist between units of the organization that operate in different locations or markets. Oddly, this boundary does not require global proportions; I have seen it consume and waste an organization's energy when units were located at two ends of the same large city. Sadly, this boundary reduces the ease at which innovative ideas can be shared and the extent to which each separated unit can learn from the other. While it may initially be seen as a time-consuming activity, I have found that geographical boundaries become more permeable when members of the "distant" organizations come together and meet personally. While electronic-based communications seems efficient and may be frequent, it does impact the reduction of boundaries as much as meaningful face-to-face meetings.

Distribute Power, Information, and Knowledge Evenly

People can make important decisions only when they have the necessary tools, skills, motivation, and authority. We have heard for the past twenty years about the importance of "empowerment." And we continue to hear management experts preach about it—not because managers don't believe in it, but because it is so hard to accomplish in the traditional hierarchy.

Organizations that are structured around products and customers, and are group-based, facilitate the notion of empowerment by providing an atmosphere in which individuals feel freedom to act because they have developed the capacity to do so. Four conditions are necessary for empowerment to become realized. First, each individual must know and understand not only the vision of the organization, but how that vision informs the mission of the group of which he or she is a part. A cluster's mission must be consistent with the organization's vision, and, since the vision is a living reality, it must be reintroduced at the cluster level. Only when members integrate the vision and understand what it means to them in the present and in the near-term future, will they be able to act with consistency.

Second, people must have the skills if they are to act on their own initiative. This requires both specific, technical skills necessary to excel at their job and a grasp of the larger picture of the organization. Ultimately, it requires an organizational commitment to continually invest in the development of people. The employees at The Container Store are provided with more than seven times the amount of training than others in the industry, resulting in extraordinary decision-making authority to address customer issues.[13] Clusters are much more dependent on the ability of their members than they are on the expertise or experience of their manager. While traditional hierarchies see training and development as a cost expense and something to be minimized, vital hierarchies treat it as an investment and lavish resources on it while ensuring that it has maximum impact.

Third, giving people power can be a cruel and potentially career-stopping tease if they are not also given information. Information is important to understand activities at the local level and to understand the broader environment in which one has to act and respond. Traditional hierarchies deny people the information they need, so they end up either operating in the dark about the context of their activities or they have to figure out how to go up and down the chain of command to accumulate it. When those in need of information have to continually go in search of it, processes will typically become too slow and fraught with potential misunderstanding to be effective.

Finally, people need to know they are trusted. This includes knowing that they will not be unfairly punished for error or failure that may accompany their ability to take initiative. When higher-level managers sit in judgment over their direct report's decision, it often amounts to scapegoating. When people quickly realize that certain actions they take will turn them into scapegoats, they will stop making decisions or taking action. Trust means knowing that when one acts in good faith, even if the desired outcome is not reached, there will be no punishment.

In the vital hierarchy, people require a considerable amount of "bandwidth" at their discretion. Within that band, error is tolerable. The bandwidth of discretion is not the same as the limits of authority often granted in the traditional hierarchy. If people are going to feel empowered, the band must be much wider for many than it is in traditional settings or there will be no additional freedom of action. Errors can (and should) be tolerated when they are made in pursuit of the vision, when something useful is learned from the error, when the error is not part of a pattern, or when the error was made within the individual's scope of discretion or—in traditional hierarchical parlance—under the individual's authority.

A criterion closely related to power and information is knowledge. Clusters and related organizational structures require a mindset about work and human behavior quite different from what is found in the traditional hierarchy. The important characteristic in the vital hierarchy is individual accountability, rather than personal responsibility. This may seem like hair-splitting, but they mean significantly different things. *Responsibility* is about doing something right; *accountability* is about doing the right thing. In a group-based setting, individuals must understand and believe in the vision and critical elements of the overall situation to understand what needs to be done.

Knowledge brings the idea of accountability to life. Those who have the knowledge to do something also have the obligation to do it. Speed of action comes from acting on one's own, and each person is accountable for the results of his or her actions.

In the traditional hierarchy, managers let employees believe that as long as they have done as instructed, they have met their obligations. Managers take responsibility for the overall success. But in vital hierarchies, every person accepts individual accountability for the success or failure of the group effort. The individual employee makes a total commitment to the group and its objectives, and accepts accountability for overall results. This turns each employee into a professional by virtue of the weight his or her decisions carry and broader ownership of responsibilities, regardless of his or her work.

The distinction between the concepts of accountability and responsibility is central to the differences between the traditional hierarchy that ultimately slows growth and the vital form that keeps the organization adaptive. For some, this is hard to comprehend and accept. The difference in attitude is a serious matter and must be understood by any leader who hopes to create a structure that supports the vision and sustains growth.

While these characteristics are all important, different configurations of people and groups may be appropriate at various levels of the organization. Any single level of an organization should be focused either on activity, outputs, or customers. While an organization may have a strategic focus in one area—technological innovation, perhaps—it will tend to also have long-term strengths in other areas such as manufacturing or marketing. It's important to maintain and capitalize on existing sources of competitive advantage while organizing to meet new strategic objectives. This can be accomplished through mixed organizational forms.

Underlying Structural Themes to Promote Sustained Growth

Sustainable growth requires a set of organization-wide qualities, collectively referred to as "culture" that I addressed in chapter 7. But culture and structure are far from independent organizational dimensions. Any structure must support the intended culture. Remember: Since structure follows strategy, and since strategy is inextricably linked to the values that provide foundation to the culture, structure must therefore support the values emanating from the vision. They depend on each other. I believe it is important to summarize here how some of those values identified as critical to successful scaling can influence the criteria for a chosen structure.[14]

Innovation

Innovation, which equals creativity plus execution, leads to new ideas that flow into the bloodstream of the organization. While the reason for innovation is obvious and has already been discussed in chapter 7, it is noted here because of its relationship to control. Traditional hierarchies are efficient mechanisms for keeping control at the top, but the consequence is a structure that fails to evoke motivation. As a result, there are fewer behaviors that lead to new and perhaps unorthodox ideas. When "control" is built into the structure, people will be motivated to avoid risk.

Structures must promote growth, facilitate creativity, enable the execution of the creative ideas, and reduce the need for systems that require approvals from others. Control in the vital hierarchy is not given up—it just changes hands from the manager to the worker. Oakley's use of a "cell" structure in their manufacturing division, for example, has led to a constant flow of new ideas to increase quality and speed while reducing costs. Kent Lane, the VP of manufacturing, remarked: "I tell everyone, 'break one rule every day.' That's the only way they're going to innovate constantly."[15]

Despite Microsoft's enormous resources and successes, Bill Gates expresses his fear of obsolescence: "We've done some good work, but all of these products become obsolete so fast. . . . It will be some finite number of years—and I don't know the number—before our doom comes."[16] What fuels Gates is not only the demise of once-successful firms that failed to innovate. It is his own vision of the future and his tremendous desire to realize that vision, to be the dominant force in software solutions for the future. He knows that innovation is key to realizing that vision, so constant innovation is not only Microsoft's creed, but it's wired into the DNA of its organizational design. His strategy consists of three critical components: hiring "very smart people," keeping a loose structure, and organizing workers in small, intense, task-oriented groups.[17] (The first component will be discussed in chapter 9.)

A tight structure may be good for an operational organization like an army or sales force, but it is deadly for a creative one like Microsoft. Tight structures inhibit creativity. Rules, whether for work routines, project approval, or project change, drain valuable energy while also blotting up initiative and creativity. Openness and spontaneity, in contrast, foster creativity. So, people like Microsoft research employees do not have fixed or formal work hours, attire, schedules, or work habits. Employees dress casually, have fun on the job, and have many opportunities for exercise on the campus.

The third structural lever that Microsoft pulls is to enhance its intense goal-oriented work ethic through task-oriented groups. People there solve tough problems, in short time frames, with limited staff, and in an intense work environment. Employees are organized into small groups with a leader and assigned to specific programming tasks. Groups tend to be intentionally understaffed. Gates believes that small groups are better able to communicate with each other, while the challenge of meeting seemingly impossible goals with limited staff motivates people to give their very best.

To be clear, Microsoft has never been a pioneer in any market in which it currently leads: operating systems, browsers, graphical user interfaces, word processors, or spreadsheets. In fact, the first few versions of Windows, Excel, and Word were flops. But innovation at this organization is about market leadership in a category, and it has not lost that leadership despite constant changes in the market. The firm's policy of relentless innovation has been fruitful and stems from recruiting, motivating, and retaining outside talent. In turn, Microsoft crafted a structure that enables talent to do their best work.[18]

Urgency

In a scaling organization, people at all levels must respond to customers with speed, bring new products to market quickly, and shift tactical strategies as needs arise. Urgency—the ability to quickly respond to internal and external demands—was not as challenging when the organization was small. Like giant oil tankers that need miles before they can stop or change direction after an order is received, large organizations require more time because of the increased "mass." The structural conundrum lies in understanding how the organization can act like a small one while simultaneously leveraging the assets that increased size provides.

The rule of thumb is for decisions to be made quickly, on the spot, by those closest to the work, and then acted on in hours or days rather than weeks or months. Customer inquiries and needs are responded to as they enter the system. New products and services are developed and launched within increasingly faster cycle times. Learning in firms like Microsoft happens across the organization, particularly in regard to what works best in one unit that may be leveraged in another. Most important, it happens quickly—regardless of geographic distance.

Flexibility

Like people, organizations that move fast have flexible limbs. How can the structure facilitate the scaling organization's requirement that individuals be proficient in multiple roles, continually learning new skills, and willing to take on new tasks and responsibilities as the needs arise? While the traditional hierarchy revels in specifying precisely each individual's static role, the clarion call of the vital hierarchy demands that people feel comfortable with a greater level of freedom and ambiguity and be prepared to learn continually.

Flexibility also requires that managers do more than manage; they dive in as needed when members of the line require more assistance. People at all levels need to master multiple knowledge and skill sets. This requires training people to handle issues and to work productively in cross-functional areas. They need the ability to think creatively and respond flexibly to new challenges that emerge in the work they and their teams are engaged in.

Adaptability

Growing organizations must execute on their ideas, leverage the diverse skill sets of employees, and continually create new ways to meld diverse people, ideas, and activities. While it would seem logical to presume innovation, urgency, and flexibility yield adaptability, the characteristics are not necessarily so related. At its essence, *adaptability* is the quality of adopting new structural forms and organizational processes as needed. It is having the collective capacity to learn what works best, as well as what is not working well anymore, and to bring those often incongruous changes into being. Adaptation is not an excuse to allow an organization to evolve in a willy-nilly fashion.

Digital Equipment Corporation (DEC), the once venerable manufacturer of mid-level computers, had an annualized growth rate of 30 percent for at least a decade.[19] It had an interesting matrix structure that suited it well and was all the rave among organizational aficionados. Its appetite for talented employees seemed insatiable, and often it hired people without a specific job in mind. New hires would discover how and where their competencies could best meet the needs of the firm. Once someone came on board, she had nine months to "find" a job within the organization, even though the firm did not keep an accurate accounting of these hires to ensure that they actually landed somewhere meaningful in the organization. Flexibility was certainly in their genetic code. During the years of growth, DEC virtually owned its market, and details like precise head counts and assignments didn't seem to matter.

But those days disappeared. DEC died a slow, painful death from the impact that powerful personal computers would have on its business. It saw the consequences of its limited strategy, to supply the increasing need for computer horsepower by depending on the mini-computer far too late, and, once it awoke to the dramatically shifting market, it was unable to make its own shift to a structure more appropriate to the external demands. During the difficult days, DEC tried restructuring several times, but it didn't matter—it was still unclear about its strategy. Structural adaptability is impossible without a clear and sound strategy.

Organizations must be simultaneously stable and changing. They must figure out how to create a structure that can maintain critical capabilities while also creating new ones. *One group of structural elements, however, must remain stable over time:* those that tell employees what skills they will need to learn to be successful, what types of career opportunities exist for them, and how they will be rewarded (more on this in chapter 9).

The general shape of the organization's structure also must remain stable. Lawler, Nadler, and Tushman's metaphorical use of architecture to describe principles of structure is helpful here as well.[20] The growing organization can be thought of, in many respects, as the metaphorical equivalent of an office building with movable walls and lots of open space. The essential structure of the building does not vary, but the space inside can be changed, fine-tuned, and reallocated based on what the occupants want and need. Organization structures must operate in the same way: The essential characteristics stay the same, but what goes on within that frame stays flexible and adapts to circumstance and need.

Delayered Structure

Simply slashing and burning hierarchical layers does not create a more adaptive and responsive organization. "Delayering" or flattening the tall organization does not automatically loosen vertical boundaries and encourage the dissemination of information, decision making, and action further down. Only when management levels are removed *and* front-line teams are given more responsibility and knowledge for managing and coordinating their own work will the impact begin to be felt. By surgically removing layers of management and replacing them with people and processes to fill the void, decisions and communications will be brought closer to customers. Lower levels of the organization will develop accountability and autonomy, and costs will decrease.

The number of management levels has traditionally depended on the "span of control"—one of those endearing terms of management that has withstood the test of time. The term of course refers to the number of people reporting to a manager, but words imply the relationship as well: one of control. In the typical hierarchy, the primary role of management is one of control.

In theory, the number of levels depends on the span of control—how many people a manager can adequately supervise and develop. But now individuals can do a considerable amount of self-management if the structure provides for horizontal groupings and processes that eliminate the need for top-down coordination and control. Lawler has found in his research over the years that flat organizations tend to have more satisfied employees.[21] Further, if an executive group can stop looking at the boxes in their organization chart as jobs and begin to assign work or tasks to *collections* of individuals or teams, then it keeps people focused on their real customer. When the customer is not their boss, employees' focus becomes far more honed to the organization's products or services that customers want.[22]

The Vital Hierarchy at Site Specific

I first met Seth Goldstein when he was twenty-six years old, and I was impressed by this young, managerially inexperienced

CEO's intrigue with, and grasp of, organizational concepts like vision and culture. Goldstein had a vision for Site Specific, and he thought the organization's culture fit the values espoused in the vision. At the onset, it did. But as the firm grew rapidly, Goldstein fell prey to the litany of entrepreneurial traps.

As the customer base increased, he expanded each functional department to keep pace. As the size of each function grew in size, people given increased responsibilities wanted to be acknowledged for it. In Goldstein's rational world of managerial growth, it seemed logical to create new managerial roles to acknowledge them. The ranks of managers increased, and those being promoted were glad to have their impressive-sounding new titles. But with the role came new responsibilities. Talented designers, for example, were now expected to manage and coordinate communications across functional areas and clients. The more they struggled with trying to figure out how to do all this "management stuff," the less they engaged in what they really enjoyed and were good at— designing. Their direct reports were becoming increasingly frustrated by being ineffectively managed, clients were beginning to feel ignored, and managers were becoming overwhelmed by the demands that were not being met to anyone's satisfaction.

Vertical boundaries were slowing communication and decisions through an increasingly steep, multilayered organization. Goldstein wanted control over some important decisions but, since he was traveling constantly to source out new business and maintain relations with current clients, he was forced to manage many production issues from a distance. The concept of "managing by remote control" had become all too real for him. Horizontal boundaries were creating possessive silos of ownership, which were becoming dangerously evident to clients. People began to fight over who did what for each client and hand-offs across functions were starting to get sloppy. External boundaries were also getting frayed. Some customers felt they were not enough in the loop regarding how their account was being managed; they weren't sure who to talk to for what.

An organizational assessment found virtually everyone was excited by his or her work and the future of Site Specific, but for various reasons related to the issues above, they were generally unhappy campers working there. Goldstein was blown away by the results; his peripatetic business trips caused him to lose touch with the daily pulse and the vision. Like the vision developed by Duncan Syme of Vermont Castings (discussed in chapter 1), Goldstein's vision was more in his head than infused within the organization. He assumed things could be improved, but he had no idea how close the place was to implosion. Great talent was ready to bolt, and some customers, feeling ignored at times, were ready to do the same.

After mulling over the assessment results with the rest of his executive group, and then feeding back the results to the entire organization, unanimity was reached on at least one thing: Something had to change. Goldstein and his executive group were at a loss as to a solution, and I was averse to recommending a wholesale restructure. But as the executive group reassessed and focused obsessively on its core strategy, it became evident to them that structure was both the problem and the solution.

They reviewed criteria, strengths, and weaknesses of the cluster model and immediately became enthusiastic about implementing it. Clusters are a frightening concept to many people accustomed to the traditional hierarchy. They believe it means surrendering the authority and power that they need to validate their worth. In many traditional hierarchies, the solution to structural-induced problems is to tighten the hierarchy even more. But since Site Specific was so young, and its management equally youthful and untarnished by more conservative hierarchies, they realized how loosening the hierarchy would help them deliver more effectively on their strategy.

Site Specific introduced the cluster model without the help of a consultant, and everyone was committed to making it work. People were accomplishing their business goals. The interaction between clusters and the rest of the organization improved dramatically while the residual hierarchy remaining served to create alignment between the clusters and the vision of the organization as a whole. Each cluster understood the vision, and they shared information about how other parts of the firm were pursuing it. Information was shared like never before, and the ultimate beneficiary, the client, was delighted. Now, clients had answers almost instantaneously about the status of their initiatives, they knew whom to speak with about what, and they felt cared for by professionals.

And what about all the folks with fancy managerial titles but not much "management" left to do? For the sake of avoiding any perception of demotion and to smooth the way for change, people kept their titles. But their jobs changed to allow them once again to do the creative stuff they were good at and loved, rather than "managing," which they were neither universally competent in nor desirous of. Clusters represented the array of functions operating within the firm, and each learned how to become self-managed.

Did this new vital hierarchy lead to continued scaling? It did, but hard measures of its effectiveness were not directly apparent. About one year after the restructuring, Site Specific was acquired by CKS Group, an integrated marketing company based in Cupertino, CA. CKS merged with USWeb in 1998, and then USWeb was acquired by Whittman-Hart in 2000. It's hard to believe this once vision-driven organization, with a new structure to successfully support the vision and growth, could maintain its uniqueness through all the merger mania.

But the executive group claimed that clusters not only saved the company but created an infrastructure strong enough to catch CKS's attention as an attractive acquisition target. In the end, many of Site Specific's professional staff ultimately left after the acquisition when they became disappointed working, once again, for a relatively traditional hierarchy.

Managing Both the Hard and Soft Dimensions of Organizational Structure

Microsoft was going into 2002 with $39 billion in cash in the bank and sales looking rosy for being in the midst of a recession. But its competitor, Sun Microsystems, found itself pulling out of a year with revenues falling nearly 50 percent, losing money for the first time in a decade. Sun Microsystems laid off employees for the first time ever, and its stock fell a heart-stopping 73 percent.[23] While an element of the culture at Sun is how people on the inside get energized by someone on the outside claiming that the firm will fail, in 2002 Sun was really feeling the screws tighten on it by IBM, Microsoft, and Dell. In the past, companies wanted two things from Sun: great hardware and stable operating systems software. Now they wanted three more things: storage, software that runs on specialized servers, and Web services.[24]

Sun spent 2001 and much of 2002 doing what it has always done: following its customers' desires and "creating seamless infrastructure that helps customers solve problems as 'The Internet Infrastructure Company.'"[25] Its business strategy and attitude remained the same. Now, success is a matter of execution. Sun's highly decentralized structure did not evolve by accident. It has been at the heart of its ability to innovate and make fast decisions. Coordinate too much, the thinking went, and you slow decision making too much. People inside Sun like to call it the "biggest little start-up in Silicon Valley."

While Sun has an extraordinarily loyal workforce, its loyalty among customers has not been as strong. To change that would mean creating divisions that operate under a single corporate umbrella. Sun tried it in 1998 and failed. But now, in 2002, to innovate, CEO Scott McNealy and his executive group must quickly and flexibly adopt a somewhat different structure that forgoes the divisional efficiency for the greater good. The challenge for Sun is not only a technical structure fix, but a change in mindset across the firm.

From a practical standpoint, as organizations grow fast, they often centralize and standardize administrative areas to handle increased transactions. They start out with simple functional structures and keep areas such as manufacturing, marketing, sales, product development, finance, and accounting all separate. As they grow, they duplicate the functional departments within divisions tied to particular products and geographic markets. Smaller units then focus on specific customer segments, and they control the resources required. Multiple businesses, for example, must determine how to manage human resources practices with a semblance of consistency. If they can normalize staffing, training, and compensation systems, then the organization can platoon people to areas where they are most needed at a given point in time rather than hire and train new employees when work in one area increases. Only a unified organization will ensure that the rapid deployment of these decentralized areas stay consistent with the growth vision.

Where there is sustainable growth, we find organizations engaged in much more than a continuous stream of attempts to restructure departments and tweak reporting relationships. They think of the entire organization and consider whether structure is aligned with the vision, whether it will get the organization closer to the vision.

This chapter has focused primarily on the formal or technical side of organization structure, and, however bizarre and nonhierarchical it may look on paper, it is what one might see on an organizational chart. But, as we have seen in the preceding chapters, organization *design* acknowledges and addresses the relationships between formal structures and the informal patterns of values, beliefs, and behavior norms that make up the organizational culture. Organizations must therefore consider both the technical and social systems in order to sustain growth.

It is that unique blend of strategy, structure, work, people, and culture that in combination give us the full picture of what an organization looks like. Even at its most basic level, effective structures are more than a chart on a piece of paper. It flows from a thorough understanding of strategy and takes into consideration both formal and informal elements of the organizational units involved.

While the eyes may not always be the window to another's soul, an organization's management practices are typically reflected in its structure. Structure, as we have seen, is more than the representation of relationships, authority, and communication on a piece of paper. It goes to the essence of what an organization believes in about its people and how people, working collaboratively with a vision as their tailwind, can be a more powerful force than structural forms like chains of command and tall hierarchies. The challenge of growing organizations is to maintain a vital hierarchy and not fall prey to "Jefferson's coat." They must adapt constantly and when a structure does not support the strategy, it must change. Box 8-1 lists some questions scaling organizations can use to evaluate a current or proposed structure.

BOX 8-1

Questions to Evaluate Current or Proposed Structure

- Does it keep the organization continually focused toward the customer?
- Does it reduce the hierarchy to ensure that those serving the customer have information, resources, and the freedom to act?
- Will it allow for flexibility to change as customer and market needs shift?
- How does it enhance partnerships with other people and organizations with whom we must have alliances?
- Does it cut the time it takes to make decisions and get work done?
- In what ways does it enhance the organization's capacity to learn?
- Does it simplify peoples' work and reduce red tape?
- Will it support individual and team accountability for results?
- Can it support fundamental and continuous process improvement and redesign?
- Are organizational boundaries minimized and made more permeable?
- Will it inspire the workforce to consider us the employer of choice in our industry and/or geographic region? Why?
- Will it promote (and not just tolerate) innovation, adaptability, and a sense of urgency among all?
- Is it consistent with, and supportive of, the desired culture?

Chapter 9

Aligning People Processes with Your Vision

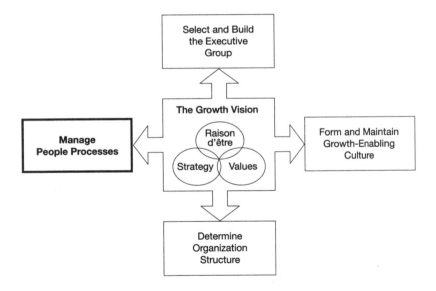

B EFORE I DIVE HEADFIRST INTO THE TOPIC AT hand, I have one small, but critical, clarification to make. The more insightful organizational trend-spotters have noted that the term "people processes" has become a stealth euphemism for the much-maligned human resources (HR) function found in most organizations. While I will comment on the role of HR in this chapter, I am not using the term "people processes" as a substitute for HR. *People processes* refers to the processes by which people are brought into the scaling organization, retained, and motivated—the focus is on what happens rather than who directs the processes at the hands-on level. In other words, if the most visible champion of these processes at your company is HR, that's fine. But don't "hand off" this chapter if that is the case; ultimately it must be the executive group who "owns" the initiation and management of these processes and ensures they are aligned with the vision.

Now, on to it.

In recent years we've seen convincing data indicating the ways in which the management of employee-related processes contribute directly to the bottom line, particularly for firms undergoing significant growth. The latest research, along with anecdotal observations from a range of industries, has created a compelling case for realizing that these processes are, in fact, a determining factor in the process of growth. Research has shown, for example, that the steep growth trajectory expected for many new ventures makes them highly dependent on key employees and especially susceptible to risks associated with people, such as tight labor markets or delays in product development.[1] And Stanford management scholar Jeff Pfeffer has argued strongly that a focus on accounting and finance without equal interest in the management of people processes can lead to dire results.[2]

If employees are indeed a critical resource that can provide sustained competitive advantage, then expertise in managing this resource—ensuring that it is aligned with the vision—may be as important to the firm's future performance as is skill in finance, marketing, or research. Being able to capitalize on the human assets of the firm, in other words—particularly during periods of rapid growth and strategy shifts—is a competency critical to the ongoing success of an enterprise.

What You Probably Didn't Learn about Competitive Advantage in Business School

I'm going to target this discussion primarily toward companies experiencing rapid growth because in a slow-growth organization, the CEO may have time to learn about and adjust to the needs created by growth by getting out and talking to employees to acquire information. This becomes increasingly difficult if not impossible as growth accelerates. While I advocate for the executive group assuming responsibility for people processes, it becomes critical as the rate of change increases, and the executive group has less time to make decisions, for a visible and credible senior executive to "own" the recruitment, motivation, and retention challenges.

Why is a "people processes strategy" so important? Let's review more conventional views of strategy. Well-established criteria that determine the ability of firms to earn above-average returns suggest that if we want to see what makes for a high-growth, high-profit organization, we should look for industries with

- barriers to entry,
- low supplier and buyer bargaining power,
- few ready substitutes, and a
- limited threat of new entrants to compete away economic returns.[3]

These strategy guidelines would point us toward industries in which patent protection of important product or service technology exists, and then we would find the major players in those industries. They would also imply that being a product pioneer in a new market would ensure longevity, if not a near-lock on that market.

In reality, the data doesn't support these widely held views. For example, if stock prices were used as a proxy measure, then our picks would be successful only if we turned these criteria upside down. The top five stocks from 1972 to 1992 (which removes effects of the Internet bubble of the mid- to late-1990s) and their percentage returns for that period were: (1) Southwest Airlines, 21,775 percent; (2) Wal-Mart (a chain store discounter), 19,807 percent; (3) Tyson Foods (poultry producer), 18,118 percent; (4) Circuit City (discount electronics and appliance chain), 16,410 percent; and (5) Plenum Publishing, 15,689 percent.[4]

Oddly, these industries were characterized by cutthroat competition, huge losses, and widespread bankruptcies. They had little if any barriers to entry, relatively insignificant proprietary technology, and a considerable array of substitute products or services.

None of the firms held a disproportionate share of the market or maintained enviable economies of scale.

Another related misconception is that becoming a market pioneer ensures long-term growth and sustainability. A recent study by Gerard Tellis of USC and Peter Goldner of NYU analyzed data going back fifty years and found that market pioneers rarely endure as leaders. Most of them end up with low market share or fail completely. "Market pioneering is neither necessary nor sufficient for enduring success," the researchers concluded.[5] What factors were found to be necessary for long-term growth and sustainability? A revolutionary and inspiring vision, a culture of persistence, and the ability to innovate relentlessly. While persistence was imbued by values set into the organizational culture, innovation in the successful firms analyzed was accomplished by *deliberate strategies*. Each organization implemented specific strategies to manage their peoples' innovation, motivation, and retention.[6]

The fact is that sources of competitive advantage migrate over time. What firms share in their ability to grow continuously is not a dependency on technology, patents, strategy position, or being a pioneer but on *the processes they've developed to manage their people*. They have developed systems that align the interests of employees, managers, and investors to the benefit of all. Put another way, companies with people processes that put investors, managers, employees, and other stakeholders on the same page with regard to vision are at a distinct advantage.

Strategies designed to align and leverage the people processes really do work. For example, a study using multiple samples and measures found that a change in one standard deviation in an index of innovative HR management practices produces increases of $20,000 to $40,000 in stock market value *per employee*.[7] Another study found that companies just one standard deviation higher in their use of high-performance work practices (tied directly to what we would consider superior HR practices) realized more than $27,000 in increased sales per employee, $18,000 in increased market capitalization, and $3,800 in profits, as well as a significant decrease in employee turnover.[8] It isn't only that these firms executed great HR practices; they were the means for accomplishing a much larger strategy.

People Processes and the Executive Group

Although capital is a crucial resource, we know that VCs provide much more than financing to their portfolio companies. The better VCs learn over time what helps rapidly growing ventures do better, and their active involvement enables them to pass along this knowledge. While VCs have helped historically with strategy, acting as sounding boards for the entrepreneurs and facilitating their development of social networks with the financial community, customers, and suppliers, I have observed them becoming more involved in the management of human capital. (In chapter 6 I discussed the importance that venture capital firms place on the presence of a complete, well-balanced senior management group.)

Research over the years has shown that if there is an executive on the top management team who understands the ways in which "people issues" can be integrated into business planning and decision making, and whose role is dedicated to implementing programs in this area, then important benefits will accrue to the firm.[9] Recently, Linda Cyr and Theresa Welbourne of Harvard and the University of Michigan, respectively, completed two groundbreaking studies that examined the relationship of growth-oriented firms and their emphasis on strategic HR practices.[10] They analyzed VC-backed firms executing IPOs during the 1990s and found that VCs influence their portfolio companies to place an HR person on the senior group *prior* to the IPO. Venture capitalist backing is a significant predictor that HR will be a family member at the strategy table. The only other variable that emerges as significant is the number of employees. Firms going into an IPO with more employees are more likely to have a VP of HR than are firms with fewer employees.

The study also measured the level of financial risk inherent in the venture. Those VC-sponsored firms executing an IPO with very high levels of risk were much more likely to have a VP of HR as opposed to those whose perceived risk was lower.[11]

When the same scholars completed a related study, they found that firms experiencing high rates of growth have better stock price performance *when their senior HR executives report directly to the*

CEO. Smaller firms have increased earnings when CEOs have HR professionals reporting directly to them.[12]

The lesson from these kinds of studies obviously goes deeper than mere reporting relationship. When there is an HR presence at the top we can extrapolate that the CEO, as well as the organization at large, acknowledges the value that people processes contribute and how the absence of these processes, or their misalignment with the vision, can lead to severe business problems.[13]

The Processes That Support Scaling

IBM didn't become a corporate behemoth until the 1950s, but the foundation was set in 1914 when forty-year-old Tom Watson Sr. joined a losing conglomerate, the Computing-Tabulating-Recording Co. During that period, manufacturers emphasized breaking tasks down to their most repetitive functions (the influence of Frederick Winslow Taylor's "Scientific Management" was taking hold). Rather than focusing on task simplification, Watson made people the focus of his organizational culture. He borrowed money to develop in-house educational programs, got rid of piecework, made the factories more attractive places in which to work, and paid above-scale wages.

With no money to afford benefit programs, he organized company picnics with bands and company songs to evoke a sense of corporate spirit. In the mid-1930s, IBM offered a group life insurance plan, survivor benefits, and paid vacations—radical stuff for its time. Perhaps most avant-garde was his "open door" (yes, this is where the term originated) policy that enabled any employee to take a complaint to Watson himself. How could they risk this? Since he ensured workers lifetime employment, even during the Depression, they felt safe enough to speak their minds. While the no-layoff policy disappeared during IBM's dark days in the early 1990s, there is much to learn from their formidable case of scaling.

IBM understood the concept of HR management long before the term came into the organizational lexicon. Like other firms, it understands the importance of taking a systems-level focus. These systems generally include rigorous recruitment and selection procedures, incentive compensation systems contingent on performance, and management development and training activities linked to the future needs of the organization. But they only have a systematic impact on the bottom line when they are embedded in the management infrastructure and help the organization accomplish such business priorities as shortening product development cycle times, increasing customer service, and lowering turnover among the people you need to keep.

Problems are different in every organization, though, and how they are handled is highly firm-specific. Unfortunately, benchmarking best practices from a generic sample of other organizations ends up playing a limited role when the practice is not aligned with the vision of the firm. While benchmarking isolated practices may keep an organization in the game, it will not provide the intellectual capital to create sustained, competitive advantage through the play-offs.

The CEO, executive group, and the senior individual responsible for championing the set of people processes must all collectively resolve one essential question: How do we create a strategy for these processes that stays aligned with the vision, business strategy, and tactical priorities, while remaining capable of rapidly adapting to changes the organizations must cope with?

Good practices are not faddish. Sadly, much of the contemporary literature on effective human-resources management tactics may give the distinct impression that the elusive enigmas for recruiting, motivating, and retaining good people are being perennially solved with new solutions all the time. The practices outlined below are admittedly overlapping and interconnected, but they are neither radical nor new. Rather, the way in which they have impact over time is through the interactive gestalt that accrues when as many practices as possible are operating simultaneously.

The IBM case and others serve as examples of how a clearly articulated and executed people-processes strategy overlaps with, and supports, the intended culture. When the vision framework is seen as a set of carefully aligned elements, each supports and sustains the others.

Recruit for Fit and Mis-Fit

Recruiting can have a powerful symbolic impact beyond getting the right people into the organization. A highly rigorous selection process evokes the feeling that one is joining an elite organization, creating high expectations for performance and sending the message that the quality of people really matters. Recruits experience the sense of accomplishment associated with completing boot camp when entering military service. But a rigorous process also magnifies a tension: There is the need to set high standards and often strict criteria, yet there is also the need to recruit people who think differently. Diversity is often not tolerated when the bar is high.

For those who manage the tension best, what do they look for in their candidates? They break away from the traditional selection practices geared toward hiring people whose knowledge, skills, and abilities (KSAs) ostensibly provide the best fit for the job. These personal characteristics rarely consider characteristics of the organization in which the job resides, and if an individual's distinctiveness is irrelevant to immediate job requirements, then his or her chance of being hired is next to nil. In this tradition-bound method, the organization is hiring "hands" or new "heads." It's only hiring parts of people, which can have a catastrophic effect on an organization that must be continually pondering how to grow from within.

Managing from a systems perspective involves multiple steps, an emphasis on finding people whose values are consistent with the vision, and clear definitions of expected attitudes and behaviors. It requires methods for identifying candidates who are likely to be drawn to the organization's culture and leveraging the importance of first impressions on candidates. While the processes of organizations adapting these hiring practices may seem peculiar and needlessly extravagant to the outsider, they make perfect sense to insiders.

During the long period when Sun Microsystems was ramping up its professional workforce, before the market for servers sputtered out at the end of the 1990s, it provided a good example of how a "rite of passage" allows for both the person and the organization to mutually assess each other. Sun was constantly changing in response to rapidly developing markets, evolving technologies, and the pace of internal growth. Employees who preferred clear job descriptions, stability, a leisurely pace, and predictability (none of which exists in scaling organizations) would have been unhappy at Sun. The hiring process was such a challenge, and so full of ambiguity, that unsuitable applicants tended to give up before the process was completed. Those hired had survived multiple interviews with many different potential coworkers. The joke at Sun was that after seven sets of interviews, it puts applicants on the payroll whether they've been hired or not. Such a process has the effect of introducing the candidates to the culture of the organization before they are hired.

At Sun's nemesis, Microsoft, an equally rigorous interview loop exists. For a huge corporation that still continues to scale despite its mature market and Justice Department attempts to contain it, Microsoft is a highly accepting place of nonconformity; there are a lot of people at Microsoft for whom being there is the key to being themselves. When it comes to finding people who can grow with the organization, Microsoft has gotten it from Day One. People there believe the organization is different from other places and that they are different from other people. It has its own mores and values, all of which stem from the conviction of its people that they are part of a new, very special group.

One tired theory about Microsoft is that everyone is—or tries to be—like Bill. If people are not already arrogant and peremptory, they learn quickly how to be. The legend is that Bill is famous for telling people that whatever they just told him is the stupidest thing he ever heard; ergo, everyone learns to—or is hired with the temperament to—grind others' ideas down to a pulp. But this is not what it looks or sounds like at Microsoft if you were a fly on the proverbial conference room wall. Managers actually talk of getting "buy in," and achieving a high level of cooperation from colleagues is an important norm. They argue and cajole. They write position papers to make their case clear and compelling to others. They do what they can to win people over to their ideas rather than bully them.

One key component of Gates's strategy is his investment in intellectual talent. He goes after the brightest minds in the industry. He says, "The key for us, number one, has always been hiring very smart people. There is no way of getting around that, in terms of IQ, you've got to be very elitist in picking the people who deserve to write software. . . ."[14] Hiring the brightest has several benefits: smarter workers ensure faster, better, or more efficient solutions to problems. Microsoft CEO Steve Ballmer claims "Smart people can learn to do most things. Workaholic, smart kids is what we're after."[15]

The community of Microsoft is not a community of bright clones. It is a group that shares a strong ethos about getting rid of software bugs, shipping software out the door, a few big concepts about work and life, and the belief that they can change the world. Just as important, they also share a belief that differences are good and that they impact the success of the company and their own enjoyment of work. Two differences—the firm's success at transcending the importance of stock options and employees' willingness to work eighteen-hour days—may enable it to continue scaling beyond the point most will have ever forecasted.

In chapter 6, I discussed the notion of "Homosocial Reproduction"—the tendency for senior managers to hire people who they perceive as similar to themselves. While it gives us a sense of comfort to work around others who think like us and have similar backgrounds, it can also be deadly for the organization if people at the executive levels have reproduced themselves. The impact of homosocial reproduction is not limited to the executive ranks, however.

About a decade ago I was engaged by a hyper-fast-growing hedge fund trading outfit to assess its management capacity and develop a program that would build leadership competencies as growth demanded. The firm was making gobs of money (investor money was pouring in), and the senior group began testing their analytic models at the beginning of what would become the longest-running economic boom. The founder and his colleagues at the top were intellectually brilliant; most had Ph.D.s in physics, mathematics, or computer sciences. They were also profoundly protective, if not paranoid, of their complex, proprietary trading models—they had me sign a one-half-inch thick agreement to never reveal that I worked for them (hence, I can't tell you who they are) or anything related to these models. I guess it was irrelevant that I wouldn't have known what to do with an analytic model if I tripped over it in the hallway.

I found the philosophy behind their employee-selection system both charming and disturbing. Charming was the practice of hiring people based on their potential to grow with the needs of the company, regardless of whether they had a specific position in mind if the person was hired. This practice reflected the understanding that a scaling organization entailed much ambiguity, that few roles had precise definitions, and that good people were a critical asset or intellectual "capital in the bank." Each person would start out in a relatively menial job, see where the business was headed, and determine how they might move into a new opportunity that attracted them once it was spotted. They learned to identify opportunities and seize them; responsibility for each career was up to the individual. And finally, each was responsible for developing the competencies required for succeeding in the position. There was an organic feel to succession planning and the way in which new positions in new lines of business were seamlessly filled from within. It really was charming and, for a while, it worked like a charm.

What I found somewhat disturbing were the criteria for initial selection into the firm—or perhaps describing the criteria as barriers to entry would be more accurate. Applicants had to be straight out of school—either at the undergraduate or graduate level—and not just any school: It was a small, elite group of schools from which the top managers would consider anybody for even the first interview. Although they had two dozen schools on their list (and you can probably guess them), this was not the disturbing part. The additional screening requirement for everybody was the need to provide SAT scores from high school days. Apply with off-the-chart SAT scores, graduate from a top school, and you had a shot at two rounds of interviews. Even as a potential consultant *I*, a relative geezer among the masses, had to show my SAT scores before they hired me for the engagement.

Here was a company doubling in size nearly every nine months and filled to the gills with overeducated people who tested well on the SAT. And here was a company that raised the notion of homosocial reproduction to a science. They were hell-bent on maintaining this philosophy regardless of the twists and turns the business took. On the surface, the philosophy made sense: Look for people who are really, really smart and have the "right" attitude. If the firm didn't know what to do with them when they were hired, they at least had the intellectual horsepower to acquire the skills they needed as the organization's needs emerged. Hiring for intellectual capacity made sense to me.

Even the SAT thing wouldn't have bothered me as much if I thought it was only a proxy for organization-specific potential. If they were looking for people with diverse skills and temperaments that might help the firm in as-yet-unknown areas, then I could have accepted it. But these folks did not have varied backgrounds, or ways of processing the world, and they certainly did not have diverse skill sets that the firm could draw from as it grew. While they were tolerant of people with personalities varying from the norm, those who did vary were referred to appropriately as "the outliers." Standardized tests like the SAT measure something, but is it enough to discern the set of diverse qualities required for a scaling organization?

After a few years, signs of implosion surfaced as the "one mindset" philosophy started to collide with inherent needs of the organization to expand in new ways. This required they become more innovative, which in turn, required that they diverge from the "one mindset" approach. Oh, did I mention that the organization had no vision? Although it did struggle to articulate one, it failed to identify its raison d'être and values.[16] It nailed the strategy, but that was not enough to guide it through a set of aligned people processes. A recent Yale English major, who happened to be a beneficiary of the tight selection criteria, ultimately developed into a great HR director. But she left after realizing that the people processes that she knew were required for fueling the firm's growth were never going to gain support from top management. Perhaps not-so-coincidentally, HR was never a member of the senior management group.

Let's turn to Oakley for comparison. Unlike the hedge fund outfit, academic degrees are not as important at Oakley—but intelligence is. "We look for people with passion squirting out of their ears," Colin Baden told me.[17] Oakley also needs people with off-the-chart creative potential and what Baden and other senior managers refer to as "street smarts." How do they assess all of that without SAT scores or Ivy diplomas? Applicants go through rigorous interviews that elicit what the individual has accomplished and learned from past experiences. Often, panels are composed of the candidate's potential manager, peers, and perhaps subordinates. What are they looking for? Not only intelligence, but entrepreneurial drive, energy level (often judged, in part, by how fast the candidate walks), and the ability to "break down barriers" to get things done. Kent Lane put it this way:

> We determine if the candidate is a builder or a maintainer during the hiring process. It is imperative to find builders. Our business evolves at hyper-speed, or direction may change 180 degrees—no 360 degrees: New systems, processes, and solutions need to be built. A maintainer will die a quick and painful death here. A builder will thrive. And these builders better not build what has already been done.[18]

Darlene Kennedy has brought the mundane task of reference checking up to a science and art form. She gets referees to really open up about the individual she's investigating to discern whether the requisite characteristics are present.

For scaling organizations, getting great people on board is worth the time, effort, and frustration it may involve. First, the process is accretive: One factor in getting great people to join an organization is letting them see all the other great people who are a part of the enterprise. Second, finding the right people makes it easier to motivate them. There is enormous power inherent in being part of a team that is expected to produce great results when everyone subscribes to the goals and has the capacity to develop. Third, if you have the wrong people on board, not much else matters. The vision may guide you in the right direction for growth, but you will never achieve much. Great vision with mediocre people still produces mediocre results.

Flood People with Feedback

One deficiency prevails across virtually every organization I have come into contact with (and I've no doubts that this is because this deficiency is tremendously difficult to overcome). It is the inability to establish a culture that provides strong encouragement for everyone to give and receive a constant flow of high-quality feedback. Building this into the culture is important because people in general avoid giving feedback that is not positive, and most cringe with the anticipation of knowing they are about to receive it. The culture must communicate, "Feedback is a way of life around here. This is how we learn, how we stay innovative, and how we create a knowledge-based organization." Feedback is information—no more, no less. Unfortunately, it is the way in which most people give it—or avoid giving it—that creates over time the aversion most have for it.

I am not talking about formal performance reviews here. The feedback provided during these sessions, which are usually no more than twice each year, is relatively worthless in helping people learn what behavior to maintain and what to change. Formal processes are delayed and, because of the time lag, the receiver of feedback has lost the clear picture of what they did (right or wrong) to elicit it.

While organizations like Oakley have regular performance review sessions with each employee, the culture more importantly demands that managers serve as coaches and give real-time feedback on a need-to-know basis. One of the primary reasons why Oakley deemphasizes the chain of command and dress codes is to establish a precedent that encourages two-way feedback: down *and* up the organization. Oakley's commitment to grow talent from within, rather than "buying" it on the market, makes it acutely aware of the need to provide people with feedback—information about how well they are learning new skills, finding new approaches to doing things, and fueling creativity.

Giving great feedback is a skill, learned and honed through practice. But unless the culture supports the constant flow of this type of communication, organizations will find themselves with people keeping inside what needs to be communicated out to others or talking *around* people rather than directly to the individual who needs to hear the feedback.

Align Performance-Based Compensation with Strategy, Structure, and Culture

Management scholars overwhelmingly agree that extrinsic rewards, including compensation, are powerful motivators. While this may seem obvious to most readers, it has been a point of debate since Frederick Herzberg shared his famous theory of the relationship between "hygiene factors" and "motivators" in a 1968 article.[19] The tide was turning back to acknowledging the powerful impact that financial incentives could have when journalist Alfie Kohn gained prominence in the practitioner literature in the 1990s with his book *Punished by Rewards*, the conclusions of which were summarized in an article titled "Why Incentive Plans Cannot Work."[20] Kohn rails against the use of extrinsic rewards to motivate—singling out compensation in particular—but he has been under fire from academic researchers in the field who have questioned much of the methodology leading to his findings.

An intense focus on paying for performance is justified for a number of reasons. It helps to attract and retain top performers, and it has been shown to be a compelling motivator that can increase loyalty over time.

But let me be clear. Pay motivates behavior when—and only when—there is a clear relationship between a significant amount of pay and the behavior desired. The figure of speech that keeps me focused on this issue was coined by Ed Lawler, an organization and HR scholar at the University of Southern California. Lawler believes all pay-for-performance plans must have a *"line of sight"* quality.[21] Each person must be able to see, with crystal clarity and ease, how his or her behavior led to the increase in their reward.

Things get muddled, however, when compensation systems are poorly planned and pay ends up motivating the wrong behavior as well as what is desired. Merit pay (pay based on level of performance), the most common form of pay-for-performance, almost always fails because it is based on poor measures and delivers such small changes in compensation that it has no meaningful effect. Merit pay has been shown consistently to have little impact in any setting. In lateral team-based organizations, which is the structure that tends to work best for scaling organizations (see chapter 8), merit pay does not fit as well as team- and organization-based pay-for-performance systems. And, when the job market is tight, the differential that great performers experience is rarely enough to serve as an inducement for loyalty.

The primary finding from decades of research on pay-for-performance is that, unfortunately, there is no "one-size-fits-all" solution. Paying for performance is critical in scaling organizations, but no single plan will fit all organizations. Nor will it be totally effective in any organization. All one can do is increase the probability that a meaningful line-of-sight exists among behavior, rewards, and the recipient—and all are aligned with the vision.

An agonizing decision in the design of pay systems is whether to reward individuals, groups, business units, or the organization as a whole. Plans that reward individuals achieve very different objectives than those rewarding the organization in total. Those that reward the organization as a whole are good at integrating individuals and encouraging them to understand the vision, the business, and developing working lateral relationships. But they are poor at motivating individuals. Team bonus plans, on the other hand, can be extremely powerful in motivating team performance and encouraging individuals to work together toward the team's objectives. But they do far too little to encourage teams to work *together*.

So, individual-, team-, and organization-based pay-for-performance plans have different impacts. All may have a place in a single scaling organization's approach to paying for performance, and this is where creativity and flexibility become critical. For example, people can be paid based on their individual performance, their team's performance, business unit's performance, and on their businesses' performance. Where individual performance can accurately be measured, using at least a merit-based pay scheme based on performance makes good sense. In organizational structures where people are part of a team, and therefore the compensations system should be aligned with, and supported by the chosen structure, team performance usually can be measured much more easily (see chapter 8). Through these systems—that carefully link employees' pay to their performance and the performance at a variety of levels within the organization—the organization is keeping people meaningfully involved in a way that encourages them to understand the business and take part in decisions that affect it.

At the base salary level, a belief held among many CEOs of growing firms is that higher wages help to recruit the best people and to retain them. Higher wages tend to attract a larger applicant pool that, in turn, allows the organization to be more selective in finding people who meet the stringent criteria. But more important, higher wages send a message that the organization values its employees. Research indicates that when people understand that their wages are higher than the prevailing market, they may perceive it as a gift and work harder as a result.[22]

When employees are educated about, and involved in, the pay-for-performance system, their line-of-sight can be easier drawn and little doubt exists about how their performance impacts on other measures of organizational effectiveness and therefore ultimately on the bonus they receive. Bonuses have to be experienced as genuinely meaningful to each person if they are expected to have a lasting impact on motivation.

In a similar vein, it's paradoxical that there is a prevailing theory that wages must be kept low to be competitive. Even in industries where margins are razor-thin and labor costs a respectable proportion of expenses, the theory doesn't hold water. If labor costs are proportionately higher—when all other conditions enumerated in this book are in place—an organization can expect enhanced service, skill, and innovation that will more than offset the difference.

The fast-food industry, notorious for keeping wages as close to the legal minimum as possible, illustrates how low wages decrease the quality of applicants and increase turnover and low job satisfaction. In the early 1990s, as the clean trajectory of growth at Wendy's stalled and its stock hit an all-time low, Dave Thomas, the late founder, and the senior executives believed the best way to bring back customers was to bring in better employees. They were hell-bent on Wendy's becoming the employer of choice for the industry. Benefits were hiked, base compensation increased, a system of quarterly bonuses implemented, and an employee stock option plan offered. Results were extraordinary: Their turnover rate for general managers fell to 20 percent in 1991 from 39 percent in 1989, while turnover among co- and assistant managers dropped to 37 percent from 60 percent. Within less than two years, Wendy's became the benchmark for the industry and, not coincidentally, sales became recharged as well.[23]

Why Alignment Is Important

The consensus of researchers falls squarely on the conclusion that compensation does motivate and satisfy people but *only* if it is aligned with organizational strategy and reinforces other systems.[24] This notion of alignment explains why compensation must be a "lag" rather than a "lead" system. For a compensation system to impact its intended targets, it must be directed by the vision. It should support the strategy, reflect the organizational structure, reinforce the culture, and be consistent with other HR systems.

Since strategy indicates how the organization will gain competitive advantage in the marketplace, it helps give direction to compensation systems by indicating the types of employee behaviors and abilities the organization needs to stay successful.

Hard data, which is easily available, helps evaluate whether innovation has already occurred, enabling the organization to leverage the power of a "lag" compensation system. Lead pay systems, which pay up-front, ahead of the actual desired performance, are generally based only on generic business strategies that do not offer competitive advantage. They also tend to be stand-alone programs unrelated to the strategy of the organization because designers of the programs don't know where to start. For example, generic job evaluation systems emphasizing general factors such as skill, effectiveness, responsibility, and working conditions may have little relationship to the core capabilities that need to be developed within the organization to support its strategy.

For example, 3M's strategy of innovation has established a goal that each business unit must derive 30 percent of its sales from products introduced within the previous four years. But when W. James McNerney Jr. took the helm after leaving GE in late 2000, he was in for a challenge. 3M's sales were anemic, and it hadn't launched a blockbuster product in years. This was an organization legendary for innovation. The language of GE (ROI, Best Practices, blunt and probing questions) didn't translate well for 3M managers accustomed to running departments with relatively free rein. McNerney was determined to find a common language, and took his executive group—the top fifteen managers—to a two-day offsite meeting to reformulate 3M's core values.[25]

Afterward, he set an ambitious goal of increasing sales and operating earnings by at least 10 percent each year; nearly twice the rate of the past decade. But he resisted barking orders and set about trying to win the hearts and minds of employees. "You can't order change," he said. "After all, there's only one of me and 75,000 of them."[26] He had a multitude of meetings with employees, discussing the new values and the prevailing vision of the firm.

And what does this have to do with people processes? McNerney and his executive group realized their strongest lever for getting people back on board to recreate an environment that fosters continual innovation was to revise the performance management system. They reminded employees about the unrest among most regarding underperformers and how the company "protected" them. In response, the option-granting program was revised from one that was essentially an entitlement program (every manager received options) to one that rewarded only better-than-average performance grades. Younger employees are now encouraged to step out of their niches. Other changes in the reward systems were implemented, and all were tied to the values, particularly those that fuel innovation, in the vision.

"3M people wake up every morning thinking about what new product they can bring to market," McNerney reflected. "Innovation is in their DNA—and if I kill that entrepreneurial spirit, I will have failed. My job is to build on that strength, corral and focus it."[27] By mid-2002, he was making progress on that through the firm's people processes.[28] A belief in encouraging experiments and discovery runs deep at 3M and has fostered the innovative products and technologies for which it is known. The "15 percent rule," for example, allows employees to spend part of their work time exploring experiments. In addition, technical employees can apply for 3M Genesis Grants, which provide corporate monies for innovative projects that are not funded through standard channels. It is through these experiments that 3M continues to be a leader in new products and technologies.

Organizational structure and culture follow from the strategy (all of which will be fundamentally established by the vision framework). These factors give direction to the organization. Without this direction, designing compensation systems that motivate behaviors necessary for growth becomes a matter of luck.

In summary, the traditional rules for paying people were based more on the worth of jobs than on how well people were doing them. That's often why people desire a promotion: Moving to a higher-level job has been the most highly rewarded organizational behavior. The old rules also paid people for the length of time they worked. While seniority-oriented pay systems do contribute to loyalty, they also develop an entitlement mentality that engenders the belief that rewards should go up because one shows up and holds down a job for a length of time.

New rules—demanded by the modern business environment—redirect the center of attention from jobs to an individual's knowledge, skills, and abilities (KSAs). People are paid relative to the market value of their KSAs and what they can actually do with them. As Lawler found in his research,

> [J]obs do not have market value—individuals do. They are the ones that add value and change employers, not jobs. . . . If individuals are to make their maximum contribution to their organization's success, they simply cannot have a static set of duties that can be described and that capture everything that they are expected to do.[29]

In addition to a focus on the person, the rewards must be tied to organizational performance in ways that support strategy and structure.

Oakley, for example, uses a "broad-banding" system that affords great flexibility in rewarding exemplary performance. Within the organization, people avoid using formal titles (and many people just make up their own title), which reinforces flexibility. For high-performers, base pay is increased, line-of-sight bonuses are awarded, and some nontraditional just-in-time rewards are offered. When people step up to the plate and go far beyond the call of duty, meaningful rewards are given. One high-performer talked about his desire for raising a particular type of dog. Voila! A puppy of that breed was waiting for him in his office area one morning. Another loved motor sports, and Oakley acknowledged his performance by renting time on a racetrack with a racecar to drive. Both of these examples demonstrate the flexibility that is so important to ensuring that rewards are *meaningful* to the recipient.[30]

Of any people process, compensation has the highest emotional content. It directly affects all employees, all the time. Virtually everyone greatly values their compensation, and they do so for many reasons: as a means to meeting basic needs, as a source of status, as a signal from the organization that they are succeeding, to name only a few. So, people monitor the pay system very closely and show a level of awareness and concern about compensation changes far above other types of organizational changes. When used in a "lag" role, rewards, and pay in particular, can be used to support significant organizational changes required to sustain growth.

Develop People and "Promote" from Within

In chapter 8, I tried to make an impassioned plea for reconfiguring the traditional hierarchy to one that is more vital. Executing on the vision-driven strategy of most growth enterprises requires a structure that is relatively flat, and emphasizes groups, teams, or clusters rather than functions. With such a structure, people develop an increasingly wide "bandwidth" of skills that makes them a more valued asset to the organization and enables them to more fully understand the scope and depth of how the place works. They become an integral part of the organizational system.

The structure of the organization has serious implications for how people are required to continually develop—not only to support the organizational growth but also for their own expectations about "moving up." In the traditional hierarchy, "moving up" does not always make people happy. Many people from technical and creative backgrounds, for example, find themselves unexpectedly unhappy when they get promoted into management. Their involvement in the "real work" that gave them satisfaction and a sense of challenge and competency has been dramatically reduced in favor of "managing," which is less appealing, something they are not good at, and may engender ill-feelings from their onetime colleagues. In today's high-growth organizations, traditional promotion to management is often a lose–lose proposition.

In the vital hierarchy, there are relatively fewer upward career movements and different expectations about what learning and leadership mean. Moving "up" can actually be moving laterally, since this is what organizations structured around lateral processes require. Research has shown clearly that if organizations are to operate laterally they need individuals who have worked in different functions and understand multiple specialties.[31]

Lateral career moves help develop strong managers and leaders. As one moves through a series of relatively slow lateral moves, more about the operations of the organization as a business is learned. In turn, the individual has a greater chance to develop better skills in managing long-term relationships with coworkers. Over time, this presents a remarkable developmental experience for those who want to take on greater managerial responsibility.

The research that led to the book *Built to Last* uncovered an interesting pattern among the visionary, and most successful, companies. Of the eighteen firms and their more than 1,700 years of combined history, the authors found only four instances in which an outsider was hired as chief executive—and that happened in only two of the eighteen firms. In contrast, the less successful comparison organizations were six times more likely to go outside for a CEO.[32] These findings do not support the widely shared belief that companies should hire outsiders to stimulate change and progress.

As great organizations grow up, promoting insiders lends continuity and order to management tenure and succession. Insiders preserve the core values, understanding them on a gut level in a way that outsiders often cannot. Yet insiders can also be change agents, building on the core values while moving the organization in exciting new directions.

Training and Development Strategy

Growing at a high rate of speed creates a paradox for senior management as it considers and evaluates a training and development strategy. The organization must develop employees in a way that's relevant to the job and business issues it faces *now*, but it simultaneously confronts the reduced time and resources available to provide such development. Everyone acknowledges the importance of development, whether formally in training or informally through coaching, but who has the time? Some high-growth firms have found the answer.

Founded in 1976, SAS Institute licenses their statistical and data-based management software to 37,000 businesses, government institutions, and universities. Among its customers are 98 percent of the Fortune 100 and 90 percent of the Fortune 500. And growth? It's been double-digit for the past twenty-four years.[33] The privately held firm not only invests significantly in training and development for all employees but believes strongly in what I call "cross-platform" skill development. This makes it easy for people to move laterally within the organization. As David Russo, the former head of HR at SAS commented:

> There are no silos of research and development, there are no silos of marketing and sales, there are no silos of technical support. Everything's based on a toolkit. If your toolkit fits this division's model for business and you want to do that, chances are pretty good you'll get to do that. And if two years later you see something else you want to do and it's across three organizational boundaries, you get to do that. . . . In an intellectual capital organization like ours, the most important thing you can do is engage the individual's energy so that they can apply it to the thing that excites them most, their work.[34]

Since data indicate that people will have three to four careers in their lifetime, SAS is doing what it can to ensure the best people have as many of those diverse careers with it.

Developing the "toolkit" to meet the needs of both the individual and the organization, for today and tomorrow, is not an easy task. Strong resistance to preparing for the future will naturally appear when rewards are based on behavior in the present. One strategy that can deal with this conundrum is to encourage people to develop cross-platform skills and competencies.

In 1999 the American Cancer Society (ACS) had some ambitious goals it was committed to achieve by 2015: slash the cancer mortality rate by 50 percent, reduce the incidence of cancer by 25 percent, and impact the quality of life of cancer survivors. It quickly became apparent that these goals would remain pipe dreams if ACS did not assemble an elite team of the best and brightest among its 6,500 employees and prepare them to lead the organization in the next phase of its war on cancer.

The ACS realized it was heading for a leadership crisis: nearly half of its senior executives were nearing retirement age and few were in line to replace them. "We hadn't done a good job of preparing people to help us achieve our 2015 goal," Ree Stanley, the national VP for HR noted.[35] In late 2000, senior leaders throughout the organization revived an e-mail announcing an unusual recruitment drive—the ACS was in need of leaders and any and all of the 6,500 employees were invited to apply for the top jobs. "We deliberately cast a wide net," said Stanley. "We couldn't afford to overlook qualified people."[36]

Candidates endured a rigorous evaluation process. It started with a detailed application in which they were asked to assess their leadership skills using fifteen separate criteria and to demonstrate how they exceeded the criteria. At this point, the cut was big. Those who made it, however, faced more hurdles. A roundtable of division managers scrutinized applications of the candidates remaining; each then went through a 360-degree review; and finally they were ranked on a talent grid alongside each other by a group of executives from the national and regional levels.

Four months after the process began, the nineteen finalists were notified that they were in the national pool of potential CEOs and COOs. Each person was given a rating ranging from "promotable within twenty-four months" to "immediately promotable." The nineteen were then assigned a management coach and directed to develop a personal plan that would take their competencies to the next level.

The goal ACS set for the recruits was straightforward: to learn to lead by leading. Those who did not make the cut would become more effective leaders when they completed the program and the ACS would have the kind of talent they wanted to reward and nurture. The ACS essentially created nineteen catalysts who would challenge the people around them to think in new ways and develop new ideas.

Unfortunately, too many organizations still plan from quarter to quarter or year to year. When the ACS set a goal (that was part of its vision) fifteen years out, it realized that if it did not build a new generation of leaders, it would never get there. Fighting cancer has taught the ACS at least one thing: Think long-term but implement the strategy now.

Create an Environment to Enhance Egalitarianism

The force that guides how SAS Institute operates is a small, consistent set of values and beliefs. One is to "create a corporation where it was as much fun for the workers as for top management."[37] This implies there is one standard for all, and everyone is treated fairly and equally. Nobody has a reserved parking spot, a more attractive health plan, a fancier dining room, or a corner office instead of a cubicle. As President and CEO Jim Goodnight explained, "Four of us started the business. When we started, there were no employees, we were all principals. What we tried to do was to treat people who joined the company as we ourselves wanted to be treated. . . . The company is characterized by an egalitarian approach."[38]

The rationale for egalitarianism is not to create a Marxist system for some social-political agenda. Rather, it makes good business sense. When egalitarianism is experienced in the workplace, people communicate more fully—and more freely—with others at all organizational ranks.

Mayor Michael Bloomberg of New York City, who was founder and CEO of Bloomberg L.P. before his foray into politics, created his Park Avenue headquarters to enhance and reinforce the strategy and culture of his corporate vision. Up until the time he left as CEO, his relatively small desk sat in the midst of the newsroom. Like everyone else in the place, he wore a photo ID around his neck (the first name large, the second name small), which eased identification and, more to the point, communication.

"What I'm selling is information," he said in 1995. "The best way to get it faster than anyone else is to create an environment of constant creativity."[39] The physical design of the workspace encourages creativity through interaction. Elevators open on *only* one of the six floors he leases—the middle one. Each time employees arrive or leave, everyone has to go through the same set of doors to get in and out, regardless of the floor on which they work. Running up the spine of the space, connecting all the floors, is a spiral staircase that many refer to as "the vertical meeting room." Employees passing on the stairs, all with name-tags, are apt to stop and chat before heading off in opposite directions. In the food court, people from all ranks gravitate to eat and talk. And, finally, there's the small space everyone—including Bloomberg—squeezes into to work. This all generates, if not forces, interaction. Interaction generates information sharing. Information sharing generates new and better ideas.

One week after being sworn in as Mayor of New York City, Bloomberg recast the central office at City Hall of the Mayor's wing to mimic what worked for him uptown: He sat at a desk in the middle of the room, surrounded by his staff who all had the same size desk and equally little elbow room. Faced on his inauguration day with a $3 billion municipal deficit as a result of the horrible double-punch of a recession and the September 11 terrorist attack, which devastated the municipal infrastructure, he made a request and a commitment. He asked that people be tolerant of the potential downsizing of municipal services. He said government would have to get smaller and do more. In the next sentence of his inauguration speech he committed to reducing the size of the Mayor's Office by 20 percent. In my twenty-five years of consulting to New York City government, I cannot recall a mayor ever offering to reduce his own office; he always orders others to downsize.

Too often, reward systems divide organizations by influencing groups of employees to focus on different goals and agendas, rather than integrating organizations by creating a sense of common direction, purpose, and involvement. For example, many organizations have special bonus plans for senior managers and different ones for those in the middle. Once people in the organization realize that what is good for senior management is not necessarily good for them, the strategy will begin to unravel. It really does not matter how much people at the top get paid; what does matter is that the direction of their performance-based rewards should be consistent with all other members of the organization.

The focus on egalitarianism at Oakley is laserlike. It's not a random consequence that everyone wears the casual clothing that Oakley designs and produces. Want to wear another brand? That's fine; just don't come in looking too corporate casual. But it doesn't stop at fashion. Oakley does not publish organization charts, which it fears might establish concerns about who is "higher" than whom. The telephone directory is listed alphabetically by *first* name because everyone is on a first-name basis with everyone else. Want the phone extension for Link Newcomb? Go to the *L*s. Of course, executive bathrooms, dining rooms, and conference rooms do not exist. The company also got rid of their "Employee of the Year" award because it found the intent was starting to backfire. It was increasingly difficult to pick one outstanding performer, and those chosen were feeling uncomfortable with the award. What was going on here? The employees were starting to realize that Oakley's success was based on everyone—whether as individuals or teams—becoming and staying high performers; singling out one person contradicted what was apparent to all.

The egalitarian environment at Oakley fosters a way of working where everyone feels comfortable speaking with anyone in the organization. There's less a sense of chain of command and more a quality of colleagueship. This encourages an enormous amount of communication and information sharing about issues and new product opportunities and enhances the need for up/down feedback I noted earlier.

Symbolic actions—like the way space is configured or the perks of executive rank are minimized—speak volumes to those in search of leadership. They evoke not just loyalty, but action.

Evoke Loyalty

While the loyalty factor may not be important to most organizations when an industry craters along with the economy, to a few, the desire is just as strong to maintain the same practices as when the War for Talent was raging. SAS Institute, the world's largest privately held software company, remains obsessed with keeping

employees satisfied—and its revenue and turnover rates substanti-
ate the payoff of this belief.

A critical element of SAS's vision is "relationships":

> The Institute was founded on a philosophy of forming lasting
> relationships with our customers, our business partners, and
> our employees. These critical relationships, combined with our
> leading-edge software and services, together form the basic ele-
> ments of our success.[40]

Jim Goodnight invokes the philosophy that he believes has been
substantiated by the firm's success: "If you treat employees as if
they make a difference to the company, they will make a difference
to the company."[41] In other words, the company's practices and
people processes are based on the premise that attracting, motivating, and *retaining* intellectual capital is paramount to its existence
and success. As the company sees it, the way to attract and retain
the best is to give them interesting work to do, interesting people
with whom to do the work, and to treat them like the responsible
adults that they are. The concept isn't radical; living it is.

What is SAS's organizational "recipe" for living out this concept? People at all levels have the potential to get involved in decision making, advance across the organization, work on projects
central to the firm's mission, and get paid above-average compensation—all in a very comfortable work environment. These factors
have contributed to annual turnover at SAS that has never nudged
over 4 percent when the industry average during tight labor markets has surged to at least 25 percent.[42]

SAS has a caring work environment that takes lifestyle issues
seriously. It demonstrates this commitment through a dazzling
array of on-site features at its Cary, North Carolina, headquarters.
The university-like campus includes two child-care centers, atrium-
like cafeterias with low-cost meals, a gym, swimming pool, and
walking trails for convenient workouts, a health care center fully
staffed with physicians and nurses, and so on. Goodnight attributes
the company's low turnover (and the minimum $50 million cost
savings from it) as proof the strategy works.[43]

The issue of loyalty is tested most when the organization hits
rough economic waters and is faced with laying people off. While

some layoffs are the result of good corporate planning and cost cutting, others are simply a matter of appeasing stockholders. A long-held axiom has been that shareholders drive the decision to trim staff in larger, publicly owned firms. With the emphasis on short-term profits, stockholders may dominate and heads can roll if companies do not make projected estimated earnings. Most of the time, a layoff is not only a wasted effort, but an action that only serves to erode loyalty.

Bain & Company examined 288 Fortune 500 firms between 1989 and 1992 to determine how stock price performance of those that reduced their workforces compared with those that did not. Over those three years, the companies laying off more than 3 percent of their total employees saw little or no gain in stock price, while those that instituted massive reductions of 15 percent or more performed significantly below average. In the end, layoffs by themselves do nothing to alter long-term stock price performance in a positive direction.

Layoffs discourage remaining employees from sticking around, especially if the process is handled crudely. The largest impact is on those who stay; layoffs that are not planned and executed well leave an organization with people who stay but who do not want to work there anymore. Such layoffs tell remaining workers there is no company loyalty to employees and no stability, and they encourage the best and brightest to start looking for new positions.

Some firms have instituted alternatives to layoffs with success. Lincoln Electric, perhaps the gold standard for decades when it comes to firms viewed as the benchmark for innovative people processes, has not laid off employees in more than forty years. Since the 1950s, the company's policy guaranteed employment for its Cleveland staff with three or more years of service regardless of economic conditions.

Through its "no-fault loss of job" program, Lincoln reserves certain rights in return for this guarantee, such as the right to reassign employees to positions in any division within the company. A reassigned employee receives the wage of the new job, which in some cases can be as much as $5 an hour less than their previous pay. When their domestic sales plunged 40 percent in the late 1980s, the company took fifty workers off the shop floor and sent them out into the field as salespeople. They became known as "the leopards" because they found spots in the market that had not been covered by the other salespeople. Some remained in the field even after sales picked up and they were offered their old positions back.[44]

But Lincoln's commitment to engender loyalty goes deeper. When the company sold an automotive division in 1999, it made the buyer agree to keep employees for at least two years. Lincoln even encouraged employees of the division under new ownership who wanted to return to Lincoln to apply for open positions. As of late 2001, 257 people had returned.[45]

Lincoln provides an enormous amount of cross-training for its three thousand Cleveland employees and transfers someone to a new position nearly every day. When the economy tightens, workers shift to adjust to the changing needs of the company. While guaranteed employment may sound like a very sweet and anachronistic deal, the company employs a rigorous performance evaluation system that leads to as many as half of first-year workers either not making the cut or deciding on a different career. Once they pass their third-year anniversaries, less than 5 percent of the workforce leaves each year.[46]

Oakley takes an upside-down view of loyalty. Rather than trying to figure out how to get employees loyal to the organization, senior management focuses on what *they* can do to earn the loyalty of their workforce. There's an intense loyalty to people and it comes through. If an individual is not succeeding in a position, management looks at what is not working and whether the job is a poor fit with the person, rather than terminating him or her. If there's an inkling that the issue is one of "fit" rather than person, a new, better-fitting (it is hoped) job is offered. At times, individuals are moved downward, but without a commensurate reduction in pay. Oakley avoids layoffs at all costs. It encourages people to take extra vacation in the dead of winter when business slows down by offering an extra paid day if one takes four consecutive days.

But tension is always on the horizon for Oakley when it comes to maintaining loyalty. It values its people, it hates turnover, and it wants to provide resources that reflect what each person is worth. But at the same time, it competes with firms who have taken production offshore and manufacture at a fraction of what it costs in

Orange County, CA. The tension is growing, and the company realizes that it must continue to find innovative ways to manage that tension.[47]

Firms such as Lincoln Electric and Oakley have realized that layoffs destroy the fabric of the culture and, in turn, the motivation and retention of their workforce. They have shown us how different people processes can work, but these alternatives require more creativity and imagination, more time, and more thought.

I *Want* to Deal with Those HR-Types!

Over the past twenty-five years, I have seen some organizations evolve from having a "Personnel" function that emphasized control, to a department of "Human Resources" that saw value in stringing together the activities of recruitment, staffing, compensation, benefits, training and development, career planning, and organization development, to a somewhat smaller, much more strategic unit of business-oriented professionals focused on designing and implementing a seamless array of "people processes" to support the business's strategy. How an organization manages its human capital could be assessed by imagining this historical evolution as a continuum, with personnel on the left side, people processes on the right, and HR somewhere in the middle. The majority of organizations in the United States probably fall somewhere in the center, and, while the term "human resources" may be in vogue, in reality many of these functions hark back to personnel departments of the 1970s.

But this is not the fault of the HR professionals in those organizations; responsibility and the negative consequences that accrue for not being right-of-center on the continuum rest with the CEO and the executive group. Poor HR strategy and execution exists in an organization because the senior-most management does not place a high enough priority on these roles and functions. This quickly translates into insufficient resources and support to those in the organization heading HR and lower expectations for the senior person managing these related functions. Is it because management doesn't understand the bottom-line impact that people processes can make? Perhaps, but considering the incontrovertible data presented in this chapter regarding the organizational impact of people processes, ignorance is no longer an excuse. For those CEOs who complain that HR is only a cost center, unable to add value and unwilling to step up to the plate to add its unique strategic detail to the vision, I would suggest that they allow—no, demand—that HR rise to the challenge.

SAS Institute, an organization that would be located on the far right of the continuum, has actually come under criticism for being anachronistic in its focus on employee satisfaction and the positive consequences that accrue from focusing on it. Maybe that's why it works. Very few organizations still provide the kind of benefits, life-cycle career opportunities, and quality of management available—and all of which are executed so well—at SAS. Critics argue that a firm can get away with this only if it makes lots of money, has the advantages of scale, and remains privately owned. While SAS remains owned by two people who are both billionaires and not accountable to anyone, the company nonetheless operates in the real world and has its own IPO in the making.

"We have an excellent business argument for investing in employees and that will not change," Goodnight says. "Anyone buying our stock will have to understand fully what they are getting into here, because that is one area of company policy that is non-negotiable."[48]

How should HR be run? Southwest Airlines sets a helpful guideline that underscores the philosophy of what HR is really about: At Southwest, if a person in HR says "no" to a line manager three times in regard to matters of HR policy creating a problem, he or she is fired. Why? Because at Southwest, the job of HR is not to tell people what they cannot do but to help them find ways to more effectively recruit, motivate, and retain great people for the organization. Human resources is given the resources to support employee training and development programs that enhance the feeling of pride and loyalty that they hope, and expect, goes along with working at Southwest. And why does HR get such support? Because the CEO and all other executives understand that Southwest's vision framework is only as effective as the day-to-day people processes in action.

Those responsible for HR-related activities in growing organizations—*and this includes line management*—should obsess over these areas. When people processes are out of alignment with the vision, the viability of the vision itself is at stake.

Left of center on the continuum is not good enough. But don't blame the HR director. In my own experience, I have found the avoidance of people process issues has at its root a CEO who does not understand the need to align these processes and to practice the key processes noted here. It has led to devastating results. Entrepreneurs may have a belief system congruent with the processes noted in this chapter, but they too often fail to ensure that the programs and policies that foster these beliefs come to life.

The demographics speak for themselves: The supply of labor is projected to grow from 2002 to 2010 between 6 and 7 percent, while the demand for labor grows between 9 and 11 percent.[49] If one analyzes further down into particular classes of talent or skill sets, the gap becomes much wider, in particular with knowledge workers. Staying viable as a growth enterprise requires the ability to attract, motivate, and retain the right talent. This requires a commitment to knowledge management and workforce planning from top management.

Chapter 10

Creating a Desired Future

I N DESIGNING THE STRUCTURE OF THIS BOOK, I HAVE tried to mimic the journey taken by those who guide organizational growth with a vision. In this chapter, I'll revisit each stage of that journey, emphasizing the points that will have the greatest influence on the successful creation and implementation of your vision.

Initial Suspicion, Core Components, and the Binary Response

Vision, for the overwhelming majority of top managers, is suspect. One CEO might have a vision (in her head, even on paper in some form) but not believe that it can truly help her company grow. Another might not even allow herself a vision, believing—as I did before 1993—that vision is nothing more than a trendy management idea.

Research suggests otherwise. There is strong support that a vision embodying a set of characteristics will increase the probability of sustainable growth. And there is just as much data to support the argument that the *absence* of a vision will decelerate growth and put the very survival of a firm at stake.

So the first step is conversion—believing that vision can and should guide your company's growth. But that's only the first step.

A vision that isn't well understood throughout the top level of the organization doesn't have a chance to positively affect the staff as a whole or customers.

Five broad categories lead to the failure of most fast-growing firms: (1) an "I'm right; the world's wrong" mindset, (2) the liability of newness, (3) uncoordinated transformations, (4) the fantasy that there's a map, and (4) a struggle to maintain the family. The common thread is an executive management group that lacks a vision.

Leading a scaling enterprise is difficult even for the most talented managers, but leading without a vision puts the executive group at great risk. When I reflect on many of the firms that flamed-out from an inability to manage their growing pains, they all had one thing in common: the executive group never agreed on a growth vision.

And so the next step toward using vision to guide and sustain growth is articulating and agreeing on the vision. And ensuring that it is robust enough to mean something when it is being used to guide the people, policies, and processes of the organization. In order for a vision to be successfully implemented, it must address three core themes: the company's *raison d'être*, its *strategy*, and its *values*.

Even conviction and articulation, however, do not ensure that a vision will become the powerful growth guide that it can be. Embracing the intellectual argument for a vision process, understanding what the vision must address, and crystal-clear articulation of the vision do not adequately protect top managers from their worst enemy: their own binary response to the vision process.

Embracing the concept of vision and knowing that it is something important that must be accomplished, yet being pulled back by the binary response, reminds me of a ritual many of us experienced as kids. We'd be taken to the local lake, the air would be warm, and we would trot up to the water's edge. Once we got wet over our ankles, though, we would have some second thoughts: from experience we knew that once we dove in, there'd be an instant of cold and our bodies would normalize to the water's temperature. But even still, we would sometime stand there, hesitating knee-deep in water and anticipation, wondering if we should take the plunge or just back ourselves out. We would be intellectually committed ("It will feel fine once I'm swimming underwater.") but our fears would hold us back ("There is *no way* this will feel okay. How could it? My body's cold and I'm not even wet yet!"). The binary response keeps us in water up to our knees; it prevents us from diving in.

Overcoming the Negative Pull of the Binary Response

How can an organization's leader overcome the binary response? He or she has to overcome three obstacles: complacency, the need for closure, and the need for control.

Overcoming Complacency. The sense of excitement and urgency at the outset of the vision development process can abate when the landscape becomes harder to navigate, when it becomes apparent that real and difficult change may be necessary. But managers who continually remind themselves of why they launched a vision process to begin with often find the energy to stay the course.

Overcoming the Need for Closure. By training and experience, many managers feel compelled to push for closure in meetings and interactions. They've learned one hundred ways to override disagreements, stifle discontent, and avoid the process of give-and-take necessary for reaching buy-in. Many have come to view getting through their agendas as progress because it's a visible sign of movement.

But that notion of progress is largely illusory. Many of us work long hours and generate reports. We have meetings, make plans, and react to problems, receiving praise and confirmation from those around us. But are we actually leading or creating anything?

When developing a creative idea, many of us fail to take into account the Zeigarnik Effect. When things get hectic or uncomfortable, we become impatient. We push for early closure and settle for less than the best possible solution. Avoiding the grip of the Zeigarnik Effect as we implement the vision involves staying aware of the discomfort of initial ambiguity and recognizing that the vision will not be in place overnight and that the notions of "closure" and "vision" may at times be antithetical to each other.

The binary response encourages managers to feel as though the hard work is behind them when they have created and distributed a carefully crafted vision statement. But once in possession of a beautifully written statement of purpose and direction, managers need to ask themselves: Are we listening to our gut instincts and actively seeking out disconfirmation of preset perspectives? How often do we deliberately refrain from premature closure and insist on keeping projects in process; stirring things up; and searching for unexpected insight, connections, and possibilities? This is what the vision process requires of us.

Overcoming the Need for Control. Many managers have a normal need for order in their organizational universe. They strive for control, since control is what has worked for them in the past. If it feels like the organization is in chaos—because torrid growth is like going through a revolution—then the easy response can be crisis management. When the sense of chaos kicks in, you may find yourself (or at least others see you) acting in counterproductive ways to retrieve some sense of control.

How can you overcome this need for control? Avoid the temptations that can derail the vision process and stay focused on the following:

- Seek contributions from people rather then directing them.
- Nurture creativity rather than compliance.
- See yourself as coaching players rather than commanding troops.
- Drive for commitment rather than settling for consent.
- Create permeable boundaries rather than confining individuals (or groups) from one another or isolating the organization from the rest of the world.
- Generate cooperation rather than fostering internal competition.
- Help others accept that ambiguity and complexity are part of the vision process instead of contriving certainties.

To a large extent, what we're seeking in business and life isn't "out there." It isn't the latest trend or technology; it's inside ourselves. It has been there all along, but many of us haven't valued or respected it, or used it as brilliantly as we are capable of.

At its essence, a meaningful and successful organizational (and personal) vision requires being attuned to what is beneath the mental analyses, appearances, control, and rhetoric. It's in the human heart, which isn't just a pump. It radiates. It activates our deepest values and ability to learn and create, transforming our values and ideas from things we think about to what we live.

The vision process requires that as we look within, we try to grasp more fully than ever what we stand for and what moves us— and how these strong feelings relate to what we want to accomplish in our organization.

Live with Disruption, Lead to Clarity

Vision is an ongoing process—a living, evolving idea that should permeate an organization at all levels and have an implicit effect on every decision made. A large part of creating a working vision, therefore, is planning how it will reach through the various levels and functions of the organization. That's where the vision framework comes in. The vision framework guides how the growth vision will be woven into the organizational fabric through four major sources: the executive group, the culture, the organizational structure, and the people processes. The vision framework, in other words, moves a vision from something that exists in people's heads (and maybe on paper in some form) to a process that shapes daily life.

As the executive group and other managers work on ensuring that the vision framework is aligned with the vision, they inevitably reach a point where they have to make a break with the past. Focusing on configuring elements of the framework is a disruptive process that can have incredibly liberating and positive outcomes. The experience of moving beyond a comfortable, sometimes constricting, context helps people open their minds and focus their energy into action. As a means of getting out of a logic where the context decides for the person, the framework can force everyone to find new ways to influence their context. And by doing so, the executive group learns how to lead change.

New beliefs, roles, time-frame perspectives, and landmarks will emerge as the vision framework unfolds. But these are also subject to change if the vision process is truly working as it should. A vision framework is a dynamic construct, not a one-time exercise that yields static "results"; it must be continuously implemented and change with the growing organization.

How should the framework be approached, applied, and measured? Senior managers from across the organization should define specific individual and group actions that will contribute toward identifying and employing the first milestones of the vision. I find an important criterion to judge the quality of application of the vision is whether it helps people act independently—to make decisions more quickly, to undertake initiatives that would have felt inappropriate before, and to take measured risks. People are more apt to break from the past when the vision is initiated through action, rather than broadcast through internal marketing blitzes that only seem to propagandize (and trivialize) the new hopes and direction.

A bit more on implementation: If implementing the vision requires new values, then it will take more than speeches from you to engage people. Even when you are at your most effective, speeches can only confirm the message sent by your daily actions. *Actions* send the clearest message. Identifying, communicating, and shaping organizational values represent perhaps the hardest prerequisites for creating or realigning the vision framework because they rely on emotion and intuition. Well-established organizations operate on a set of beliefs that usually remains implicit. But when you assert boldly what you and the organization stand for, then the people on the inside identify with the values and become more deeply committed to the organization that personifies them.

Andy Grove, former CEO of Intel, was characteristically blunt about his disdain for vision "statements," but both he and his close-knit top-level executives nonetheless worked relentlessly to embed a common ambition into the thinking of every person at Intel, while still giving each individual the freedom to interpret the company's expansive objectives creatively. Defining an organization's vision so that it has personal meaning for employees, and leading its implementation across the organization, is hard. It requires action with a sense of urgency.

Stay Focused on the Vision;
Don't Let Growth Distract You

A study by Deloitte & Touche Consulting examined organizations attempting long-term growth and separated those who had achieved their growth goals from those who did not. Those firms who had crafted and communicated a clear message about how the firm saw its future, and why growth was critical to that future, were *four times* more likely to be fast-growing and high-performing companies than those who only articulated the need for "growth."[1] In other words, the study found the firms that continually reinforced their vision, along with reinforcing the need for growth, were much more likely to grow fast. Missing from the firms that failed to reach their targets was an unambiguous message clarifying not only the commitment to growth but also a future-oriented picture of what the organization would be like and feel like. While some organizations have survived without employees knowing where they were heading, those attempting to scale long term have generally been unable to sustain that growth without a beacon.

Firms can be so single-minded in their need to grow, and so driven to fuel growth by generating revenues, that they frequently take on additional business simply because it is there. The impact on profit margins, working capital, and cash requirements can easily become less a priority than growth for its own sake.

The consequences of growth for the sake of growth are most obvious among rising entrepreneurial rockets where everyone feels impervious to the frenzy of success. Unfortunately, success may be poorly defined. When Dell Computer grew from a $550 million company to a $2 billion one in less than two years, life seemed blissful. Unfortunately, poor production planning left it without notebook computers just when the market wanted them. At the same time, Dell was being hammered by security analysts about their accounting practices. "Growth had been pursued to the exclusion of all else, but no one knew how the numbers really added up," Michael Dell told *Fortune* magazine.[2]

"One of the things that is confusing and intoxicating when you are growing a business is that you really have little way of determining what the problems are," he said. "You had different parts of the company believing they were making their plan, but when you rolled up the results of the company, you had a big problem." He learned a valuable lesson from the experience, which was "to change the orientation of the organization away from growth, growth, growth, to liquidity, profitability, and growth, which has become a real mantra for the company."[3]

In early 2002, Dell and his executive group set out criteria that had to be met for the development of any new peripheral products: They must be (1) PC-related, (2) sizable, (3) profitable, and (4) increasingly a commodity.[4]

In the midst of torrid growth, you may lack direct or even comparable competitors against which you can set performance norms, so your own internal performance standards are unclear. Without accurate ways to assess performance, overconfidence can set in and senior management can become entrenched in false confidence: "We seem to be doing well, the competitors are not clobbering us, so why bother fixing something that isn't broken?"

Success can breed failure, but it doesn't have to. Don't stop scanning for new opportunities. Growing industries mature for the existing players because new entrants change the rules of the game. Customers develop new needs different from the ones the organization has become so good at satisfying. "Success is a lousy teacher," Bill Gates said. "It seduces smart people into thinking they can't lose. And it's an unreliable guide to the future."[5]

Firms with vision-guided growth avoid the traps set by the myopic orientation of growth-for-growth's-sake. For them, growth is in pursuit of the raison d'être—the firm's overarching purpose as reflected in the vision. When the vision process is enacted, you won't be looking at your business environment only through the lens of your internal products and processes. In other words, you won't look at what you make and simply try to figure out how you can sell more of it. Your firm and your people won't become trapped in the past. You avoid becoming stuck defining the organization within a narrow industry and viewing your core competencies as static.

"There is no such thing as a growth industry," wrote Theodore Leavitt in the *Harvard Business Review* over forty years ago.

"There are only companies organized and operated to create and capitalize on growth opportunities."[6] Dell, for example, realizes its success lies in commoditization because it is the master of the direct model. Its manufacturing structure allows it to make more money selling more computers at lower prices that it can selling fewer computers at higher prices. So, what did Dell do during the downturn starting in 2000, going all the way through 2002? They created a price war, of course. While Dell's manufacturing model is the key to its vision, it refuses to be easily swayed into manufacturing items where healthy margins cannot be reaped.

When innovation is hard-wired into organizational processes from the beginning, the maturing organization will be able to avoid the normal inertia that sets in to protect the status quo, to not challenge the process, and to avoid risk. Innovation requires institutionalizing risk and giving license for others to take measured risks—and fail. Maintaining it requires that well-developed innovation processes be in place, with accurate metrics to track them.

In organizations where there is an explicit orientation to growth emanating from the vision, innovation is typically encouraged and supported through the establishment of innovation processes, leaders who are directly involved in new product development, a continual stream of fresh ideas, a conscious and continual means of removing barriers to innovation (particularly those that creep in to create boundaries across divisional lines), and accurate ways to measure innovation performance. With this kind of infrastructure, rapid growth should not easily lull people into complacency or create a mentality that anything touched will turn to gold.

Reinforce the Vision, Continually

Repetition is powerful. Think about a time when the lyrics or melody of a song got stuck in your head. Even a song you may not have particularly liked. After listening to it for six or eight times on the radio, you find yourself mumbling or humming it to yourself; it becomes wired into part of our memory, unconsciously, without any effort to learn it. Research on persuasive communication consistently emphasizes the power of repetition.[7] While I have discussed the effectiveness of stories and metaphors, other means for reinforcing the messages in the vision must be tailored for the audience that needs to embrace it.

Return to the three core themes (raison d'être, strategy, and values) and consider ways in which they can be repeated until they sink in and take root throughout the organization. As an architect of the vision, you understand how it reflects these core themes. But others in the organization may not—even with the vision framework taking shape. You know you're successful when employees who have not been part of the vision development or implementation process start invoking—and acting on—the core themes without being aware of it.

Owen Harris points out in his "Primer for Polemicists" that reinforcement helps ensure that support doesn't slip away. It expands the executive's persuasive reach: "Preaching to the converted, far from being a superfluous activity, is vital. Preachers do it every Sunday. Strengthening the commitment, intellectual performance and morale of those already on your side is an essential task, both in order to bind them more securely to the cause and to make them more effective exponents of it."[8]

Putting a vision into practice consists of articulation, images that emerge from the use of metaphors and stories, constant reiteration, and communication at all levels, over and over again. You spread it among the executive group and then they have to go down—way down—with it in their organizations.

Establish Markers of Progress

If the vision is to be taken seriously, then there had better be measurements to indicate whether progress toward it is being made. This is where the management of measurements becomes important. It's the organizational equivalent of the kids screaming from the backseat on their daylong trip to grandma's house, "Are we *there* yet?"

How does Oakley, for example, know that its vision is successfully guiding growth? Its obsession with style is not about getting the masses to buy its products. In fact, it designs and manufactures things it doesn't expect anyone to buy (take a look at its Over-the-Top eyewear frames that sprinters wore in the 2000 Olympic Games). It never holds focus groups to determine whether the general population likes its designs, and it abhors marketing studies. Clearly, sheer volume of sales would not be an accurate indicator of whether the vision was working. But one of its important metrics is whether the people who buy and wear its products are emblematic of the style-as-sculpture genre that is part of its culture. Oakley takes risks, so it looks carefully to see if famous people (in the sports or performing arts, for example) are seen wearing Oakley stuff. If they are perceived as risk takers, that's good. If they represent Middle-America, not so good.

And Always Carry the Torch

Remember the quote from Martin Luther King Jr. in chapter 1? To paraphrase, King said that people need a great leader to become devoted to a cause. For the vision to be effective, it needs a champion. You—and every member of the executive group—need to be a torchbearer for the vision. You have to live the vision by making all your actions and behaviors consistent with it, and you need to create a sense of urgency and passion for reaching it.

Those who guide growth with a vision do not have to be great speech-makers or possess the charm of a television personality. It is not equivalent to charisma. Rather, such leaders are able to emotionally engage their organization at whatever level they operate. Senior managers at Oakley, the founders of The Container Store, and those like Elisabet Eklind who use their personal passion to guide small nonprofit organizations—all influence their colleagues' values, goals, needs, and aspirations through their relentless attention to shaping interpretations and creating a sense of purpose.

How can you be a torchbearer for the vision? You can face the challenges other organizations face, but with sharper instinct and greater creative engagement. You can respond creatively when your sense of time is not stuck in the present. You can develop exceptional tolerance for ambiguity and leave things "in play," creatively speaking. You can accomplish objectives and still stay open and imaginative. And you can encourage such capabilities in others, especially if you bypass the tendency to label possibilities and challenges as "right" or "wrong" and "good" or "bad."

You can energize your organization and find ways to motivate your members to achieve its goals. You can demonstrate empathy, listen, understand, and share the feelings of others in the organization. You can create events to signal and celebrate transitions and turning points, expressing support for those grappling with the pressures of stressful change efforts and reinforcing the new vision.

You can express your confidence in your own ability and in the ability of others to succeed.

Appendix

Exercise 1: Deciphering Your Organization's Culture

An Executive Group Activity (Allow at least 4 hours)

Management owns this process because they *are* the process. It helps the executive group—or managers within a division—articulate what they are trying to achieve, translate these challenges into tasks, identify the cultural elements required to support the tasks, define the existing culture, and, finally, determine the gaps between what exists and what is required.[1]

Define the "Business Problem"

Meet in a room with lots of wall space and a bunch of flipcharts. Start with a "business problem": something you would like to fix, something that could work better, a particular organizational challenge, or some new strategic intent tied to the vision. Focus on concrete areas for improvement, or else the culture analysis may seem pointless and stale.

Determine the tasks and behaviors required for meeting these challenges:

- What are the dozen most important tasks that must be accomplished, and the behaviors that everyone must be consistently engaged in, if the organization is to fully execute the vision?

- What is the degree of interdependence required among units if these tasks and behaviors are to be coordinated? What will people have to do to achieve this level of interdependence?

- Does everyone fully understand the end-to-end "flow" required to accomplish the work? If not, why not?

Ask "what if" questions. Imagine who in the world could be your toughest competitor if they decided to go into your business. How would you have to change to survive?

Review the Concept of Culture

Once you agree on the strategic or tactical goals—the thing you want to change or improve—review the concept of culture as existing at three levels: visible "artifacts," espoused values, and shared but unspoken assumptions. (Below is an outline of the concept, but reading through the entire activity will bring greater clarity.)

Level One: Artifacts

The easiest level to observe when you go into an organization is that of artifacts: what you see, hear, and feel as you hang around. Note your observations and emotional reactions to the architecture, decor, and the climate, based on how people behave toward you and toward each other. The level of "artifacts culture" is very clear and has immediate emotional impact. But you don't really know why the members of the organization are behaving as they do and why each organization is constructed as it is. Just by hanging around and observing, you cannot really decipher what is going on. You have to be able to talk to insiders and ask them questions about the things you observe and feel. That takes you to the next level of culture.

Level Two: Espoused Values

Imagine yourself as a new employee or manager being offered a job at your organization. Do you know enough about its culture from experiencing the artifacts and behavior patterns, or should you dig deeper? To dig deeper means asking questions about the things the organization values. *Why* does it do what it does? Why, for example, does your organization create open office areas, while other firms like yours put everyone behind closed doors? These questions have to be asked especially about those observed artifacts that puzzle you or that seem somehow inconsistent with what achieving the vision would require and what you would expect. For this purpose, you may need to find other insiders who can explain the organization to you. Anthropologists call such insiders "informants" and depend heavily on conversations with them to decipher what's going on. Even if you've conducted your cultural "due diligence," by looking at the "two cultures" (culture expressed through the artifacts and the culture based on the values you believe the organization promotes) you may not conclude that you understand the two cultures. Don't give in to temptation. You still may not capture either of these cultures at the level required.

The typology may actually be misleading. All you know is that while your artifacts may seem inconsistent, your espoused values may be paradoxically quite similar. That is, the artifacts may appear to contradict each other with respect to getting a handle on the culture, but your "values inventory" may find that all the values are quite consistent. In addition, the longer you hang around, the more questions you ask, the more you see observable inconsistencies between some of the espoused values and the visible behavior. If you are to understand the culture, you must decipher what is going on at the deepest level.

Level Three: Shared but Unspoken Assumptions

To understand this deepest level, you have to think historically about the organization, even if its history is relatively short. Throughout the life of the organization, what were the values, beliefs, and assumptions of the founders and key leaders who brought it to where it is today? Every organization is started by individuals or small teams who initially impose their own beliefs, values, and assumptions on people whom they hire. If the founder's values and assumptions are out of line with what the environment of the organization allows or affords, the organization will fail and never develop a culture in the first place.

Make sure that all the members of the working group understand this model.

Identify Artifacts (Step 1)

Start by brainstorming about the artifacts that characterize your organization. "Artifacts" refers to the overt behavior, policies, rules, and practices—the tangible stuff you can see and hear. Ask the relatively new members of the organization what it is like to come to work there. What artifacts do they notice? Write down all items that come up. Use the list and the following "trigger questions" as thought-starters and to make sure you cover all of the areas in which cultural artifacts are visible. You generally will find that as the group gets started, all the participants chime in with things they notice. You might fill five to ten pages of newsprint. Tape them up so the culture's manifestations are symbolically surrounding you.

> *Notice peoples' behavior.* Make a list of behaviors you see frequently, whether it contributes to or detracts from achieving the vision. For example, if people tend to shoot down new ideas, pointing out why they will not work, then that would be a characteristic of the culture. Alternatively, if people tend to openly appreciate each other, then that would also describe the culture.

> *Get fresh feedback.* Check with those who have "stranger's eyes." Ask the newest managers in your organization to tell you what they observe in the culture that's different for them. Ask them to describe what they see. What did they first notice as strengths and challenges? Do the same with longtime trusted vendors and any consultants working on projects within the organization. Who else can provide a set of stranger's eyes?

Consider the following questions:

- Is more effort spent on internal competition or external?

- When a goal or deadline is missed or a result not accomplished, do people tend to make excuses and blame others or are they highly accountable? Is it okay to make a mistake around here?

- Do the prevailing values, beliefs, and norms tend to encourage new ideas or shoot them down?

- Are important and controversial issues openly discussed in meetings or afterward in the hall? What are the current levels of trust and openness in the organization?

- What does it actually take to get ahead in this organization?

- Imagine that a friend joins your organization and asks you what she should do to be noticed as a top performer. What advice would you give her?

- What is the prevailing dress code?

- What dominates the stories or legends that people tell about the organization? What messages are they conveying?

- What is the level of formality in authority relationships?

- What are meetings like? How frequently are they held, how are they run, and how long do they take?

- How are decisions made?

- Is there a consistent character to the social events linked to the organization?

- What are the primary ceremonies and rituals held with some regularity? What purposes do they serve? Are some of the purposes unintended?

- How are disagreements and conflicts handled?

- What reward systems are in place? What messages get sent with respect to activities or accomplishments that are valued—and which are not?

- Think of three influential people in the organization. In what ways do they symbolize the character of the place?

Physical Space

How is space occupied by the group? Is it shared? Do people defend their space? Culture can be read in evaluating the ways people carve out territories for themselves. Are doors closed? Are departments starting to "police" their boundaries with gatekeepers and ferocious assistants? Space can tell you something about status, power, and connections. Consider who gets the most space and how precisely that space is allocated. Think about your office space and other areas (e.g., game rooms, cafeterias, and other common zones). Think about ways people decorate their space. Are the walls bare? Are there family pictures? Think about the functionality of the space. Is everything used for work-related activities? Or is space allocated for social interaction?

Communications

How do you learn stuff? How do people prefer to exchange ideas and information—e-mail, phone, face-to-face? How much time do people spend talking face-to-face? Walk into some organizations and you are overwhelmed by the rich buzz of conversation, and in others there is a deadly silence. In some firms you would not think of sending an e-mail without copying it to at least half a dozen others. Think about the ease in which you can get ahold of others in your organization. Does hierarchy or function get in the way of effective communication? Or is it simply a matter of busy schedules? Do people deliberately make themselves unavailable—including you? In some organizations you may have experienced the infuriating feeling of speaking to five voice-mail systems before you hear a human voice. How does your organization cope with communication across geographic distance? Do you recognize this as a challenge? Finally, when people meet and talk face-to-face, is it in groups or primarily one-to-one? And are these formal meetings, or do they just happen around some gathering space? When there is a formal group meeting, do individuals have separate conversations afterwards to discuss reactions that could not be discussed during the "official" meeting? Who is involved in the meetings—is it insiders only, or might customers and suppliers be involved? Imagine a picture of your communication network. Who are the main players, and who is not in it? What's the nature of language that dominates everyday discourse—buzzwords, clichés, catch phrases? What are the favorite topics of informal conversation?

Time

How do people manage it? How long do people stay at work? Are long hours the norm and, if they are, who feels comfortable leaving first? Is it okay to leave before the boss? How carefully does your company measure time at work? When do you know when you're wasting time? Does someone have to tell you? How long does it take before you are "found out"? If you go out for coffee or a drink with your group, is it considered a waste of time? Think about how long it takes to get to know someone in your organization. Are people quickly open about their personal lives, or do you have colleagues whose family situations you still do not know?

Identity

How do people express their personal identities? Do people try to look alike with common dress codes and manners of speech? Is there only one way to present yourself or does the culture encourage expressions of individuality? Within the organization, do people identify with their team, their function, their division, the whole organization, their profession, or perhaps their customers? When people identify with the organization, what are they identifying with? Is it their colleagues? Or is it the vision and values of the organization, its traditions? The broader organization's strategy? Or, do they identify with being part of the best marketing or sales team (at the department or divisional level)? Is it winning that binds people to the organization? And how encompassing is this identification? Think about what happens when people leave your organization. Is it honored by a celebration? Do these people still see themselves as part of a family? Would people who leave ever return or do they disappear without a trace? Could you imagine a thriving "Former [YOUR ORGANIZATION]' ers" club?

Rewards

Rewards are the monetary and nonmonetary things that the organization gives employees for behavior consistent with the company's culture and goals. Are rewards managed well? Or do they communicate values and beliefs, and promote norms, that are at odds with the firm's vision and goals? Do those who receive public awards/rewards become the company's heroes? Do they truly exemplify the firm's values, beliefs, and norms?

Identify Your Organization's Values, Beliefs, and Norms (Step 2)

After an hour or so, shift gears and ask the group to list some of the *espoused* values that your organization holds. Some of these may have already been mentioned, but list them on pages separate from the artifacts. Often these have been written down and published. Sometimes they have been reiterated as part of the "vision" of how the organization should be operating in the future to remain viable and competitive.

What really gets rewarded in the organization (which is not to be confused with what management says is rewarded)? For example, are there comments at the beginning of a meeting, by those running the meeting, that people should "speak their mind"? Yet, when an individual offers information conflicting with the meeting leader's position, is he or she admonished verbally or nonverbally?

Compare Values with Artifacts (Step 3)

Next, compare the *espoused* values with the artifacts in those same areas. It is helpful to first go back to the original newsprint pages where the group identified artifacts (Step 1). Group those that seem to relate to similar themes and, if everyone agrees, label the themes. Don't force a label on each cluster or theme if there is not complete agreement. This "clustering" will refamiliarize you with the information from that prior step. Now, compare the newsprint notes from Step 1 with the notes relating to Step 2. For example, if "pushing the limits" is an espoused value, see what systems of reward or accountability you have identified as artifacts and whether they truly support it. At Oakley, the Annual Review Form asks each manager to assess his or her direct reports on a number of criteria directly tied to the company's values. Each employee is evaluated, for example, on the extent to which he or she is "obsessed with excellence, doesn't accept the status quo, is adaptable to change, has compulsion for innovation and pursues cutting edge technology."[2] This shows, at least in one arena, how Oakley is reinforcing a value (pushing the limits) with an artifact (the performance review process).

If your firm doesn't provide artifacts that support the values, you have identified an area where a deeper unspoken assumption is operating and driving the systems. You now have to search for that deeper assumption.

Let's use another example: You may espouse the value of open communication and open-door policies with respect to bosses, yet you may find that whistle-blowers and employees who bring bad news are punished. You may have detected, among your artifacts, that employees are not supposed to mention problems unless they have a solution in mind. These inconsistencies suggest a shared unspoken assumption that your culture is really closed, that only positive communications are valued, and that if you cannot come up with a solution you should keep your mouth shut.

As a general principle, the way to understand deeper cultural levels is through identifying the inconsistencies and conflicts you observe between overt behavior, policies, rules, and practices (the artifacts) and the espoused values as formulated in the vision, policies, and other managerial communications. Then, identify what is driving the overt behavior and other artifacts. This is where the important elements of the culture are embedded. As you uncover deeply shared assumptions, write them down on a separate page. You will begin to see what the patterns are among those assumptions, and which ones seem to really drive the system in the sense that they explain the presence of most of the artifacts that you have listed.

Assess the Shared Assumptions (Step 4)

It's now time to assess the pattern of shared basic assumptions you have identified in terms of how they aid or hinder you both in your role in the organization and for the organization broadly in accomplishing the goals you set out in the first step of this process (defining the business problem). Define the gaps between current and desired culture. Are the norms required for realizing the vision—and future scaling—the same as those identified in the culture now? Where do you have inconsistencies?

Are there inconsistencies between what the organization says is important and what the culture "says" is important?

Are there norms identified as important to accomplishing the critical tasks that are not currently valued by the culture?

What are the "hero stories?" The behaviors and actions that become legend within an organization are strong signals of the way things should be done. Who do people stand around and talk about with pride and respect? What behaviors do these people exhibit? Who gets applauded at meetings—and why? Within all strong cultures the sharp observer will find dozens of stories that clearly point to the behaviors considered by many to be critical to success, yet they may not be integrated into the culture.

Conclusions: Determine Actions Required to Reduce the Gaps (Step 5)

(end of activity)

Exercise 2: Thinking about Vision before the Planning Group Meets

A Planning Group Activity (Allow at least 4 hours)

A. Vision Needs Assessment

In your opinion:

1. Is there a need to take command of our organization's future?

   ☐ Yes   ☐ No   ☐ Not sure

2. Is our organization's long-term reason for existence clearly understood (and that does not mean maximizing profit or shareholder value)?

   ☐ Yes   ☐ No   ☐ Not sure

Is there agreement:

3. Across our organization on which customers/users have priority?

   ☐ Yes   ☐ No   ☐ Not sure

4. On which of our organization's products, services, and strategies are most important?

   ☐ Yes   ☐ No   ☐ Not sure

5. On the most significant challenges facing our organization's growth and survival?

   ☐ Yes   ☐ No   ☐ Not sure

6. On the most significant opportunities available to our organization?

   ☐ Yes   ☐ No   ☐ Not sure

7. Are people in our organization unhappy or confused about its current direction?

☐ Yes ☐ No ☐ Not sure

8. Is our organization losing its reputation for:
   a. Quality products/services?

   ☐ Yes ☐ No ☐ Not sure

   b. Innovation/creativity?

   ☐ Yes ☐ No ☐ Not sure

   c. Ability to attract and retain the best talent?

   ☐ Yes ☐ No ☐ Not sure

9. Do you think our organization is not responding to:

   a. New technology?

   ☐ Yes ☐ No ☐ Not sure

   b. Socioeconomic changes?

   ☐ Yes ☐ No ☐ Not sure

   c. Political changes?

   ☐ Yes ☐ No ☐ Not sure

   d. Other external changes or conditions?

   ☐ Yes ☐ No ☐ Not sure

10. Are we losing our:

    a. Unique and distinctive reputation?

    ☐ Yes ☐ No ☐ Not sure

    b. Sense of pride and commitment among employees?

    ☐ Yes ☐ No ☐ Not sure

    c. Desire to change to remain competitive and stay at the top of our game?

    ☐ Yes ☐ No ☐ Not sure

11. Are we faced with significant issues or problems that require a new vision?

    ☐ Yes ☐ No ☐ Not sure

12. Where do you think we'd be in one to three years if we refuse any changes. Would you like such an outcome?

    Brief thoughts:

B. Organizational Strengths

1. Consider the values that you think are part of our culture. Which of these, in your judgment, significantly influence the daily interaction/behavior of employees, for better or worse.

2. What do you consider as our unique strengths?

    Please list:

3. Do we enjoy any of these strengths to an extent significantly greater than does someone whom we may perceive as a "competitor"?

    ☐ Yes   ☐ No   ☐ Not sure

    Please list:

4. Can you think of any current organizational traits or elements that could become future strengths?

    ☐ Yes   ☐ No   ☐ Not sure

    Please list:

5. As you experience us trying to implement our current strategy, does it reveal to you significant under-utilized strengths and/or weaknesses?

☐ Yes ☐ No ☐ Not sure

Briefly explain:

C. Organizational Weaknesses

1. Do we have any *unique* weaknesses?

☐ Yes ☐ No ☐ Not sure

Please list:

2. Do you think we have greater weaknesses than our "competitors"?

☐ Yes ☐ No ☐ Not sure ☐ Not applicable

Please list:

3. Do we have any current traits that may become future weaknesses?

☐ Yes ☐ No

Please list:

4. Do you think our current strategy requires greater competencies and/or resources than it now possesses?

☐ Yes ☐ No ☐ Not sure

Briefly explain:

Notes

Introduction

1. M. Lipton, "Demystifying the Development of an Organizational Vision," *Sloan Management Review* 37, no. 4 (1996): 83–92.

2. J. C. Collins and J. I. Porras, *Built to Last: Successful Habits of Visionary Companies* (New York: HarperCollins, 1994).

3. Lipton, "Demystifying the Development of an Organizational Vision."

4. Lipton, "When Clients Make you Crazy," *Journal of Management Consulting* 8, no. 4 (1995); "When Clients Resist Change," *Journal of Management Consulting* 9, no. 2 (1996).

5. A. Campbell and S. Yeung, "Do You Need a Mission Statement?" *Ashridge Strategic Management Centre, Special Report No. 1208* (London: Economist Publications, 1990), 6.

Chapter 1

1. H. Mintzberg, *The Rise and Fall of Strategic Planning* (New York: The Free Press, 1994), 209.

2. M. Lipton, "Demystifying the Development of an Organizational Vision," *Sloan Management Review* 37, no. 4 (1996): 83–92.

3. D. S. Pottruck and T. Pearce, *Clicks and Mortar: Passion Driven Growth in an Internet Driven World* (San Francisco: Jossey-Bass, 2000), 288–289.

4. Lipton, "Demystifying the Development of an Organizational Vision."

5. J. C. Collins and J. I. Porras, *Built to Last: Successful Habits of Visionary Companies* (New York: HarperCollins, 1994), 56.

6. Korn/Ferry International and Columbia University Graduate School of Business, *Reinventing the CEO* (New York: Korn/Ferry International and Columbia University Graduate School of Business, 1989), 90.

7. Corporate Leadership Council, The Corporate Executive Board, *Voice of the Leader: A Quantitative Analysis of Leadership Bench Strength and Development Strategies* (Washington, D.C.: Corporate Leadership Council, The Corporate Executive Board, 2001), 36.

8. G. Hamel and C. K. Prahalad, *Competing for the Future* (Boston: Harvard Business School Press, 1994).

9. Weekly Insider Periscope Web site <http://www.cda.com/investnet/periscope/011121.html> (accessed 30 June 2002). L. Newcomb, personal conversation with author, 22 October 2001.

10. Oakley, Inc. corporate profile <http://investor.oakley.com/ireye/ir_site.zhtml?ticker=oo&script=2100> (accessed 30 June 2002).

11. M. L. King, Jr., as quoted in L. Bennett, *What Manner of Man* (Chicago: Johnson, 1964), 127.

12. P. Lawrence and J. Lorsch, *Organization and Environment* (Cambridge, MA: Harvard University Press, 1967).

13. Ibid.

14. H. Mintzberg, *The Rise and Fall of Strategic Planning* (New York: Free Press, 1994), 273.

15. Mintzberg, *The Rise and Fall of Strategic Planning,* 321.

16. Mintzberg, 222–320.

17. L. Downes, "Strategy Can Be Deadly," *The Industry Standard,* 7 May 2001, 75; <http://www.thestandard.com/article/0,1902,24138,00.html> (accessed 30 June 2002).

18. Ibid.

19. L. Downes, "Strategy Can Be Deadly," *The Industry Standard,* 7 May 2001, 75; <http://www.thestandard.com/article/0,1902,24138,00.html> (accessed 30 June 2002).

20. H. Mintzberg, *The Rise and Fall of Strategic Planning,* 210.

21. L. Greiner, "Evolution and Revolution as Organizations Grow," *Harvard Business Review,* May–June 1998, 55–67.

22. eBay Web site <http://www.shareholder.com/ebay/releases-earnings.cfm> (accessed 30 June 2002).

23. "Corporate Strategy Board Study," noted in J. Rich, "The Growth Imperative," *The Journal of Business Strategy* 20, no. 2 (1999): 27–31.

Chapter 2

1. Whole Foods Market Web site <http://www.wholefoodsmarket .com/company/> (accessed 10 July 2002).

2. M. Lipton, "Demystifying the Development of an Organizational Vision," *Sloan Management Review* 37, no. 4 (1996): 83–92.

3. D. Kirby and K. Lewis, eds., D. Packard, *The HP Way: How Bill Hewlett and I Built Our Company* (New York: HarperBusiness, 1996), 172.

4. Taco Bell Web site <http://www.tacobell.com> (accessed 12 July 2002).

5. R. Charan and N. Tichy, *Every Business Is a Growth Business* (New York: Random House, 1998), 71.

6. Roz Chast, "The Tunnel of Why," *New Yorker,* 21 May 2001, ID# 45580.

7. See, e.g., R. Barrett, *Liberating the Corporate Soul* (Woburn, MA: Butterworth Heinemann, 1998), 112.

8. Whole Foods Market Web site <http://www.wholefoodsmarket .com/company/declaration.html> (accessed 25 June 2002).

9. Ibid.

10. Ibid.

11. E. Schonfeld, "The Total Package," *Ecompany,* June 2001, 92.

12. Whole Foods Market Web site <http://www.wholefoodsmarket .com/company/corevalues.html> (accessed 25 June 2002).

13. Ibid.

14. Personal conversations with various store managers, New York, NY and Cambridge, MA, February 2002.

15. Schonfeld, "The Total Package," 92.

16. Presentation by G. Bethune (Stanford University Business School, Stanford, CA, 2 May 2001).

17. Lipton, "Demystifying the Development of an Organizational Vision," 88.

18. D. Roth, "My Job at The Container Store," *Fortune,* 10 January 2000; <http://www.fortune.com/indexw.jhtml?co_id=359&doc_id=201104 &channel=artcol.jhtml&_DARGS=%2Ffragments%2Ffrg_top_story_body .jhtml.1_A&_DAV=artcol.jhtml> (accessed 25 June 2002).

19. The Container Store slipped to Number 2 on the list in 2002, *Fortune* Web site <http://www.fortune.com/lists/bestcompanies/index.html> (accessed 30 June 2002).

20. It's worth noting here that visions can be created for the organization as a whole or built first in a local context—for example, in one department. If successful during a test period, it can then be implemented across the organization. If we think of visions as elements that define a framework, it makes sense to want the framework to be stable and reliable over time; local tests in certain circumstances make sense.

21. J. Conger, *Charismatic Leader: Behind the Mystique of Exceptional Leadership* (San Francisco: Jossey-Bass, 1989).

22. Whole Foods Market Web site <http://www.wholefoodsmarket .com/company/declaration.html> (accessed 25 June 2002).

Chapter 3

1. S. Goldstein, interview with author, January 2001.

2. S. Goldstein, personal conversations with author, February 1998–November 2001.

3. Ibid.

4. D. Kirby and K. Lewis, eds., D. Packard, *The HP Way: How Bill Hewlett and I Built Our Company* (New York: HarperBusiness, 1996), 141.

5. Ibid.

6. Ibid.

7. Ibid.

8. Kirby and Lewis, 52.

9. Personal conversation with employees, 12 December 2000.

10. Wall Street Research Net Web site <http://www.wsrn.com/apps/ companyinfo/fund.xpl?s=AMZN&f=FUND> (accessed 30 June 2002).

11. Schumpeter also addressed the impact of aggressive growth. He alleged that a certain level of failure is part of "a perennial gale of creative self-destruction" in an industry. Destruction is thus the price of innovation. But is this an adequate rationale to explain the crushing failure of firms that have scaled quickly? Major innovations usually evolve through many steps rather than through a single discontinuity. Schumpeter's model ignores important variables such as the technical difficulties and the learning-by-doing that major innovations require. A more contemporary spin takes us off the trail blazed by Schumpeter and on to one discovered by Clayton Christensen of Harvard University. And, Edith Penrose, for instance, argued in *The Theory of the Growth of the Firm* (White Plains, NY: M.E. Sharpe, 1959), that the optimal size of a firm represents a moving target because of ongoing increases in its managerial capabilities.

Organizations that do not grow tend to require less and less managerial capacity because managers' jobs are increasingly routinized. A firm must find a way to continue growing so as to best utilize this ever-increasing overcapacity. And as Stanford economist Nathan Rosenberg explains in *Perspectives on Technology* [(Cambridge, England: Cambridge University Press, 1976)], it must continue innovating to sustain its growth. How do they remain innovative? Christensen, who studied product evolution in the disk drive industry, concluded in *The Innovator's Dilemma: When New Techniques Cause Great Firms to Fail* [(New York: HarperBusiness, 2000), 128–129] that new firms need to grow quickly and plan strategically to attend to the internal nuances of torrid growth. He contends that, during the start-up stage of an organization, much of what gets done is attributable to its resources—its people. Over time, Christensen found, an organization's competencies must shift away from resources, and far greater emphasis must be placed on organizational processes and values (160). One reason why so many soaring young companies experience success with a strong initial product then ultimately flame out after they go public is because they failed to create processes that weave the desired core values into the fabric of the organization's culture.

These three theories, when linked together, provide an important foundation for establishing the organizational need for a vision, as it is defined here.

12. "Morningstar Quicktake Report," Morningstar.com Web site <http://quicktake.morningstar.com/stock/Snapshot.asp?Country=USA& Symbol=PSFT> (accessed 30 June 2002).

13. J. Case, "The Wonderland Economy," *Inc.*, 16 May 1995, 14–29.

14. Ibid.

15. A. U. Bhide, *The Origin and Evolution of New Business* (New York: Oxford University Press, 2000), 98.

16. A. L. Stinchcombe, "Social Structure and Organizations," in *Handbook of Organizations*, ed. J. G. March (Chicago: Rand McNally & Company, 1965), 142–193. J. Brüderl, P. Preisendörfer, and R. Ziegler, "Survival Chances of Newly Founded Business Organizations," *American Sociological Review* 57 (1992): 227–242. D. Krackjhardt, "Social Networks and Liability of Newness for Managers," in *Trends in Organizational Behavior*, vol. 3, eds. C. L. Cooper and D. M. Rousseau (New York: John Wiley & Sons, 1996), 159–173.

17. Bhide, *The Origin and Evolution of New Business*, 245.

18. Ibid.

Chapter 4

1. L. Kellaway, "Beware: Vision and Values Can Damage Your Company," *Financial Times*, 15 September 1997.

2. Bain & Company. Survey published in *Le Mensuel Consulting* (Paris), July/August 1995.

3. D. C. Hambrick and L. M. Crozier, "Stumblers and Stars in the Management of Rapid Growth," *Journal of Business Venturing* 1 (1985): 31–45.

4. Ibid.

5. P. F. Drucker, "Leadership: More Doing than Dash," *Wall Street Journal,* 6 January 1988.

6. Ibid.

7. E. Eklind, conversation with author, 18 March 2001, New York, NY.

8. S. Wells, *From Sage to Artisian* (Palo Alto, CA: Davies-Black, 1997), 62.

9. As quoted in *Bartlett's Familiar Quotations* 16th ed. (Boston: Little, Brown and Co., 1992), 571—from play "Back to Methuselah" [1921], pt. I, act I.

10. C. De Ciantis, *Using an Art Technique to Facilitate Leadership Development* (Greensboro, NC: Center for Creative Leadership, 1995).

11. J. R. Baum, E. A. Locke, and S. A. Kirkpatrick, "A Longitudinal Study of the Relation of Vision and Vision Communication to Venture Growth in Entrepreneurial Firms," *Journal of Applied Psychology* 83, no. 1 (1998): 43–54.

12. Ibid.

13. M. H. Erikson and E. L. Rossi, "Two-Level Communication and the Microdynamics of Trance," *American Journal of Clinical Hypnosis* 18 (1976): 153–171.

14. Ibid.

15. M. Lipton, "Demystifying the Development of an Organizational Vision," *Sloan Management Review* 37, no. 4 (1996): 84–85.

16. In T. Richman, "Identity Crisis," *Inc.,* October 1989, 100.

Chapter 5

1. *Fortune,* 16 May 1994, 101.

2. E. Eklind, personal conversation with author, 1 May 2002, New York, NY.

3. Ibid.

4. Quoted in D. Goleman, R. Boyatzis, and A. McKee, *Primal Leadership: Realizing the Power of Emotional Intelligence* (Boston: Harvard Business School Press, 2002), 204–205.

5. Quoted in Goleman, Boyatzis, and McKee, *Primal Leadership,* 205–206.

6. A. Zaleznik, "Managers and Leaders: Are They Different?" *Harvard Business Review,* May–June 1977, 67.

7. Zaleznik, "Managers and Leaders: Are They Different?" 77.

8. A. S. Grove, *Swimming Across* (New York: Warner Books, 2001).

9. Goleman, Boyatzis, and McKee, *Primal Leadership,* 206.

10. W. Bennis and B. Nanus, *Leaders: Strategies for Taking Charge* (New York: Harper and Row, 1985), 134.

11. E. Eklind, personal conversation with author, 1 May 2002, New York, NY.

12. E. C. Smith and P. M. Smith, *A History of the Town of Middlefield, Massachusetts* (Middlefield, MA: Middlefield History Fund, Inc., 1988), 167.

13. D. Pierce, "Keystone Arches," Seeourtown.com Web site <http://www.seeourtown.com/arts/Museums/ChesterFoundation/chesterfound2.cfm> (accessed 22 June 2002).

Chapter 6

1. A. U. Bhide, *The Origin and Evolution of New Business* (New York: Oxford University Press, 2000), 145.

2. L. Weinzimmer, P. C. Nystrom, and S. J. Freeman, "Methods of Measuring Organizational Growth: Issues, Consequences, and Contingencies," *Journal of Management* 24, no. 2 (1998): 235–262.

3. Johnson & Johnson, "2001 Annual Report," <http://www.jnj.com/2001_annual_report/2001_Report.htm> (accessed 22 June 2002).

4. D. C. Hambrick, "Corporate Coherence and the Top Management Team," in *Navigating Change,* eds. D. C. Hambrick, D. Nadler, and M. C. Tushman (Boston: Harvard Business School Press, 1998), 123.

5. See, e.g., C. A. Bartlett and S. Ghoshal, *Managing Across Borders: The Transnational Solution* (Boston: Harvard Business School Press, 1989).

6. D. Ancona and D. Nadler, "Top Hats and Executive Tales: Designing the Senior Team," *Sloan Management Review* 3, no. 1 (1989): 19–28.

7. According to *Bartlett's Familiar Quotations,* 14th ed., this is from *Huis-Clos (No Exit)* [1944].

8. Ancona and Nadler, "Top Hats and Executive Tales."

9. D. Robson, "Nike: Just Do . . . Something," *Business Week*, 2 July 2001, 70; <http://www.businessweek.com/magazine/content/01_27/b3739181 .htm> (accessed 12 July 2002).

10. Ibid.

11. Ibid.

12. Ibid.

13. M. Lipton, "Successful Women in a Man's World: The Myth of Managerial Androgyny," in *Not As Far As You Think: The Realities of Working Women,* ed. L. Moore (Lexington, MA: Lexington Press, 1986), 128–161.

14. W. E. Moore, *The Conduct of the Corporation* (New York: Random House, 1962).

15. "In Times of Trouble, The Best Leaders Listen to Dissenters," *The Wall Street Journal,* 13 November 2001.

16. K. M. Eisenhardt, J. L. Kahwajy, and L. J. Bourgeois, "Conflict and Strategic Change: How Top Management Teams Disagree," in *Navigating Change,* eds. D. C. Hambrick, D. Nadler, and M. C. Tushman (Boston: Harvard Business School Press, 1998), 151.

17. Ibid.

18. Ibid.

19. Ibid.

20. A. Amason, "Distinguishing the Effects of Functional and Dysfunctional Conflict on Strategic Decision Making: Resolving a Paradox for Top Management Teams," *Academy of Management Journal* 39, no. 1 (1996): 123.

21. K. Back, "Influence Through Social Communication," Journal of Abnormal and Social Psychology (1951), in *Social Conflict: Escalation, Stalemate, and Settlement,* eds. D. Pruitt and J. Rubin (New York: Random House, 1986).

22. Ibid.

23. W. Green, "How EDS Got Its Groove Back," *Fast Company,* October 2001, 106–117.

24. Ibid.

25. Ibid.

26. Ibid.

27. Ibid.

28. C. A. O'Reilly and J. Pfeffer, *Hidden Value* (Boston: Harvard Business School Press, 2000).

29. L. Tolstoy, *Anna Karenina* (New York: Oxford University Press, 1998), 1.

Chapter 7

1. Continental Airlines, "Annual Report," 1994.

2. Presentation by G. Bethune (Stanford University Business School, Stanford, CA, 2 May 2001).

3. K. Cameron and R. E Quinn, *Diagnosing and Changing Organizational Culture* (Reading, MA: Addison-Wesley, 1999), 4.

4. J. P. Kotter and J. L. Heskett, *Corporate Culture and Performance* (New York: The Free Press, 1992).

5. Fortune Web site <http://www.fortune.com/lists/bestcompanies/index.html> (accessed 30 June 2002).

6. J. C. Collins and J. I. Porras, *Built to Last: Successful Habits of Visionary Companies* (New York: HarperCollins, 1994), 114–139.

7. C. Baden, President, and L. Newcomb, COO, personal conversation with author, 22 October 2001, Foothills Ranch, CA.

8. Ibid.

9. Ibid.

10. Ibid.

11. Ibid.

12. W. Daily, interview with author, 23 October 2001, Foothills Ranch, CA.

13. C. Baden, President, and L. Newcomb, COO, personal conversation with author, 22 October 2001, Foothills Ranch, CA.

14. Ibid.

15. Ibid.

16. K. Lane, interview with author, 19 October 2001, Foothills Ranch, CA.

17. D. Kennedy, interviews with author, 19, 22, and 23 October 2001, Foothills Ranch, CA.

18. C. Baden, President, and L. Newcomb, COO, personal conversation with author, 22 October 2001, Foothills Ranch, CA.

19. A number of cases can be seen in B. Vedin, *Management of Change and Innovation* (Alderhot, England: Dartmouth, 1994).

20. See A. Kakabadse, F. Nortier, and N. Abramovici, eds., *Success in Sight: Visioning* (London: International Thomson Business Press, 1998), 12.

21. C. Baden, personal conversation with author, 22 October 2001, Foothills Ranch, CA.

22. Presentation by G. Bethune (Stanford University Business School, Stanford, CA, May 2, 2001).

23. Ibid.

Chapter 8

1. S. Salsbury, *The State, the Investor, and the Railroad: The Boston & Albany, 1825-1867* (Cambridge, MA: Harvard University Press, 1967), 186–187.

2. W. Bounds, "Traditional Publisher Meets Internet Start-up: Can the Marriage Survive?" *Wall Street Journal,* 30 September 1996.

3. H. de Lesser, "More Entrepreneurs Take Help of Executive Coaches: CEOs Hope to Gain Edge as Their Businesses Burgeon Amid Sea of Changes," *Wall Street Journal,* 5 September 2000.

4. W. G. Dyer Jr., *Cultural Change in Family Firms: Anticipating and Managing Business and Family Transitions* (San Francisco: Jossey-Bass, 1986).

5. T. Jefferson, "Letter to Samuel Kercheval," 12 July 1816.

6. For example, F. Ostroff, in his book, *The Horizontal Organization* (New York: Oxford University Press, 1999).

7. For an additional view on this perspective, see S. F. Dicter, C. Gagnon, and A. Alexander, "Memo to a CEO: Leading Organizational Transformations," *McKinsey Quarterly* no. 1 (1993): 104.

8. K. Lane, personal conversation with author, 23 October 2001, Foothills Ranch, CA.

9. D. Q. Mills, *Rebirth of the Corporation* (New York: John Wiley & Sons, 1991), 66.

10. S. A. Mohrman, S. G. Cohen, and A. M. Mohrman, *Designing Team-Based Organizations* (San Francisco: Jossey-Bass, 1995).

11. E. D. Lawler III, *From the Ground Up: Six Principles for Building the New Logic Corporation* (San Francisco: Jossey-Bass, 1996), 82–101. D. Nadler and M. C. Tushman, *Competing By Design: The Power of Organizational Architecture* (New York: Oxford University Press, 1997).

12. See R. Ashkenas, D. Ulrich, T. Jick, and S. Kerr, *The Boundaryless Organization* (San Francisco: Jossey-Bass, 1995), 11–13.

13. National Retail Federation Web site, STORES online <http://www.stores.org/archives/jan01sidebar_5.html> (accessed 25 June 2002).

14. While these criteria were developed independently, virtually identical "Success Factors" were identified by Ashkenas, Ulrich, Jick, and Kerr in *The Boundaryless Organization,* 7–9.

15. K. Lane, personal conversation with author, 23 October 2001, Foothills Ranch, CA.

16. "ASAP Interview Bill Gates," *Forbes ASAP,* 7 December 1992, 63, 74.

17. Other sources: P. E. Ceruzzi, *A History of Modern Computing* (Cambridge, MA: MIT Press, 1999); J. Lowe, *Bill Gates Speaks: Insight from the World's Greatest Entrepreneur* (New York: John Wiley & Sons, 1998).

18. "ASAP Interview Bill Gates," 63, 74.

19. Lawler, *From the Ground Up*, 84. Nadler and M. Tushman, *Competing By Design*.

20. Ibid.

21. Lawler, *From the Ground Up*, 90.

22. Ibid.

23. F. Vogelstein, "Sun on the Ropes," *Fortune*, 7 January 2002, 87.

24. Ibid.

25. Ibid.

Chapter 9

1. J. Pfeffer, *The Human Equation* (Boston: Harvard Business School Press, 1998), 31.

2. Ibid.

3. Pfeffer, "Producing Sustainable Competitive Advantage Through the Effective Management of People," *Academy of Management Executive* 9, no. 1 (1995): 55–69.

4. "Investment Winners and Losers," *Money*, October 1992, 133.

5. G. Tellis and P. Goldner, *Will and Vision: How Latecomers Grow to Dominate Markets* (New York: McGraw-Hill, 2002), 41.

6. Ibid.

7. B. E. Becker and M. A. Huselid, "High Performance Work Systems and Firm Performance: A Synthesis of Research and Managerial Implications," *Research in Personnel and Human Resources Management* 16, no. 1 (1998): 53–101.

8. Huselid, "The Impact of Human Resource Management Practices on Turnover, Productivity, and Corporate Financial Performance," *Academy of Management Journal* 38 (1996): 891–919.

9. See, e.g., L. Baird and L. Meshoulam, "Managing Two Fits of Strategic Human Resources Management," *Academy of Management Review* 13, no. 1 (1988): 116–128.

10. T. M. Welbourne and L. A. Cyr, "The Human Resource Executive Effect in Initial Public Offering Firms," *Academy of Management Journal* 42, no. 61 (1999): 616–629. See also Cyr, Welbourne, and D. E. Johnson, *Entrepreneurship Theory and Practice* (Waco, TX: Baylor University, 2000), 71–91.

K. M. Eisenhardt and S. L. Brown, "Time Pacing: Competing in Markets That Won't Stand Still," *Harvard Business Review,* March–April 1998, 59–69.

11. Welbourne and Cyr, "The Human Resource Executive Effect in Initial Public Offering Firms," 616–629.

12. Eisenhardt and Brown, "Time Pacing: Competing in Markets That Won't Stand Still."

13. Cyr, Welbourne, and Johnson, *Entrepreneurship Theory and Practice,* 71–91. Eisenhardt and Brown, "Time Pacing," 59–69.

14. D. Allison, "Bill Gates Interview," National Museum of American History, Smithsonian Institution, <http://www.americanhistory.si.edu/csr/comphist/gates.htm> (accessed 22 January 2002).

15. J. Young, *Greatest Technology Stories* (New York: John Wiley & Sons, 1998), 258.

16. For a somewhat disguised chronicle of how this firm struggled with the process of vision development, see Lipton, "Demystifying the Development of an Organizational Vision," *Sloan Management Review* 37, no. 4 (1996): 87–92.

17. C. Baden, personal conversation with author, 22 October 2001.

18. K. Lane, personal conversation with author, 23 October 2001.

19. F. Herzberg, "One More Time: How Do You Motivate Employees?" *Harvard Business Review,* January–February 1968, 53–62.

20. A. Kohn, *Punished by Rewards* (Boston: Houghton Mifflin, 1993); "Why Incentive Plans Cannot Work," *Harvard Business Review,* September–October 1993, 54–63.

21. E. D. Lawler III, *From the Ground Up: Six Principles for Building the New Logic Workplace* (San Francisco: Jossey-Bass, 1996), 210.

22. G. Akerlof, "Gift Exchange and Efficiency Wage Theory," *American Economic Review* 74 (1984): 79–83.

23. J. W. Near, "Wendy's Successful 'Mop Bucket Attitude'," *Wall Street Journal,* 27 April 1992.

24. See the meta-analysis conducted by G. D. Jenkins Jr., A. Mitra, N. Gupta, and J. D. Shaw, "Are Financial Incentives Related to Performance? A Meta-analytic Review of Empirical Research," *Journal of Applied Psychology* 83 (1998): 777–787.

25. "How Leader at 3M Got His Employees to Back Big Changes," *Wall Street Journal,* 23 April 2002.

26. Ibid.

27. Ibid.

28. Ibid.

29. Lawler, *From the Ground Up,* 201.

30. D. Kennedy, personal conversation with author, 19 May 2001.

31. J. R. Galbraith, *Competing with Flexible, Lateral Organizations,* 2d ed. (Reading, MA: Addison Wesley, 1994).

32. J. C. Collins and J. I. Porras, *Built to Last: Successful Habits of Visionary Companies* (New York: HarperCollins, 1994), 169.

33. D. F. Russo, transcript from a talk given at Stanford University Graduate School of Business, 15 May 1998. In C. A. O'Reilly and J. Pfeffer, *Hidden Value* (Boston: Harvard Business School Press, 2000) 105–108.

34. Ibid.

35. W. Breen, "The American Cancer Society's Next Crusade," *Fast Company,* October 2001, 58.

36. Ibid.

37. A. Walker, "A Walk in the Park," *Human Resources Executive,* April 1997, 64.

38. J. Pfeffer, "SAS Institute: A Different Approach to Incentives and People Management Practices in the Software Industry," Case HR-6 (Stanford, CA: Graduate School of Business, Stanford University, 1998), 1.

39. N. Haas, "The House that Bloomberg Built," *Fast Company,* November 1995 <http://www.fastcompany.com/online/01/bberg.html> (accessed 22 January 2002).

40. SAS Institute, Inc. Annual Report (Cary, NC: 1996), 1.

41. Ibid.

42. C. A. O'Reilly and J. Pfeffer, *Hidden Value* (Boston: Harvard Business School Press, 2000), 108–117.

43. SAS Institute, Inc. Annual Report (Cary, NC: 1996), 1.

44. J. Pfeffer, *The Human Equation,* 66.

45. Ibid.

46. Ibid.

47. D. Kennedy, personal conversation with author, 22 October 2001.

48. SAS corporate Web site <http://www.sas.com/news/feature/25dec00/fortune100.html> (accessed 22 January 2002).

49. Bureau of Labor Statistics Web site <http://www.bls.gov/news.release/ecopro.nr0.htm> (accessed 30 June 2002).

Chapter 10

1. T. Doorley and J. Donovan, *Value-Creating Growth* (San Francisco: Jossey-Bass, 1999), 36.

2. J. Rahul, "The Resurrection of Michael Dell," *Fortune,* 18 September 1995, 118.

3. Rahul, "The Resurrection of Michael Dell," 120.

4. A. Serwer, "Dell Does Domination," *Fortune,* 21 January 2002, 74.

5. W. Gates, *The Road Ahead* (New York: Viking, 1996), 35.

6. T. Leavitt, "Marketing Myopia," *Harvard Business Review,* September–October 1975, 28. (Originally printed in 1960.)

7. P. G. Limbardo and M. R. Lieppe, *The Psychology of Attitude Change and Social Influence* (New York: McGraw-Hill, 1991).

8. O. Harris, "A Primer for Polemicists," *Commentary* 78, no. 3 (1984): 40.

Appendix

1. This exercise draws heavily on the concepts developed by E. H. Schein and presented in two of his books: *The Corporate Culture Survival Guide* (San Francisco: Jossey-Bass, 1999) and *Organizational Culture and Leadership* (San Francisco: Jossey-Bass, 1997).

2. Oakley, "Annual Review Form," February 2002.

Index

About the Author

Mark Lipton is Chair of the Organization Change Management program at the Milano Graduate School of Management and Urban Policy, New School University, in New York City. He was formerly also Chair of the Graduate School's Human Resources Management program (the country's largest masters degree program in this field), Associate Dean of the Milano Graduate School, and Founder of The Leadership Center.

Mark holds a Ph.D. from the School of Management at the University of Massachusetts at Amherst, where he also taught. He has held senior management positions in both the corporate and government sectors.

His research and opinions on management and strategy have appeared in the *Harvard Business Review, Sloan Management Review, The Journal of Management Consulting, Executive Excellence, Human Resources Management, Management Review, Management World, Human Resources Professional, Organization Development Journal,* and *Human Resources Annual,* and he has contributed chapters to several books. Mark currently serves on the editorial board of *The Journal of Management Consulting,* and he is a frequent presenter at conferences and management seminars in the United States, Europe, South America, and Africa.

Mark's private consulting practice, Lipton & Co., has focused for over twenty-five years on helping organizational leaders manage large-scale change. He works personally with CEOs and senior managers one-on-one, with divisional teams, and with entire organizational systems to develop unique solutions. His work spans the breadth of publicly owned global organizations to medium-sized family businesses.

His client engagements have typically focused on facilitating organization-wide initiatives for managing growth. Working with executive groups, he helps them define comprehensive organizational visions and determine strategies for implementing them. Often, he coaches executive management through difficult change initiatives that impact—or are impacted by—growth. Lipton & Co. also works closely with executive management to integrate merged and acquired organizations.

A sample of the diversity of organizations to which he has provided recent consulting support includes Schieffelin & Somerset Co., Cap Gemini-Ernst & Young Management Consulting, Citibank, Sun Microsystems, Landor Associates, Flatiron Partners, Marriott International, The Ford Foundation, Cotton Incorporated, UNICEF, American International Group, Oslo Energi, The Port Authority of New York and New Jersey, United States Office of Federal Housing Enterprise Oversight, The City of New York (Mayor's Office, Departments of Personnel, Probation, Consumer Affairs, Parks & Recreation, Housing Preservation and Development, Corrections, Office of Management and Budget), and many nonprofit organizations.

He is the architect of the Leadership Institute, the longest-running development program for high-potential senior managers working for the City of New York. Other leadership development programs he has designed for regional and foreign governments, corporations, and large nonprofit organizations continue to enhance the skills and insight of senior managers.

Mark's home and business are based in the Berkshire Hills of Western Massachusetts.

lipton@newschool.edu
mark@liptonandcompany.com